BIOGRAPHY AND CRITICISM

General Editors
A. NORMAN JEFFARES
R. L. C. LORIMER

1

JAMES HOGG
A Critical Study

LOUIS SIMPSON

JAMES HOGG
A Critical Study

OLIVER & BOYD
EDINBURGH AND LONDON
1962

OLIVER & BOYD LTD
Tweeddale Court
Edinburgh 1

39A Welbeck Street
London W1

First published 1962

PRINTED IN GREAT BRITAIN
AT THE PRESS OF THE PUBLISHERS

Preface

Hogg vacillated from one kind of writing to another, and from good to bad; there is no clear development of his art. I have therefore not dealt with his works in the order of their appearance. Instead, I have begun with a description of his life; then I have considered his verse; and last, at greater length, I have discussed his prose. This, I believe, is the right balance and the right order of going, for the Ettrick Shepherd, poet of *The Queen's Wake*, is a less important figure than James Hogg, author of the *Justified Sinner*. This work, which towers above the rest, I have treated last of all. It was the climax of his art, though not of his life. Everything that came before was a preparation for the writing of this novel; nothing that came after was as original or powerful.

Hogg has never been entirely forgotten. Some of his poems and the *Justified Sinner* have always found a few readers. But, confronted with the mass of mediocre writing in which his original tales and poems are embedded, most readers have been content to hurry by. Also, his performance as the Ettrick Shepherd has been a cause of his obscurity. We are likely to think of him as he often represented himself, a self-educated peasant, uncouth or comic in his conversation, imprudent in his behaviour, tolerated in society only because he had a gift for song and for uttering whimsical monologues, in short, nearly a buffoon. This character has repelled some critics who have assumed that it represents Hogg adequately. In the margin of the index to Lockhart's *Memoirs of the Life of Sir Walter Scott, Bart.*, in the volume that I have consulted, opposite the name of Hogg a hand has pencilled "should have been whipt out of society." This extreme judgement is echoed in the apologies offered by the biographers of the Ettrick Shepherd. However, as I have read Hogg himself, I have come to think that in many ways he was superior to those who patronised him. The purpose of this study is criticism, not

v

biography; yet to understand the works of James Hogg, I have had to deal with the Ettrick Shepherd. I have tried to keep him in his place.

There is no selection of Hogg's best writings, nor is there a complete collected edition. I have read his works where they are scattered, in incomplete collections, periodicals, and volumes that have never been reprinted. In the course of this study I have referred either to editions which follow Hogg's original texts or to the originals. For Hogg's poetry I have drawn largely upon Thomson's edition of 1865, *The Works of the Ettrick Shepherd*; the text is satisfactory—unlike Thomson's edition of the prose. For the tales and sketches I have drawn upon the edition of 1837, which Hogg himself revised shortly before his death. The 1947 edition of the *Justified Sinner* follows the original, unmutilated text, and is one of the few attractive editions of Hogg available to the public; besides, it contains André Gide's introduction; I have therefore used it. For the "Autobiography" I have gone to Thomson rather than to the several, fragmentary editions of Hogg's memoirs. For the rest—the *Scottish Pastorals*, *The Spy*, *The Three Perils of Woman*, *Altrive Tales*, *The Domestic Manners and Private Life of Sir Walter Scott*, *A Series of Lay Sermons*, and other works— I have been compelled to refer to texts which may not be available to the reader.

I am grateful to Dr James C. Corson, Deputy Librarian of the University of Edinburgh, for permitting me to use the Library, and to the Staff of the National Library of Scotland, for their unfailing courtesy and assistance. I am also most grateful to Professors Jerome H. Buckley and David A. Robertson, Jr., and to Mr R. L. C. Lorimer, who, by their advice, have enabled me to improve this work considerably.

L. S.

Berkeley,
California

Contents

Part I

GENIUS AND NECESSITY

Then what are houses, goud, or land,
To sic an heirship left in fee ?
An' I think mair o' auld Scotland,
Than to be fear'd for mine or me.

"The Monitors"

I

Genius and Necessity

IN James Hogg's lifetime many of his contemporaries—among them Byron, Scott, and Wordsworth—considered him a writer of power and originality.[1] His books were read in Europe and America, and at the end of his life, when he visited London, he was lionised. But, a hundred years after the publication of his *Private Memoirs and Confessions of a Justified Sinner*, André Gide, having read the novel "with a stupefaction and admiration that increased at every page," was unable to find a cultivated Englishman, American, or Frenchman who had read it or knew anything about the author. How, Gide wondered, could such a work have failed to become famous?[2]

Reasons for the neglect of the *Justified Sinner* and of Hogg's other writings, though they were not quite so forgotten as Gide suggests, are not hard to find. He wrote carelessly and too much; his better works are buried in his worse; and his virtues as a writer have been obscured by the eccentricity, sometimes verging on absurdity, of his behaviour.

It is the object of this study to examine and to evaluate the writings of James Hogg apart from his personality. Only

---

[1] Byron (to John Murray, 3 Aug. 1814) : ". . . surely he [Hogg] is a man of great powers." Thomas Moore, *The Life of Lord Byron with his Letters and Journals*, London 1854, p. 259. In a footnote to this letter Moore gives his own opinion of Hogg : "this ingenious and remarkable man."

Scott : "Hogg called this morning to converse about trying to get him on the pecuniary list of the Royal Literary Society. Certainly he deserves it, if genius and necessity could do so." Walter Scott, *The Journal of Sir Walter Scott*, edd. J. G. Tait and W. H. Parker, Edinburgh 1950, p. 106.

Wordsworth (to R. P. Gillies) : "Mr Hogg has too much genius to require that support." (Wordsworth means by "support" Hogg's modelling his style on Scott's.) Rydal Mount, 23 Nov., 1814, in Gillies' *Memoirs of a Literary Veteran*, London 1851, II.146.

[2] André Gide, "Introduction" to *The Private Memoirs and Confessions of a Justified Sinner*, by James Hogg, London 1947, p. ix.

one lengthy critical study of Hogg's works has been attempted —Edith C. Batho's *The Ettrick Shepherd* (1927).[3] But Miss Batho condescends to Hogg and to his works; she concentrates upon explaining his labours as an editor and anthologist, to the neglect of criticism; her opinions are superficial, and, for the most part, are not supported by a reading of the texts.[4]

A review by Francis Jeffrey, the reported comments of Sir Walter Scott, a letter written by Wordsworth, essays by John Wilson, George Gilfillan, and George Saintsbury, comments by Thomas Thomson, the editor of Hogg's *Works*, and by Sir George Douglas, which are mingled with and hard to extricate from biography, an introduction by Gide, and a few pages by Kurt Wittig—these are the noteworthy criticisms of Hogg.[5] Most of the comments that do exist deal with his verse; the prose is rarely mentioned.

For the purpose of criticism, the following account of Hogg's life is limited to matters that bear upon his writings. The primary source of information is Hogg's "Autobiography," expanded from a memoir first published with *The Mountain Bard*. Though not trustworthy as a record of fact, in its very errors and exaggerations the "Autobiography" casts light upon Hogg's mind. The self-portrait is amplified by Hogg's sketches, the footnotes appended to his works, his memoir of Sir Walter

[3] Edith C. Batho, *The Ettrick Shepherd* (henceforth cited as Batho), Cambridge (England), 1927.

[4] The most valuable part of Miss Batho's "Critical Study" is the "Bibliography," and for this I am grateful. Her survey of Hogg's work as an editor and compiler is thorough. But her criticism is inferior. Her method is, for the most part, only to quote amusing passages or offer a short opinion not supported by discussion. "Of the longer tales *The Renowned Adventures of Basil Lee* is easily the worst" (*The Ettrick Shepherd*, p. 131) ; "*The Edinburgh Baillie* is not good" (p. 122)—statements like these are substituted for criticism. Moreover, though she seems accurate when dealing with the relatively unimportant matter of Hogg's use of old ballads, her statements are open to question when she undertakes criticism. "The Long Pack is . . . a good murder story" (p. 131)—but a reading of the text will show that it is not a murder story. In the course of this study I have taken exception to her opinions. Miss Batho's criticism is often mixed with biography, and it is evident that she had no high opinion of Hogg himself.

[5] I have not included H. T. Stephenson in this list, for though he has some acute minor comments—as in his comparison of Hogg with Defoe—his major judgements are absolutely wide of the mark. He finds Hogg's "Skylark" equal in quality to Burns and he thinks *The Three Perils of Woman* Hogg's best book. H. T. Stephenson, *The Ettrick Shepherd. A Biography*, Indiana University Studies, Vol. IX, Study No. 54 (Sep. 1922), pp. 69, 70, 85.

Scott, and his *Lay Sermons*. The writings of his contemporaries provide further material. He figures largely in John Gibson Lockhart's *Memoirs of the Life of Sir Walter Scott, Bart.*, and in the memoirs of John Wilson, Robert Pierce Gillies, John Morrison, and others. His correspondence and accounts of his dealings with William Blackwood, Archibald Constable, and John Murray appear in the histories of their publishing houses.

In the *Noctes Ambrosianae*, the dialogues first published in *Blackwood's Edinburgh Magazine*, Hogg is presented in the character of the Shepherd; and though the *Noctes* are largely the work of John Wilson, and certainly should not be read as verbatim reports of Hogg's conversation, they may be consulted as a mixture of truth and fiction. Several of Hogg's letters are preserved in the archives of the National Library of Scotland. The earliest biography is Thomson's, published thirty years after Hogg's death; there are biographical studies by Hogg's daughter Mrs Garden, by Sir George Douglas, H. T. Stephenson, Edith C. Batho, Alan Lang Strout, and Donald Carswell.[6]

James Hogg was born in 1770, in the parish of Ettrick, in the Scottish Border Country.[7] He was the second son of Robert Hogg, a shepherd, and Margaret Laidlaw. Robert Hogg, having saved a little money and taken a lease on the farms of Ettrickhouse and Ettrickhall, was then residing at the "humble homestead of Ettrickhall."[8] There James was born.

J. G. Lockhart derives the name Hogg from *hog*, signifying in the vernacular a young sheep that has never been shorn. Hogg, he comments, came of a long line of shepherds.[9] Veitch

---

[6] The texts here referred to are listed in the Bibliography.

[7] For a discussion of the date of Hogg's birth, see Mrs Garden, *Memorials of James Hogg, the Ettrick Shepherd* (henceforth cited as Garden), 1885, pp. 2-4. Until nearly the end of his life Hogg thought that he had been born in 1772, on 25 January—Burns' birthday—but the parish register gives 9 Dec. 1770 as the date of his baptism. There was, it seems, no conscious effort by Hogg to deceive ; he came to believe that he was born on the same day as Burns, because he wanted it so.

[8] Garden, pp. 10-11.

[9] J. G. Lockhart, *Memoirs of the Life of Sir Walter Scott, Bart.*, Edinburgh 1837, v. 9.

suggests a more heroic ancestry for the author: Hogg might have descended from the Viking invaders, whom he resembled in "features, hair, and frame of body." For the name Hogg, he argues, was derived not from the shepherds' *hog* (a young sheep), but from the Scandinavian *haug* or *haig* (meaning a hill or mound).[10] Hogg himself inclined to this view, as is shown by his celebration of his supposed Viking ancestor in *The Pilgrims of the Sun.*

The Hoggs were vassals of the Scotts of Harden on the lands of Fauldshope, in a feudal relationship noted in folk rhyme:

> If ye *a*reive the Hoggs of Fauldshope   *a* rob
> Ye *a*harry Harden's *b*gear.[11]   *a* plunder   *b* goods

The Hoggs were also said to have been tenants of the lairds of Oakwood, the traditional residence of the wizard, Michael Scott.[12] Hogg himself claimed that "several of the wives of Fauldshope were supposed to be rank witches."[13]

Margaret Laidlaw, his mother, came of a family known for their shrewdness and cleverness. Her father, the famous shepherd Will o' Phaup, had excelled in "feats of frolic, strength and agility." [14] In his sketch, "Odd Characters," Hogg describes Will o' Phaup's triumphs as a runner and assures the reader that he was "the last man of this wild region who heard, saw, and conversed with the Fairies."[15] Margaret Laidlaw was a repository of folklore; she knew the old ballads and legends of the Border and would recite them to her children. But, according to William Hogg, the author's older brother, she did not care for poetry. In a letter written in

[10] John Veitch, *The History and Poetry of the Scottish Border* (henceforth cited as Veitch), Glasgow 1878, p. 41.

[11] Hogg tells that at "a great festival at Bowhill" Sir Walter Scott requested that the Duke of Buccleuch permit Hogg to come to Scott's table, quoting this rhyme to win his point. Hogg found himself placed at the right of Scott of Harden. James Hogg, *The Domestic Manners and Private Life of Sir Walter Scott*, Glasgow. John Reid & Co. Edinburgh and London 1834, p. 73.

[12] Sir George Douglas, *James Hogg* (henceforth cited as Douglas), Edinburgh 1899, p. 16.

[13] Batho, p. 3.

[14] James Hogg, *Tales and Sketches* (henceforth cited as *Tales*), Glasgow 1837, VI, 209-10.

[15] *Tales*, p. 215.

1818 he says: "I have often read some of the best pieces of English poetry to her, but she was altogether insensible to their beauties."[16]

In the framework of his tale "The Marvellous Doctor," Hogg renders passages of his mother's speech which show that, to his mind at least, she was witty and curious.[17] Having listened to the Doctor's anecdotes of his adventures with a love-elixir, of which he claimed to be the "sole and original inventor," she maintained that a love-elixir

> was known to the chiefs of the gypsy tribes for centuries bygone; and as proofs of her position, she cited Johnie Faa's seduction of the Earl of Cassillis's lady, so well known in Lowland song, and Hector Kennedy's seduction of three brides, all of high quality, by merely touching the palms of their hands, after which no power could prevent any of them from following him.[18]

Hogg's father is described by Mrs Garden as "not a man in any way remarkable. A hard-working shepherd, a well-meaning, well-living man."[19] But he was also, by William Hogg's account, an enthusiastic reader of the Bible. If we can ascribe James Hogg's interest in ballads and legends to his mother's influence, we may credit to Robert Hogg something of his son's understanding of Puritanism. "Our father," says William Hogg, "is perfectly enamoured with a fine description, whether in prose or verse; and even at this time, the sublime descriptions of Isaiah, the plaintive strains of Jeremiah, or beautiful imagery of Ezekiel, form his principal reading."[20]

"The one grand ambition of Scottish peasants," says Mrs Garden, was to make a boy a minister; but Hogg's parents were too poor to do this.[21] Though he had little schooling,

---

[16] Letter from William Hogg to James Gray, 1818. Quoted in Alan Lang Strout, *The Life and Letters of James Hogg, the Ettrick Shepherd* (henceforth cited as Strout), Texas 1946, p. 9.

[17] *Tales*, IV, pp. 145-73.

[18] *Op. cit.*, iv. 172.

[19] Garden, pp. 10-11.

[20] Letter from William Hogg to James Gray, 1818. Quoted in Strout, pp. 9-10.

[21] Garden, pp. 12-13.

he received an informal education, of which his brother William gives an account:

> He was remarkably fond of hearing stories, and our mother to keep us boys quiet would often tell us tales of kings, giants, knights, fairies, kelpies, brownies, etc., etc. These stories fixed both our eyes and attention, and our mother got forward with her housewifery affairs in a more regular way. She also often repeated to us the metre psalms, and accustomed us to repeat them after her ; and I think it was the 122nd which Jamie . . . could have said. I think this was before he knew any of the letters. I am certain before he could spell a word. After he could read with fluency, the historical part of the Bible was his chief delight, and no person whom I have been acquainted with knew it so well.[22]

At the age of six, Hogg relates in his "Autobiography," he was sent to school at the schoolhouse near Ettrickhall, and "had the honour of standing at the head of a juvenile class, who read the Shorter Catechism and the Proverbs of Solomon."[23]　But then, Robert Hogg, having failed as a dealer in sheep, was evicted with his family from Ettrickhall, and the child was obliged to "go to service."[24]　He was hired by a neighbouring farmer as a cowherd, his wages for the half year being a ewe lamb and a pair of new shoes. Fortunately, the family was befriended by a Mr Brydon of Crosslee, who took a short lease of the farm at Ettrickhouse, and placed Hogg's father there as his shepherd. In the next year, during the winter, James was brought home and put to school "with a lad named Ker, who was teaching the children of a neighbouring farmer."[25]　Here, Hogg says, he got into the class that read the Bible. "I had likewise, for some time before my quarter was out, tried writing; and had horribly defiled several sheets of paper with copy lines, every letter of which was nearly an inch in length. Thus terminated my education.

[22] Garden, p. 13.

[23] James Hogg, "Autobiography of the Ettrick Shepherd" (henceforth cited as "Autobiography"), in *The Works of the Ettrick Shepherd*, ed. Rev. Thomas Thomson (henceforth cited as *Works*), Glasgow 1865, II. 441.

[24] "Autobiography," p. 441.

[25] *Ibid.*, p. 442.

After this I was never another day at any school whatever. In all, I had spent about half a year at it."[26]

His brother, William, adds something to the picture of Hogg's schooldays:

> He was a quick and ready scholar, not however, much excelling his schoolfellows in aptitude for learning. He got his lessons very easily, but I am not sure if his memory retained them well. . . . In the play-ground he was every day entering into competitions which gave me uneasiness, as I knew he had no chance with his competitors in racing, wrestling, etc. They were frequently far above his age, and above his strength, yet his frequent defeats did not discourage him.[27]

Of Hogg's boyhood little is known. He herded lambs and cows; at the age of eight, he tells us, he was strongly attracted to a girl named Betty; before he was fifteen, he had served a dozen masters, "working with horses, thrashing &c."; and he learned to play the fiddle.[28]

He went to work for a distant cousin, Laidlaw, at Elibank upon Tweed; he stayed there for "three half years," then went to work as a shepherd for Laidlaw's father at Willenslee.[29] It was at this time, the "Autobiography" relates, at the age of eighteen, that Hogg first read Blind Harry's *Life and Adventures of Sir William Wallace* (paraphrased by Hamilton of Gilbertfield) and Allan Ramsay's *Gentle Shepherd*.[30] The latter work, as Veitch remarks, had made famous the pastoral scenery of the Lowlands, and the valleys of the Tweed, the Teviot, and the Yarrow, in particular.[31] Hogg admired not only Ramsay's use of idyllic scenery, but also his manner; Hogg's first book of verse, *Scottish Pastorals*, would be filled with echoes of Ramsay.

Though he was "immoderately fond" of these rhymed tales in vernacular Scots, Hogg regretted that they were not in prose, "that everybody might have understood them," or at least in the familiar metre of the Psalms.[32] He read slowly, for his little ability at reading had been nearly lost, and the

---

[26] "Autobiography," p. 442.   [27] Garden, p. 14.
[28] "Autobiography," pp. 442-3.   [29] *Ibid.*, p. 443.
[30] *Ibid.*   [31] Veitch, pp. 443-4.
[32] "Autobiography," p. 443.

language was an obstacle. "Before I got to the end of a line, I had commonly lost the rhyme of the preceding one; and if I came to a triplet, a thing of which I had no conception, I commonly read to the foot of the page without perceiving that I had lost the rhyme altogether."[33] He also read James Harvey's *Meditations among the Tombs* aloud to his father.[34]

Mrs Laidlaw lent the shepherd books to read while tending the sheep. These were mostly theological, and the only one Hogg could later remember was Bishop Burnet's *Theory of the Conflagration of the Earth*. He was happy that he had not understood it completely, for "all the day I was pondering on the grand millennium and the reign of the saints; and all the night dreaming of new heavens and a new earth—the stars in horror, and the world in flames."[35] From that lady he also had newspapers, which he pored over earnestly, reading them straight through from the date, through "advertisements of houses and lands, balm of Gilead, and everything."[36] At this time, he relates, having to write a letter to his brother William, he found he had forgotten how to write the letters of the alphabet.

From Willenslee he went to work as a shepherd for another Laidlaw, at Blackhouse, where he stayed for ten years. William Laidlaw, one of the sons of Hogg's employer, offers a striking portrait of the shepherd at the age of nineteen:

> . . . his face was fair, round, and ruddy, with big, blue eyes that beamed with humour, gaiety, and glee. And he was not only then, but throughout his chequered life, blessed with strong health, and the most exuberant animal spirits. His height was a little above the average size, his form at that period was of faultless symmetry, which nature had endowed with almost unequalled agility and swiftness of foot. His head was covered with a singular profusion of light brown hair, which he usually wore coiled up under his hat. When he used to enter church on Sunday (of which he was at all times a regular attendant), after lifting his hat, he used to raise his right hand to his hair to assist a shake of his head, when his long hair fell over his

---

[33] "Autobiography," p. 443.   [34] Batho, p. 8.
[35] "Autobiography," p. 443.   [36] *Ibid.*

loins and every female eye at least was turned upon him as with a light step he ascended to the gallery, where he usually sat.[37]

The "Autobiography" tells us that he first attempted to write verses in the spring of the year 1796, but this is an error, and we may move the following description of his beginning struggles as a writer back to the years between his coming to the Laidlaws at Blackhouse and his first publication, "The Mistakes of a Night"—that is, between 1791 and 1794.

Mr Laidlaw having a number of valuable books, which were all open to my perusal, I about this time began to read with considerable attention—and no sooner did I begin to read so as to understand, than, rather prematurely, I began to write. For several years my compositions consisted wholly of songs and ballads made up for the lasses to sing in chorus ; and a proud man I was when I first heard the rosy nymphs chaunting my uncouth strains and jeering me by the still dear appellation of "Jamie the poeter."

I had no more difficulty in composing songs then than I have at present; and I was equally well pleased with them. But then the writing of them !—that was a job ! I had no method of learning to write, save by following the Italian alphabet; and though I always stripped myself of coat and vest when I began to pen a song, yet my wrist took a cramp, so that I could rarely make above four or six lines at a sitting. Whether my manner of writing it out was new, I know not, but it was not without singularity. Having very little spare time from my flock, which was unruly enough, I folded and stitched a few sheets of paper, which I carried in my pocket. I had no ink-horn; but in place of it I borrowed a small phial, which I fixed in a hole in the breast of my waistcoat; and having a cork fastened by a piece of twine, it answered the purpose fully as well. Thus equipped, whenever a leisure minute or two offered, and I had nothing else to do, I sat down and wrote out my thoughts as I found them. This is still my invariable practice in writing prose.[38]

Was the "poeter" also trying his hand at prose? Though Hogg's description of his start as a writer mentions only

---

[37] Garden, pp. 21-2.   [38] "Autobiography," p. 443.

song-writing, yet he claims that most of *The Winter Evening Tales* were written "in early life, when [he] was a shepherd among the mountains."[39] However, this may be an error of memory, or an attempt to make the writing of the *Tales* seem more glamorous.

His method of writing poetry was different from his method of writing songs or prose. Whatever the length of the piece, he composed and revised it in his head, or with the help of a slate; then wrote it down "as fast as the A, B, C." And once the verses were written, he would not correct them. This practice he followed throughout his life.[40]

He had, with little assistance, taught himself to read, and he was learning to write; he had, for his own pleasure mostly, begun to compose songs and ballads; and it is possible that he had written some prose. To make him an author, something more was needed. The decisive influence was hearing of Robert Burns. One day, he tells us, in the summer of 1797, the year after Burns' death, a "half-daft man named John Scott" came to him while he was watching his flock, and amused him with a recitation of "Tam o' Shanter."[41] Hogg was ravished with delight, and right then learned the poem from beginning to end. (It would remain his favourite poem.) Scott told him that it was made by "one Robert Burns, the sweetest poet that ever was born; but that he was now dead, and his place would never be supplied." This, says Hogg, formed a new epoch in his life. Every day he pondered on the genius and fate of Burns:

> I wept, and always thought with myself—what is to hinder me from succeeding Burns? I too was born on the 25th of January, and I have much more time to read and compose than any

---

[39] "Autobiography," p. 457.

[40] *Ibid.*, pp. 443-4. John Wilson (as Christopher North) describes Hogg in later life "poetizing on a slate, from which he transfers his inspiration to paper, in a fine Roman hand." *Noctes Ambrosianae*, ed. R. Shelton Mackenzie, New York 1863, IV. 142. A similar description is given by R. P. Gillies in *Memoirs of a Literary Veteran*, II. 128. Mrs Garden states: "Hogg learned to write fluently and well, and in his manuscripts scarcely an error of grammar or spelling is to be found." (*Memorials*, pp. 23-4.) She also states that he subscribed to a library "kept by Mr. Elder, in Peebles." But when this was, exactly, she does not say. Perhaps she had the information from Hogg himself.

[41] *Ibid.*, p. 444.

ploughman could have, and can sing more old songs than ever ploughman could in the world. But then I wept again because I could not write. However, I resolved to be a poet, and to follow in the steps of Burns.[42]

Donald Carswell thinks this anecdote "a . . . bare-faced lie." It is unlikely, he argues, that Hogg had never heard of Burns, for "every intelligent peasant in Scotland" had heard of him, and certainly the Laidlaws, with whom Hogg was living, would have known of Burns.[43] Miss Batho takes exception to the end of Hogg's story. At that time, she says, not only could he write, but he had published.[44] Certainly, Hogg may be exaggerating—he was never loath to exaggerate—but the story seems acceptable in the main. It is perfectly possible for a self-educated man to have gaps in his knowledge; and among people who are not literary, though poems and tales may be read, the names of authors are not particularly noted. Also, in saying that he could not write, Hogg may only mean that he found it difficult to do so.

The young author was slow to be recognised. He joined a literary society of shepherds; he submitted his writings to his friend William Laidlaw, who alone encouraged him; and he collected his poems and songs.[45] "Donald M'Donald," one of his songs, became very popular and was sung every day in the mess of a general named M'Donald who thought it had been written in praise of him, yet "no one ever knew or inquired who was the author."[46]

In 1801, believing that he had become "a grand poet," Hogg decided to publish a pamphlet of poems, at his own expense. The idea came to him while he was in Edinburgh to sell sheep; he wrote down the poems from memory and

---

[42] "Autobiography," p. 444. Compare this adulation of Burns with Hogg's later remarks in the tale "The Mysterious Bride." He calls Burns "a certain, or rather uncertain, bard," whose best songs were sung "one hundred and fifty years before he was born" (*Tales*, IV. 336).

[43] Donald Carswell, *Sir Walter: A four-part Study in Biography*, London 1930, p. 180.

[44] Batho, p. 9.

[45] See "Storms," in *Tales*, II. 129, for a description of the Shepherds' Literary Society, and "Autobiography," pp. 444-5, for Hogg's own account of his beginnings as an author.

[46] "Autobiography," p. 445.

delivered them to the printer. A thousand copies were printed. Hogg, on receiving a copy and comparing it with the manuscripts he had at home, was disappointed to find many stanzas omitted, others misplaced, and numerous typographical errors. All of these poems, he remarks, were "sad stuff," although he thought them exceedingly good. He was so anxious about the "fate of his poems" that he fell ill, shut himself up in his house, and spent much of his time in bed, waiting to hear something.[47]

In Miss Batho's opinion, Hogg did not have this pamphlet printed from memory. For how could he have remembered the long poems, such as the "Dialogue in a Country Church Yard" and the "Death of Sir Niel Stuart and Donald M'Vane, Esq.," which appear in the pamphlet, and not have been able to recall his songs? The anecdote, she implies, is merely an excuse for his poor judgement, or another example of Hogg's romancing. She surmises that, planning to have a pamphlet published, he had copies of what he thought were his most imposing works in his pocket when he went to Edinburgh.[48]

This pamphlet is the *Scottish Pastorals, Poems, Songs, Etc.*, published by John Taylor in the Grassmarket in January 1801 at the price of a shilling.[49] The *Scots Magazine* included the entire poem, "Willie and Keatie," in the issue of January 1801, as "no unfavourable specimen" of the work, and listed the pamphlet under "New Publications" in the issue of February.[50]

In 1801, Walter Scott, then Sheriff-Depute of Selkirkshire, was gathering old ballads for his collection entitled *The Minstrelsy of the Scottish Border*.[51] Hogg's friend William Laidlaw was asked to help and, knowing that Hogg's relations had preserved ballads and stories, he asked Hogg to supply them. Hogg obliged, making an effort to take down the ballads

---

[47] From "The earliest letter we have of his . . . dated January, 1801, and . . . addressed to Mr. William Laidlaw." Garden, p. 36.

[48] Batho, p. 14.

[49] James Hogg, *Scottish Pastorals, Poems, Songs, Etc.* (Edinburgh: Printed by John Taylor, 1801). There are copies of this rare pamphlet in the British Museum, the National Library of Scotland, and the Library of the University of Edinburgh.

[50] *Scots Magazine*, LXIII (Jan. 1801), pp. 52-4, and (Feb. 1801), p. 119.

[51] *Minstrelsy of the Scottish Border*, ed. T. F. Henderson, Edinburgh and New York 1902.

exactly as he heard them, and passing them along to Laidlaw, who in turn sent them to Scott.[52]   One evening in the summer of 1801, as Hogg tells it, he was hoeing in the fields at Ettrick-house when old Wat Shiel came "posting over the water" and told him to go to Ramseycleuch as fast as his feet could carry him, for there were some gentlemen there, "the Shirra an' some o' his gang," who wanted to see him.   Hogg hurried home to put on his Sunday clothes, but on the way he met Scott and William Laidlaw, who were coming to visit him.   The visitors stayed at the cottage of the Hoggs for nearly two hours.[53]

But Hogg's memory is unreliable.   In his account of the meeting, he says that it was after he had seen the first volumes of the *Minstrelsy*—and they were published in January 1802. Also, as Miss Batho points out, the meeting took place the day before Scott visited the Hoggs at home.   Hogg went to Ramseycleuch, where Scott and Laidlaw were spending the night, bringing his ballad manuscripts with him.   He stayed until nearly three in the morning.   The next day they repaid the visit.[54]   However, though Hogg's account of the facts is mistaken, his memory of his first impressions rings true.   He and the "Shirra" were friends "on the very first exchange of sentiments."[55]   It was the beginning of a friendship that would last, with one interruption, until Scott's death.

While Scott was visiting the Hoggs, Margaret Laidlaw sang the ballad of "Old Maitlan" and cleared up some doubts the Sheriff had about its authenticity.   He asked her if she thought it had ever been printed.   Her answer was, in Hogg's recollection:

> "Oo, na, na, sir, it was never printed i' the world, for my brothers an' me learned it frae auld Andrew Moor, an' he learned it, an' mony mae, frae auld Baby Mettlin Maitland, that was house-keeper to the first laird o' Tushilaw."
>
> "Then that must be a very auld story, indeed, Margaret," said he.

---

[52] Batho, pp. 18-22 ; and Robert Carruthers, "Abbotsford Notanda," in Robert Chambers, *Life of Sir Walter Scott . . . with Abbotsford Notanda*, by Robert Carruthers, ed. W. Chambers, Edinburgh 1871, p. 129.

[53] "Autobiography," pp. 461 ff, and James Hogg, *The Domestic Manners and Private Life of Sir Walter Scott*, Glasgow 1834, pp. 59-61.

[54] Carruthers, *Abbotsford Notanda*, pp. 129-31.   [55] *Domestic Manners*, p. 60.

"Ay, it is that ! It is an auld story ! But mair nor that, except George Warton and James Steward, there was never ane o' my sangs prentit till ye prentit them yoursell, an' ye hae spoilt them a'thegither. They war made for singing, an' no for reading ; and they're nouther right spelled nor right setten down."

"Heh—heh—heh ! Take ye that, Mr. Scott," said Laidlaw.

Mr. Scott answered by a hearty laugh, and the recital of a verse . . . and my mother gave him a rap on the knee with her open hand, and said, "It is true enough, for a' that."[56]

On the appearance of the *Minstrelsy*, Hogg tells us, he was dissatisfied with the imitations of the ancient ballads that it contained, and himself set about imitating ballads. He selected traditional stories and put them in metre, "by chanting them to certain old tunes."[57] In these, he says, he was more successful than in anything he had hitherto tried, "although they were still but rude pieces of composition."[58]

In 1801, Hogg had travelled into the Highlands—apparently on a holiday—as far as the sources of the Dee. In the following year he visited Edinburgh, saw two plays, *The Heir at Law* and *Hamlet,* and went to the races at Leith. He proceeded to Perth, then into Athol, and further still into the Highlands, as far as Rannoch. A record of the journey is given in letters from "A Shepherd" published in the *Scots Magazine*—which was the first periodical to publish a poem by Hogg and the only one to notice the *Scottish Pastorals*—under the title, "A Journey through the Highlands of Scotland in the Months of July and August 1802, in a Series of Letters to ——, Esq." A covering letter signed "S.W.," printed in preface to Hogg's article, states that the author is in fact a shepherd, and commends his natural powers of observation. The benefactor, it is fairly certain, was Scott.[59]

Lockhart has an anecdote which, though touched with the distaste he often shows for Hogg, draws an amusing portrait of the shepherd in 1803. On one of his visits to Scott in Edinburgh, Hogg was invited to dinner at Castle Street.

---

[56] "Autobiography," p. 461.   [57] *Ibid.*, p. 446.
[58] *Ibid.*   [59] *Scots Magazine,* LXIV (Oct. 1802), pp. 812-18.

When Hogg entered the drawingroom, Mrs. Scott, being at
the time in a delicate state of health, was reclining on a sofa.
The Shepherd, after being presented, and making his best bow,
forthwith took possession of another sofa placed opposite to
hers, and stretched himself thereupon at all his length; for,
as he said afterwards, "I thought I could never do wrong to
copy the lady of the house." As his dress at this period was
precisely that in which any ordinary herdsman attends cattle
to the market, and as his hands, moreover, bore most legible
marks of a recent sheep-smearing, the lady of the house did
not observe with perfect equanimity the novel usage to which
her chintz was exposed. The Shepherd, however, remarked
nothing of all this—dined heartily and drank freely, and, by
jest, anecdote, and song, afforded plentiful merriment to the
more civilized part of the company. As the liquor operated,
his familiarity increased and strengthened ; from "Mr. Scott,"
he advanced to "Sherra," and thence to "Scott," "Walter,"
and "Wattie,"—until, at supper, he fairly convulsed the whole
party by addressing Mrs. Scott as "Charlotte."[60]

A few days later Hogg wrote to Scott to apologise for his
conduct—blaming it on the liquor, but hoping it could not
have been so bad after all, as Mrs Scott had stayed in the
company. He assured the Sheriff that he would bear in mind
his parting advice not to be "ensnared by the loose women in
town." He had an "utter abhorrence . . . at those seminaries
of lewdness." He went on to ask Scott's advice as to how to
go about getting his songs published. He had enough to make
a hundred closely-printed pages. Would Scott be his patron
and accept the dedication? Failing that, what did Scott think
of Lady Dalkeith? Neither word nor sentiment, he assured his
prospective benefactor, would offend the most delicate ear.[61]

Scott accepted the dedication, wrote a prefatory letter to
the Memoir (the nucleus of Hogg's "Autobiography") and
persuaded Constable to take the book. But *The Mountain Bard*
was not published until 1807.

In 1803 Hogg travelled into the Western Highlands and the
Isles. Again, in 1804, he visited the Highlands, this time with
the purpose of arranging to emigrate to the Island of Harris,

[60] Lockhart, *The Life of Sir Walter Scott*, I. 408-9.
[61] *Ibid.*, pp. 409-11, *passim.*

B

for his lease of Ettrickhouse had expired.[62]   His poem, "Fare-well to Ettrick," relates to this:

> Fareweel green Ettrick, fare-thee-weel !
> I own I'm something wae to leave thee ;
> Nane kens the half o' what I feel,
> Nor half the cause I hae to grieve me ![63]

But the Harris plan was abandoned; thanks to a legal technicality Hogg lost his savings, which he had invested in buying a farm there.   He spent a few months in Cumberland, and on his return to Scotland went to work as a shepherd for a Mr Harkness, at Mitchelslack in Nithsdale, where he stayed until 1807.[64]   In 1808 he began the valuation of land (a part-time job he kept until 1811).[65]   It was while he was at Nithsdale that the young poet Allan Cunningham made a journey especially to see Hogg, and recited his poems to him.[66]   The episode, Douglas remarks, shows that Hogg's fame was spreading.[67]

He was contributing frequently to the *Scots Magazine*; a score of his ballads and songs were published in it between May 1803, and January 1806.   When *The Mountain Bard* appeared, it contained several of these pieces with some revisions, and also work that had not yet been published. Lockhart witnesses to the popularity of the book and states that "James Hogg was by this time beginning to be generally known and appreciated in Scotland."[68]   Hogg even made money out of *The Mountain Bard*—about £214.   In this year, too, he published *The Shepherd's Guide: being a Practical Treatise on the Diseases of Sheep*, a manual that was awarded a prize by the Highland Society.[69]

[62] "Autobiography," p. 446.   Hogg's resolution to emigrate was not as unusual as it may seem.   Many Border shepherds had already migrated into the Highlands, and had even penetrated into the Islands, during the last twenty-five years or so.

[63] *Works*, II. 98.

[64] "Autobiography," p. 446.

[65] Concerning Hogg's work as a land agent, see the letter to his brother William (Edinburgh, 8 Oct. 1811) quoted in Garden, *Memorials*, p. 51.

[66] "Autobiography," pp. 464-65.

[67] Douglas, p. 45.

[68] Lockhart, *Life of Sir Walter Scott*, II. 177.

[69] James Hogg, *The Shepherd's Guide : being a practical treatise on the diseases of sheep*, Edinburgh 1807.

According to Lockhart, at about this time Hogg's "prime ambition was to procure an ensigncy in a military regiment." Scott objected that the pay was small. There was another objection, says Lockhart, that Hogg's friends considered but did not mention to him: his nerves were "not heroically strung." This, Lockhart states, "was in truth no secret among his early inmates, though he had not measured himself at all exactly on that score, and was even tempted, when he found there was no chance of the militia epaulette, to threaten that he would 'list for a soldier' in a marching regiment."[70]

Nothing came of his military plans. But from *The Mountain Bard* and *The Shepherd's Guide* he had nearly £300. He therefore decided to set up as a farmer. He went into partnership with a friend, Adam Brydon, and leased the farm of Locherben in Yarrow.

Now, as throughout his life, Hogg was plagued by mismanagement and money troubles; he was not a good manager —though he was not always to blame. He undertook to lease the farm of Cofardine about seven miles to the west, and it appears that he tried to run both farms at the same time.[71] His partner Brydon was a hard drinker, or reputed to be, and between them they produced a state of affairs of which there is a lively account in the reminiscences of John Morrison, the land-surveyor.[72] Morrison visited Hogg's farm at Locherben and, Hogg being absent, was entertained by his housekeeper, "a very good-looking girl."[73] Morrison told Scott, as they talked about it later, that the expedition had been "more like a scene in romance than an adventure in real life," and had given him a high opinion of Hogg's taste. "Happy rogue!" said Scott. "I am well informed that he has put more pretty girls through his fingers than any fellow in Ettrick Forest."[74] In a subsequent visit to Hogg's farm at Cofardine, Morrison found all the sheep on the wrong side of the hill and the master

[70] Lockhart, *Life of Sir Walter Scott*, II. 177.
[71] "Autobiography," p. 446.
[72] John Morrison, "Random Reminiscences of Sir Walter Scott, of the Ettrick Shepherd, Sir Henry Raeburn, etc.," in *Tait's Edinburgh Magazine*, x (Sep. 1843) p. 573.
[73] *Ibid.*
[74] *Op. cit.*, p. 574.

absent, "feasting, drinking, dancing, and fiddling, etc."[75] When Hogg turned up, Morrison advised him to leave farming, come to Edinburgh, and attend to literary business. Hogg agreed, for, he told Morrison, "he had in contemplation a long poem about Queen Mary."[76]

For three years Hogg struggled on, dividing his efforts between writing, farming, and fiddling. His schemes failed, his property was taken by his creditors, and he found that no one, now that he had been a farmer, wished to employ him again as a shepherd. In February 1810, he tells us, "in utter desperation, I took my plaid about my shoulders, and marched away to Edinburgh, determined, since no better could be, to push my fortune as a literary man."[77]

He was forty years old.

In Edinburgh Hogg had two good friends, John Grieve and his partner, a man named Scott, hatters by trade. For six months he lived with them; they helped him with money and clothes, and through them he made acquaintances. One of these was James Gray, a master in the High School. Hogg fell in love with Gray's sister-in-law, Margaret, but it was ten years before he could afford to marry her.

Early in the summer of 1810 he published *The Forest Minstrel*, a collection of poems by various writers, dedicated to the Duchess of Buccleuch. His was the largest contribution. In general, Hogg says, the songs were not good, but the worst were his own, for he inserted "every ranting rhyme that [he] had made in [his] youth, to please the circles about the fireside in the country."[78] Besides, he knew no more of human life or manners than a child. The book was published to make money, but did not.

His next venture was to publish a weekly paper. *The Spy* first appeared on 1 Sept. 1810. It was edited and mostly written by Hogg, and published by James Robertson, a bookseller in Nicholson Street. In the third and fourth numbers, the publication of a *risqué* prose tale, "On Instability

---

[75] John Morrison, "Random Reminiscences of Sir Walter Scott, of the Ettrick Shepherd, Sir Henry Raeburn, etc.," in *Tait's Edinburgh Magazine*, x (Sep. 1843) p. 574.

[76] *Ibid.*   [77] "Autobiography," p. 446.   [78] *Ibid.* p. 447.

in One's Calling" (later revised and republished as "The Adventures of Basil Lee") lost him half his readers. The "literary ladies," Hogg says, agreed "that [he] would never write a sentence which deserved to be read." He despised "the fastidiousness and affectation of the people."[79]

Besides "Basil Lee," there were other good tales in *The Spy* which Hogg would revise and publish again, among them: "Story of the Ghost of Lochmaben" (reprinted as "The Wife of Lochmaben"), "The Country Laird" ("The Wool-Gatherer"), "Love of Fame" ("Adam Bell") and "Duncan Campbell." The verse included songs such as "Lock the Door Lariston," "What gars the parting Daybeam blush?" "Could this ill Warl' hae been contriv'd," and poems, among them "Macgregor" and "King Edward's Dream." The stories and poems were interspersed with essays.

The Spy failed after fifty-two numbers. In his last editorial the author took an acerbated farewell of his readers. His efforts, he said, had without doubt met with at least as much encouragement as they deserved; he frankly acknowledged that the encouragement had not been much to boast of. As his name had become known the number of subscribers had diminished. "The learned, the enlightened, and polite circles of this flourishing metropolis, disdained to be either amused or instructed by the ebulitions of humble genius."[80] He had had spiteful enemies; but, worse, he had had pretended friends, "liberal in their advices, and ardent in their professions of friendship, [who] yet took every method in their power to lessen the work in the esteem of others, by branding its author with designs the most subversive of all civility and decorum, and which, of all others, were the most distant from his heart."[81] The editorial terminated with reflexions upon mortality and an expression of confidence in the Christian faith.

As a young shepherd, Hogg had been member of a literary society and had found the discussions valuable. In Edinburgh, with a few other young men, he formed a debating society, "The Forum." The meetings were held weekly; the public was admitted for sixpence, and for three years attendance

---

[79] "Autobiography," p. 447.   [80] *The Spy*, LII (24 Aug. 1811), p. 409.
[81] *Ibid.*

was large. Hogg was appointed secretary, though never paid; he spoke every night, and was, he says, "a prodigious favourite." This public testing, in his opinion, helped to form his taste.

> Of this I am certain, that I was greatly the better for it, and I may safely say, I never was in a school before. I might and would have written "The Queen's Wake" had the Forum never existed, but without the weekly lessons that I got there I could not have succeeded as I did.[82]

But the meetings were sometimes ludicrous, especially in the formality of the presidents, and Hogg wrote a musical farce, "The Forum, a Tragedy for Cold Weather," in which the members, including himself, were satirised.

In 1811, being advised by Grieve to return to poetry, he prepared *The Queen's Wake* for publication:

> . . . having some ballads or metrical tales by me, which I did not like to lose, I planned "The Queen's Wake," in order that I might take these all in, and had it ready in a few months after it was first proposed.[83]

According to Hogg, he took the book first to Constable, who received him coldly, saying that if Hogg obtained two hundred subscribers to protect the publisher against loss, he would put up £100, and print a thousand copies. Hogg set about this reluctantly. But then "one George Goldie, a young bookseller in Princes Street," whom Hogg had met at the Forum, asked to see the manuscript. Hogg, though "predetermined to have nothing to do with him," let him see the book. The next time Hogg met him, Goldie wanted to publish it, outbidding Constable and the amount offered by the subscribers. But Hogg, loath to leave Constable, went to see him again. He was in a bad humour, having quarrelled with Scott, and "would do nothing further than curse all the poets, and declare that he had met with more ingratitude from literary men than all the rest of the human race." Goldie got the book, and published it in the spring of 1813.[84]

That is Hogg's account. Goldie himself declared later that

---

[82] "Autobiography," p. 448.   [83] *Ibid.*
[84] *Ibid.*, p. 449.

he had never been to the Forum, and that Hogg, having been rejected by Constable, waited upon him, and expressed his opinion of Constable in terms "too coarse and vulgar to be repeated."[85]

The Queen's Wake, published in 1813, with a dedication to Princess Charlotte of Wales, was Hogg's most ambitious work to date—not a collection of songs and ballads, but a book with a plan. The subject, a wake, or celebration, held by Mary Queen of Scots at Holyrood, during which various minstrels competed for a prize, allowed Hogg to show his ability on a large scale and in various forms. The poems of Scott and Byron had formed a taste for long narratives in verse, and Hogg might hope for great rewards, if successful.

No one but Grieve had seen the poem, and he had only assured the author "it would do." Hogg walked about the streets of Edinburgh, looking at his book in the bookshop windows, but not daring to go in. "I was like a man between death and life, waiting for the sentence of the jury." A man he knew, the whisky-merchant William Dunlop, came up to him and, by Hogg's account:

> "Ye useless poetical deevil that ye're !" said he, "what hae ye been doing a' this time ?"—"What doing, Willie ! what do you mean ?" "Ye hae been pestering us wi' fourpenny papers an' daft shilly-shally sangs, an' bletherin' an' speakin' i' the Forum, an' yet had stuff in ye to produced a thing like this !"— "Ay, Willie," said I, "have you seen my new beuk ?"—"Ay, faith, that I have, man ; and it has cheated me out o' a night's sleep. Ye hae hit the right nail on the head now. Yon's the very thing, sir . . . ."[86]

With the observation that no one would have thought there was so much in that sheep's head of Hogg's, Dunlop parted from him.

From that day, Hogg tells us, everyone spoke well of the work. Every review, except the *Eclectic*, praised it.[87] "The reading public," in Mrs Garden's words, "was taken by storm. 'Who,' they asked, 'was this poet who sang the beautiful lay of "Kilmeny," and the incomparable "Witch of Fife ?" Under what bushel had he been hiding his talents all these

[85] Batho, p. 69.   [86] "Autobiography," p. 449.
[87] *Ibid.*

years?' " From that hour "James Hogg was acknowledged as a man of genius." He was introduced to literary celebrities; eminent men and women wished to know him, and it became the fashion in Edinburgh to have him to supper. His writing-table was covered with notes of invitation.[88] The "Auto-biography" informs us that he made himself "rather scarce," except to a few friends.[89]

On the other hand, there were those who asserted "that it was impossible that a work possessing so high and so varied excellencies could be produced by a man who had actually spent the greater part of his life in the character of a shepherd."[90]

Within the year *The Queen's Wake* went into a second edition, and in 1814 into a third—whereupon Goldie, who had also published Hogg's *Hunting of Badlewe*, became bankrupt. The remainder of the third edition was published in 1814 by William Blackwood, one of the trustees of the bankrupt estate: this publication is regarded as the fourth edition. A fifth edition was got out by subscription in the spring of 1819, and a sixth in the summer.[91]

Francis Jeffrey reviewed the third edition in the *Edinburgh*

[88] Garden, *Memorials*, pp. 55-7, *passim*.   [89] "Autobiography," p. 450.
[90] Letter from James Gray to William Hogg (Edinburgh, 21 Oct. 1813) in Garden, *Memorials*, p. 62.
[91] Hogg's dealings with Constable, Goldie, and Blackwood, with all of whom at one time or another, he quarrelled, are of interest to Hogg's biographer, but add little to our understanding of his works. In the "Autobiography" Hogg himself shows a lively concern over disputes of literary business which, in his opinion, affected his good name, and the "Autobiography" declines in interest accordingly. Hogg's biographers take sides, but the results show mainly their own prejudice. Miss Batho finds that Hogg used Goldie badly. When there were rumours of Goldie's failing, Hogg "went behind his back" to Constable to ask him to publish the third edition of *The Queen's Wake*. She approves of Goldie's public castigation of Hogg (Batho, p. 70). On the other hand, Douglas finds that an examination of Hogg's quarrel with Goldie "fails to bring forward any-thing against Hogg which tends in any respect to lower him in our estimation" (Douglas, p. 74). Miss Batho admits the unimportance of these matters when, in speaking of Hogg's disputes with Blackwood and the *Blackwood's Magazine* group, she concludes, "all the quarrels, with one exception, were made up and forgotten" (Batho, p. 103).
For information about Hogg's dealings with his publishers, the reader may refer to these works : Thomas Constable, *Archibald Constable and His Literary Correspondents*, Edinburgh 1873 ; Mrs Oliphant, *Annals of a Publishing House ; William Blackwood and His Sons*, Edinburgh 1897 ; Samuel Smiles, *A Publisher and His Friends. Memoirs and Correspondence of the Late John Murray*, London 1891.

Review, quoting liberally from the poems "Kilmeny" and
"The Abbot M'Kinnon." He gave a short account of Hogg's
career and congratulated him upon preferring to starve for
poetry rather than to seek ease and affluence by renouncing
it. The poet, said Jeffrey, had sought success by the fairest
and most manly means; neither poverty nor ambition had
made him obsequious. He offered an analysis of the merits
and faults of Hogg's poetry, and concluded with the opinion:
"Mr. Hogg is undoubtedly a person of very considerable
genius."[92] But the panegyric was slightly marred by Jeffrey's
comment that the success of *The Queen's Wake* had not gone
beyond the narrow sphere to which the personal influence
of the author or the publishers extended. Perhaps it was this
that drew from Hogg the seemingly ungrateful observation
that Jeffrey had not ventured to review the work until its
success was sure.[93]

Hogg was famous and until the end of his life would remain
so. He might have thought that, from this time forward, fame
would go hand in hand with prosperity. It did not.

R. P. Gillies draws an interesting, if somewhat exaggerated,
picture of Hogg's effect in Edinburgh society. Gillies claims
that he was the first who brought Hogg "into repute as a
welcome guest among what are called the upper classes of
society," and adds that in this purpose Lady Williamson
assisted "by her dinner parties."[94] The rustic Hogg, like his
great predecessor Burns, pleased the literati.

> I think the appearance of the good honest Shepherd in our
> Edinburgh society, acquired by degrees a marked influence on
> the tone of that society, and even gave a new impetus to our
> literature. Numberless were the convivial parties at dinner
> and supper which, but for him, would never have taken place
> at all, and but for his quaint originality of manners and in-
> exhaustible store of good songs, would have been comparatively
> so *fade* and lifeless, that no one would have desired a repetition.
> Farther, I am thoroughly convinced that his example gave a

---

[92] *Edinburgh Review*, xxiv (Nov. 1814-Feb. 1815), p. 173.

[93] "Autobiography," p. 449.

[94] This is contradicted by Hogg's own statement (in *The Domestic Manners
and Private Life of of Sir Walter Scott*, p. 106) that Scott ensured him "a welcome
among all the genteel company of the kingdom. . . ."

new impulse to literature. There were individuals who, observing with wonder the facility and pertinacity with which he composed, and the undeniable merit of his productions, became ashamed that, with all their book knowledge, they should allow themselves to be outdone, and cast utterly into shade by an illiterate shepherd, a man also who seemed to give himself no thought nor care about his own works, but to be engaged day after day, or rather night after night, in scraping on the fiddle, singing his own ballads, and, with the help of Glenlivat, making himself and others uproariously merry! In truth, after his appearance, the number of aspirant authors increased wonderfully.[95]

Besides being busy as a cause of wit in other men, Hogg plunged headlong into authorship. Like his contemporaries, we may be astonished at his "facility and pertinacity"; even by the standards of the age he was prolific. He wrote books— some of them very long indeed; poems, sketches, tales, and articles, which were published in various periodicals. He lent his hand to "calendars" and compilations. He gathered his periodical writings and hurried them into covers, sometimes revising, sometimes not. By his own count, made at the end of his life, between 1813 and 1819 he published fifteen "volumes," including *The Queen's Wake*; and eleven "volumes" before and after that period. "Making in all thirty volumes, which, if the quality were at all proportioned to the quantity, are enough for any man's life."[96]

The Queen's Wake and *The Hunting of Badlewe*—which had helped to founder Goldie—were followed by *The Pilgrims of the Sun* (1815), a lengthy narrative poem. In 1816 Hogg published another long narrative poem, *Mador of the Moor*—which had actually been written before *The Pilgrims of the Sun*—and also *The Poetic Mirror*, a collection of imitations and parodies in verse. Hogg, by his own account, had conceived the *Mirror* as an anthology of famous poets; but as they had failed to send poems he had written imitations instead.[97] The book was published anonymously. In the "Autobiography" he entertains the curious thought that, had the parodies of

---

[95] R. P. Gillies, *Memoirs of a Literary Veteran*, II. 130, 133-4.
[96] "Autobiography," p. 458   [97] *Ibid.*, p. 454.

Wordsworth been a little less obvious, his work might have passed as the genuine productions of the poets and had greater popularity.[98]

None of these works brought Hogg the affluence that the success of *The Queen's Wake* might have led him to expect. For a while he toyed with the idea of writing for the stage, and in 1817 published *Dramatic Tales*, a collection of poetic dramas. Though "Sir Anthony Moore" was submitted "to the players," Hogg informs us that he "shrunk from the idea of intrusting [his] character as a poet in the hands of every bungling and absurd actor."[99] Whether this is true, or the drama was rejected, the incident was decisive. At this time, he relates:

> I had . . . commenced an epic poem on a regular plan, and I finished two books of it, pluming myself that it was to prove my greatest work. But seeing that the poetical part of these dramas excited no interest in the public, I felt conscious that no poetry I should ever be able to write would do so; or if it did, the success would hinge upon some casualty, on which it did not behove me to rely. So from that day to this, save now and then an idle song to beguile a leisure hour, I determined to write no more poetry.[1]

The "epic poem," *Queen Hynde*, was finished and published in 1825. Some of the "idle" songs of which he speaks are among his best poetry; but from 1817 to the end of his life, most of his writing was in prose.

Hogg—as we have noted—had dedicated *The Forest Minstrel* to the Duchess of Buccleuch; she gave him a hundred guineas in return. On 17 Mar. 1814, he wrote her a letter in which, apologising for his "applications for this and that," and acknowledging that he had again and again received her "private bounty," he requested the continuance of her patronage. The letter goes on to say there is a farm on her estate of which "a certain poor bard, who has two old parents, each of them upwards of eighty-four years of age," could make good use. "A single line, from a certain very great and very

---

[98] "Autobiography," p. 454.   [99] *Ibid.*   [1] *Ibid.*

beautiful lady, to a certain Mr. Riddell [the Duke's Chamber-
lain at Branksome Castle] would insure that small pendicle
to the bard at once."[2]   The Duchess mentioned the matter to
her husband; five months later she died, and the Duke, feeling
himself obligated by her query on Hogg's behalf, offered him
the farm of Altrive in Yarrow at a nominal rent.

It is sometimes difficult to fix the dates of Hogg's movements.
On points that would seem easy to determine the evidence is
often confusing.   When did Hogg move to Altrive?   The
"Autobiography" states that from 1809 to 1814 he resided in
Edinburgh.[3]   On receiving the farm from Buccleuch, Hogg
says, "I then began and built a handsome cottage on my new
farm, and forthwith made it my head-quarters."[4]   Douglas
says that Hogg "entered upon possession of the little farm"
in the spring of 1815, and from the description that follows it
seems that he was living at Altrive from that time forward.[5]
On the other hand, Miss Batho states flatly: "Hogg moved to
Altrive in 1817."[6]

It seems that between May 1815 and April 1820, when he
married, Hogg lived sometimes at Altrive and sometimes in
Edinburgh.   We know that he was at Altrive in June 1815, for
Wilson visited him there and surprised him in his cottage
bottling whisky.   The house itself was, in Wilson's opinion,
"not habitable," but the situation was good and might be
made "very pretty."[7]   According to Gillies, Hogg found that
at Altrive he was too often visited by friends, and was compelled
to stay in Edinburgh, at John Grieve's house in George Square,
as a place of "retirement and refuge."[8]

Whatever difficulties his new situation brought, the gift
of Altrive enabled Hogg to realise certain pleasures on which
he had set his mind.   Writing to John Murray in May 1815,
he declared his intention of leaving Edinburgh in a few
days for his "little farm on Yarrow."   There he would

[2] Lockhart, *Life of Sir Walter Scott*, III. 293-5, *passim*.
[3] "Autobiography," p. 458.
[4] *Ibid.*
[5] Douglas, pp. 77 ff.
[6] Batho, p. 104.
[7] Mrs Gordon, *"Christopher North,"* a Memoir, London 1879, p. 133.
[8] Gillies, *Memoirs of a Literary Veteran*, II. 241-2.

have a confused summer, for he had as yet no house to live in. But:

> I hope by-and-by to have some fine fun there with you, fishing in Saint Mary's Loch and the Yarrow, eating bull-trout, singing songs and drinking whisky. This little possession is what I stood much in need of—a habitation among my native hills was what of all the world I desired; and if I had a little more money at command, I would just be as happy a man as I know of; but that is an article of which I am ever in want.[9]

During these years he also made short holiday journeys into the Highlands and journeys to visit Wordsworth and other acquaintances.[10] Meanwhile, he was saving to build a new, habitable cottage at Altrive to replace the "auld clay biggin," and to marry Margaret Phillips. Hogg's mother died before he could bring her to Altrive, but he installed his old father there. In 1819, the new cottage was built—at a cost that ate into Hogg's funds.[11] In April 1802, Hogg and Margaret were married, and set up housekeeping at Altrive.

About this time, Hogg had a thousand pounds owing to him, from his several publishers.[12] He also expected a dowry from his wife's father, a prosperous man. On these expectations, he "determined once more to farm on a larger scale," and took a nine-year lease on the large farm of Mount Benger, adjoining his own. This farm had already ruined two men in six years.[13]

Soon after, his father-in-law suffered financial losses, and Hogg found himself, instead of receiving help, obliged to give it. Referring to an earlier disappointment, Mrs Garden has said: "No pecuniary results of a satisfactory nature followed."[14] The same might be said of all Hogg's schemes.

Stocking Mount Benger with sheep, cows, and horses; buying farm tools, crop, and manure; draining, fencing, and building; writing to pay for all this, and getting into debt;

[9] Hogg (to John Murray, 7 May 1815), in Samuel Smiles, *A Publisher and his Friends*, i. p. 349.
[10] Hogg (to Mrs Bald "Maggernie [sic] Castle," 18 Jun. 1816), in Garden, pp. 69-72.
[11] Hogg (to Margaret Phillips, Aug. 1819), in Garden, p. 121.
[12] "Autobiography," p. 459.   [13] *Ibid.*   [14] Garden, p. 48.

and at the end of the nine-year lease being left "without a
sixpence in the world"—this might have soured another man.
But Hogg remained cheerful. None of his reverses, he assures
us, ever preyed on his spirits. He has done all for the best,
acted honestly, and laughed at the futility of his calculations,
still hoping to make more money as soon as possible. "I never
knew either man or woman who has been so uniformly happy
as I have been," he claims, and attributes this to a good
constitution and to "the conviction that a heavenly gift,
conferring the powers of immortal song, was inherent in [his]
soul."[15]   His married life has been so smooth and happy that
he cannot distinguish one part from another, "save by some re-
markably good days of fishing, shooting, and curling on the ice."[16]

He was now a celebrity, and his house was open to the many
friends and strangers who dropped in. For these he provided
food, drink, entertainment, and, sometimes, a bed. He might
take them over to the hostel kept by a famous old lady, Tibby
Shiels, on St Mary's Loch; or get up an expedition with rod
or gun. On his visits to Edinburgh, once or twice a year on
business—when he seized the chance to entertain and be
entertained—he would stay at Watson's Selkirk and Peebles
Inn in the Candlemaker Row, and on the night before
returning to Yarrow he would give a party. Robert Chambers,
who was present at one of these occasions, says that when the
word got round, "something like a Highland host" descended
upon Hogg. "Each of the men he had spoken to came, like
a chief, with a long train of friends, most of them unknown to
the hero of the evening, but all of them eager to spend a night
with the Ettrick Shepherd."[17]

As a celebrity in his own right, Hogg was acquainted with
several of his famous contemporaries. Southey knew and
admired the Shepherd.[18]   Washington Irving, while visiting

[15] "Autobiography," p. 459.   [16] *Ibid.*
[17] William Chambers, *Memoir of Robert Chambers*, Edinburgh 1872, p. 248.
[18] ". . . what I say of the Ettrick Shepherd ever since I have known him and
his writings, is that I admire and esteem and like him." Letter from Southey to
Hogg—"Keswick, 19 Oct. 1821"—Ms. 2245, p. 72, National Library of Scotland.
See also Southey's letter to Hogg (Keswick, 1 Dec. 1814) in Garden, *Memorials*,
p. 74 : ". . . the 'Wake' has equalled all that I expected. . . . The 'Witch of
Fife' is a rich work of fancy. 'Kilmeny' a fine one of imagination, which is a
higher and rarer gift. . . ."

at Abbotsford, wished to see him; but Hogg was busy with his farming.[19]   Byron corresponded with Hogg, urged his own publisher, John Murray, to "make out an alliance" with Hogg, and supported the project of Hogg's *Miscellany*.[20] Writing to Murray from Ravenna, Byron thanks him for sending Hogg's tales, which he finds "rough, but RACY, and welcome."[21]   On the occasion of Byron's marriage Hogg wrote to him saying that he hoped Miss Milbanke "might prove a good *mill* and a *bank* to him," to which his Lordship replied with a "satirical bitter" letter.[22]   The pseudo-Hogg of the *Noctes* tells how he once accompanied Byron on an expedition to Rydal, and spied on Wordsworth "grumblin out some of his havers, and glowering about him like a gawpus," but the story, unfortunately, is not true: Hogg and Byron never met.[23] Hogg's relations with Wordsworth are more notable, and their behaviour in the scene of the Triumphal Arch makes one of the livelier anecdotes of literary life.

As he tells it in the "Autobiography," Hogg had always admired Wordsworth's poetry, and when he met him at John Wilson's house he listened to the English poet "as to a superior being, far exalted above the common walks of life."[24]   Together with Hogg and old Dr Anderson, editor of *The British Poets*, Wordsworth and his wife visited the house of Hogg's father, and the party proceeded to view the Yarrow landscape—an episode commemorated in Wordsworth's "Extempore Effusion Upon the Death of James Hogg":

> When first, descending from the moorlands,
> I saw the stream of Yarrow glide
> Along a bare and open valley,
> The Ettrick Shepherd was my guide. . . .[25]

---

[19] Strout, p. 130.
[20] Moore, *Life of Byron*, Letter 197 (to Murray, Newstead Abbey, 2 Sep. 1814), p. 109.
[21] *Ibid.*, Letter 391 (to Murray, Ravenna, 12 Oct. 1820), p. 458.
[22] "Autobiography," p. 453.
[23] *Noctes*, II. 11.
[24] "Autobiography," p. 463.
[25] *The Poetical Works of William Wordsworth*, ed. E. de Selincourt and Helen Darbishire, Oxford 1946, IV. 276-8.

Hogg visited Wordsworth at Rydal Mount several times, "and certainly never met with anything but the most genuine kindness."[26] But, on one visit to Rydal, Hogg was insulted— or thought he was insulted—by Wordsworth, and thereafter bore a grievance. The episode is related by Hogg in the "Autobiography," and there is a similar version in the *Noctes*.[27] Hogg, Wordsworth, Dorothy Wordsworth, De Quincey, and others had walked out to view the aurora borealis. Dorothy Wordsworth, who was leaning on Hogg's arm, expressed a fear that the phenomenon might prove ominous. Hogg answered: "Hout, me'em! it is neither mair nor less than joost a treumphal arch, raised in honour of the meeting of the poets." Thereupon, Wordsworth grunted and, drawing De Quincey aside, said to him: "Poets? poets? What does the fellow mean? Where are they?"

Who could forgive this, Hogg exclaims. For his part, he never will. He admires Wordsworth, but has a lingering ill-will he cannot get rid of. "It is surely presumption in any man to circumscribe all human excellence within the narrow sphere of his own capacity." Still, he hopes that De Quincey was lying, for he himself did not hear the words.[28]

Hogg's resentment of Wordsworth accounts for the excellence of his parodies of Wordsworth in *The Poetic Mirror*; they are honed to a fine edge. Also, the gibes at Wordsworth uttered by the Shepherd of the *Noctes* echo the grievance.[29]

But Hogg's relations with Wordsworth, Byron, and Southey,

---

[26] "Autobiography," p. 464.   [27] *Noctes*, II. 10.

[28] "Autobiography," pp. 463-4. Miss Batho, in her account of Hogg's and Wordsworth's behaviour in the "triumphal arch" scene, and their relations in general, hastens to tip the balance in Wordsworth's favour. Hogg, she says, once called Wordsworth's lakes "dubs," but Wordsworth took it in good humour. Also, Wordsworth was not offended by *The Poetic Mirror*—if he ever read it. And Wordsworth's "Extempore Effusion on the Death of James Hogg" might have been recognised by "even the Shepherd's vanity" as sufficient amends (Batho, pp. 92, 93). Miss Batho is never unwilling to assume that Hogg is in the wrong in such matters, though she is good enough to say that his "impudence" is "so simple that it rouses rather kindly laughter than wrath . . .," and he is "not undeserving, in spite of some lapses, of the affection which he received from better men" (p. 168). However, the reader who does not share Miss Batho's superiority to her subject may feel that in the "triumphal arch" scene Hogg had cause to be indignant, and that Wordsworth's vanity was no better than the Shepherd's.

[29] *Noctes*, I. 363 ; III. 273, etc.

and with numerous other literary acquaintances, were peripheral. Of far greater importance was his friendship with John Wilson. On reading Wilson's poem, *The Isle of Palms*, Hogg had been "taken with many of his fanciful and visionary scenes, descriptive of bliss and woe." He reviewed the book, and made efforts to meet the author. At length he invited Wilson to dinner—Hogg was then lodging in the Road of Gabriel. "I found him," says Hogg, "so much a man according to my own heart, that for many years we were seldom twenty-four hours asunder, when in town." Hogg returned the visit, going to Wilson's house in Westmorland, "where [they] had some curious doings among the gentlemen and poets of the lakes."[30]

Hogg's friendship with Wilson was instrumental in plunging him into journalism. Hogg, Wilson, and Lockhart became the leading spirits of William Blackwood's new monthly magazine, which would publish Tory opinions and literary criticism, opposing the *Edinburgh Review* and competing with the *Quarterly Review*. On 1 Apr. 1817, the first number of *Blackwood's Edinburgh Magazine* appeared, edited by Thomas Pringle and James Cleghorn. The first number included a tale "Of Pastoral Life" by Hogg.[31] After three numbers the editors went over to Constable—who had lost Scott's Waverley novels to Blackwood and was now his antagonist—taking the list of subscribers with them. Constable set up a magazine of his own, which soon collapsed. Blackwood thereupon undertook to be his own editor. To assist him, he enlisted Hogg, Wilson, Lockhart, and R. P. Gillies. The immediate result of the Blackwood-Constable quarrel was an article in *Blackwood's Magazine* entitled "Translation from an Ancient Chaldee Manuscript."[32] In Biblical language, divided into chapter and verse, the "Chaldee Manuscript" satirised Constable, Jeffrey, Pringle, Cleghorn, and the notable Whigs of Edinburgh. Though Hogg's fellow journalists denied it later, there is no doubt that he wrote most of the articles: the first two chapters, part of the third, and part of the last. By Hogg's

---

[30] "Autobiography," p. 450.
[31] This tale was never reprinted.
[32] *Noctes*, i. xx-xxii.

C

account, Blackwood, on first reading it, did not wish to publish the manuscript; he was persuaded to do so by the others—Lockhart in particular—who made it offensive by adding "a good deal of deevilry of their own." The article that Hogg had written was innocuous, and he would have willingly shown it to Constable and Pringle.[33]

The "Chaldee Manuscript" was received with execration throughout Edinburgh, prosecutions were begun against Blackwood, and he had to pay £1,000 in costs and damages in two years.[34] But the magazine was off to a smashing start; readers looked for more sensations, and the writers did their best to oblige. To the original group were added Thomas Hamilton, William Maginn, John Galt the novelist, D. M. Moir, Thomas Sym, and correspondents.

In 1819, John Wilson began to assume the main editorial work of *Blackwood's Magazine*. Blackwood carried on the business management, but Wilson gradually became recognised as editor.[35] In March 1822, the magazine presented the first of the *Noctes Ambrosianae*, a series of dialogues on which has been founded the popular idea of Hogg as a quaint, uncouth, boozing, strangely talented shepherd—in effect, the Shepherd of the *Noctes*.

Between December 1822 and February 1835, when the series closed, Hogg—in the role of the Shepherd—frequently appeared in the *Noctes*; indeed, second to Wilson—appearing under the pseudonym "Christopher North"—the "Shepherd" is the most frequent actor in the dialogues. The Shepherd speaks on every topic and serves as a foil to Wilson and the other wits of *Maga*, as they styled themselves. But whether the words put into the Shepherd's mouth were uttered by Hogg is another matter. It has pleased some readers to think so. The portraits of Hogg rendered by Edith Batho and Donald Carswell are much the same as that presented in the *Noctes*. Miss Batho informs her reader that the *Noctes* contain "the accent of Hogg with a smaller proportion of valueless matter

---

[33] "Autobiography," p. 455.

[34] For an account of the "Chaldee manuscript" affair, see "Autobiography," pp. 455-6, and "History of Blackwood's Magazine," by Dr. R. Shelton Mackenzie, in *Noctes*, I. x-xi.

[35] "History of Blackwood's Magazine," in *Noctes*, I. xv, xvii.

than Hogg's own prose writings."[36] It is a strange observation, for only in the writings signed with Hogg's name can we know that we have his "accent." In this opinion Miss Batho follows Saintsbury, who declared: "Out of the *Confessions of a Sinner*, Hogg has never signed anything half so good as the best prose passages assigned to him in the *Noctes*. They are what he might have written if he had taken pains: they are in his key and vein; but they are much above him."[37] Carswell says that Hogg, remembering Edinburgh's treatment of Burns, decided to exaggerate his egoism and rusticity in every way. "The result was the low-comedy character of 'The Ettrick Shepherd,' a roaring, swearing, drinking, quarrelsome, vainglorious, impudent, innocent, affectionate, fantastical humorist."[38]

Sir George Douglas attacks this conception:

> In these celebrated dialogues the principal part was borne by the Shepherd. The situation thus brought about was probably unique in literature, for here was a writer of established reputation made to figure month after month as the mouth-piece of remarks and opinions of which he had generally as little previous knowledge as any other member of the public.[39]

Douglas points to the evidence in J. F. Ferrier's Preface to the *Noctes*. Ferrier, eager to show that Wilson was a "consummate artist," states that Hogg in his conversation "never . . . attempted any colloquial display, although there was sometimes a quaintness in his remarks," which

> supplied to the consummate artist who took him in hand the hints out of which to construct a character at once original, extraordinary, and delightful—a character of which James Hogg undoubtedly furnished the germ, but which, as it expanded under the hands of its artificer, acquired a breadth, a firmness, and a power to which the bard of Mount Benger had certainly no pretension.[40]

---

[36] Batho, p. 101.

[37] George Saintsbury, *Essays in English Literature, 1780-1860*, First Series, London 1890, p. 45.

[38] Carswell, pp. 190-1.

[39] Douglas, p. 86.

[40] The source of this is given by Douglas (p. 87) as Ferrier's Preface to the *Noctes Ambrosianae*, p. xvii. I have been unable to locate this edition.

"So, then," Douglas concludes, "it is acknowledged by the advocate of the other side that the real and ideal Shepherds are two very different persons."[41]

To give the *Noctes* a semblance of validity, there were descriptions in the dialogues of the way they were reported. A "short-hand writer," Gurney, was supposed to be concealed in a closet where, himself unobserved, he could jot down the conversations. Then the stenographer's notes were "extended."[42] That Gurney took down some actual conversations there is no reason to doubt. The catch is in the extension, the work of John Wilson. And the style of the *Noctes* throughout is closer to the sentimentality of Wilson than to the style of Hogg's prose. There is a frantic poeticising in the language of the Shepherd that can be found nowhere in Hogg's works.[43]

But can we agree with Douglas that the Shepherd is very different from Hogg? There is evidence that, in fact, Hogg sometimes spoke and behaved like the Shepherd; and Hogg himself seemed to think so. Only when he felt that he was being held up to ridicule did he object to the representation; at other times he positively enjoyed it. Dr Shelton Mackenzie relates an anecdote told to him by "one who knew [Hogg] well, and loved him dearly as a brother."[44] One autumn at Mount Benger, when this friend was staying with Hogg, the Peebles carrier delivered a package of reading matter:

> "The *gleg* eye of the Shepherd singled out *Blackwood*, just issued for the month. The Noctes were laid open in a moment, and presently Hogg's mirth exploded in a loud guffaw, as he exclaimed, slapping his thigh, 'Gad, he's a droll bitch, that Wulson ! an' as wonderfu' as he's droll !' He had alighted upon one of Wilson's raciest personifications of himself, and could not restrain his appreciation of its skill and genius."[45]

The anecdote illustrates two points: that Hogg did not always think that the *Noctes* were a travesty; and that Wilson was, if not always, at least sometimes the author of the Shepherd's conversation.

But Hogg had reason to regret his part in the *Noctes*. He

---

[41] *Ibid.*   [42] *Noctes*, II. 352.   [43] See Appendix B.
[44] Shelton Mackenzie, in *Noctes*, IV. xviii.   [45] *Ibid.*

was complacent and, by all accounts, willing to be the butt
of a good joke. But Wilson, Lockhart, and the other lights of
Maga sometimes pushed him too far. On several occasions
Hogg had a real grievance against *Blackwood's*. It would be
hard to imagine a more insulting review than that of *The
Mountain Bard* published in *Blackwood's* in 1821. The reviewer
was, in all probability, Wilson. A postscript to the review,
signed "C.N.," expressed the hope that "by this tickling the
public sympathy may be awakened, so as to occasion a most
beneficial demand for his [Hogg's] works, and put a few cool
hundreds in his pocket."[46] The tickling consisted of such
remarks as these, levelled at the memoir of Hogg's life which
preceded his poems:

> I take the liberty of sending back Hogg, which has disgusted
> me more severely than anything I have attempted to swallow
> since Macvey's Bacon. . . . Pray, who wishes to know anything
> about his life ? Who, indeed, cares a single farthing whether he
> be at this blessed moment dead or alive. . . . He could not
> write, he says, till he was upwards of twenty years of age. This
> I deny. He cannot write now. . . . The Poetic Mirror is
> now lying before me, and two of the imitations of Wordsworth
> are admirable. But Hogg never wrote one syllable of them.
> They were written by Lord Byron . . . no more did he write
> the Chaldee Manuscript than the five books of Moses. . . .[47]

With a friend such as Wilson, Hogg may have felt he had no
need of enemies.

In 1828 he was still being irritated. Now it was the portrayal in the *Noctes*. Writing to William Blackwood, he said:

> I am exceedingly disgusted with the last beastly "Noctes,"
> and as it is manifest that the old business of mocking and
> ridicule is again beginning, I have been earnestly advised by
> several of my best and dearest friends to let you hear from me
> in a way to which I have a great aversion. But if I do, believe
> me, it shall be free of all malice, and merely to clear my charac-
> ter of sentiments and actions which I detest, and which have
> proved highly detrimental to me.[48]

---

[46] *Blackwood's Edinburgh Magazine*, x (Aug. 1821), p. 52.
[47] *Op. cit.*, x (Aug. 1821), pp. 43 ff.
[48] Hogg (to William Blackwood, Mount Benger, 28 Mar. 1828), in Mrs
Oliphant, *Annals of a Publishing House*, I. 355-6.

In the *Noctes* of March 1831, we see that the representation of the Shepherd had created an unfortunate impression of the life of James Hogg. Lockhart, writing in the *Quarterly Review*, had denied that Hogg was the "boozing buffoon" he was represented to be in the *Noctes*. North and the Shepherd discuss the matter:

> NORTH : Have you read the last number of the Quarterly Review, James ?
>
> SHEPHERD : Na. It hasna come our length yet.
>
> NORTH : 'Tis therein said, James, that in these our Noctes you are absurdly represented as a "boozing buffoon."
>
> SHEPHERD : What ? In the Quarterly ? Na—na—sir. I can swallow a gude deal frae you—but that's bacon I canna bolt.[49]

Had the impression not been current, thanks to the *Noctes*, there would have been no need to deny it.

The Shepherd is conspicuously absent from the *Noctes* between November 1831 and May 1834, when he is welcomed back with *hurrahs*. In the reconciliation the Shepherd declares he will never breathe a word of any misunderstanding that has happened, and that he forgives North (Wilson) absolutely.[50] He remains the principal figure of the dialogues until Hogg's death, when the *Noctes* cease.

It remains to be determined how close the Shepherd is to Hogg, and how far we may accept the Shepherd's conversation as an accurate report of Hogg's. Hogg's own attitude to the *Noctes* must be discounted, for, as we have seen, it varied.

The truth is, it seems, in the middle. The Shepherd is not an absolute misrepresentation, nor is he James Hogg.

In spite of Ferrier's comment, Hogg *did* frequently speak in the vernacular. There was no reason at all why he should not. In Hogg's time, many of the gentry still spoke Scots, and it was not yet regarded as a sign of social inferoirity to do so.[51] Besides, there is evidence that Hogg spoke in Scots not unlike

---

[49] *Noctes*, IV. 262.   [50] *Op. cit.*, V. 218.
[51] However, the Broad Scots spoken in Edinburgh drawing rooms differed considerably from "vulgar" Scots.

that attributed to the Shepherd. Gillies, who knew him at first-hand, reports his conversation thus:

> "Eh, man !" said he one morning, "ye're a grand critic, nae doubt, wi' your Greek, and Latin, and logic, and metapheesics ! *Yon* story that you and Jeems Wilson baith leuch at yestreen, is *gaun to turn out* just the very best and maist curious thing that ever I composed in a' my life—and that's no little to say !"[52]

Though this is a revision of the conversation as Gillies first published it in *Fraser's Magazine*, neither the substance nor the dialect of the passage has been refined.[53]

Hogg's thoughts, says Gillies, "flowed freely, and he gave them as they arose, with the energy of a man, and almost the naïveté of a child. . . ."

> He would argue readily enough if people were disposed for contradiction, but to make him lose temper was utterly impracticable. If others got angry, he only "guffawed"; and the grotesque manner in which he sometimes illustrated his own positions, made his antagonist laugh also. He had great enjoyment of life. . . .[54]

Lockhart, also, in *Peter's Letters to his Kinsfolk*, furnishes specimens of Hogg's "picturesque and characteristic" conversation. Once, says Lockhart, when Dr Spurzheim, a phrenologist, "began to feel out the marks of genius in the cranium of the pastoral poet," Hogg expressed his opinion of phrenology in these words: ". . . if a few knots and swells make a skull of genius, I've seen mony a saft chield get a swapping organization in five minutes at Selkirk tryst."[55]

And Thomas Carlyle, having met Hogg, adds to the evidence with a few dour observations in his "Note Book." Hogg, he remarks:

> Behaves himself quite easily and well ; speaks Scotch, and mostly narrative absurdity (or even obscenity) therewith. Appears in the mingled character of zany or raree show. All

---

[52] Gillies, *Memoirs of a Literary Veteran*, II. 121-2.
[53] *Fraser's Magazine*, XX (Oct. 1839), p. 422.   [54] *Op. cit.*, p. 420.
[55] J. G. Lockhart, *Peter's Letters to His Kinsfolk*, Edinburgh 1819, II. p. 341.

bent on bantering him, especially Lockhart; Hogg walking through it as if unconscious, or almost flattered. His vanity seems to be immense, but also his good-nature.[56]

At times Hogg may have spoken more "correctly"—there is no trace of Scots in the reported exchange between Wilkie and Hogg at Altrive [57]—but it is apparent that Douglas has over-stated his case. Hogg was, in fact, not very different from the Shepherd in his behaviour. On the other hand, the *Noctes* belong in the collected works of John Wilson, Professor of Moral Philosophy of the University of Edinburgh, not among the works of Hogg. The opinion of Miss Batho and Saintsbury may be repudiated; the conversation of the Shepherd, being largely the work of Wilson, may not be compared to Hogg's prose—and, indeed, to compare them is pointless. Hogg spoke Scots, but in prose (except often in dialogue) he set out to write English. And Douglas is right in this, that an entire dimension of Hogg's mind, the part from which his best work springs, is not represented in the Shepherd.

The last word on the authenticity of the dialogues is, perhaps, expressed by Christopher North in the *Noctes* of June 1829: "Inaccurate as these reports generally are, they yet convey somewhat the substance of what we say."[58]

From the time of his first meeting with Scott, in 1802, Hogg had been befriended by his famous contemporary— then Sheriff-Depute of Selkirk, later Sir Walter Scott, author of the Waverley Novels. The friendship did not always run smooth; for a whole year they were not on speaking terms. But in general they were fast friends. Scott respected Hogg's talent and had great affection for the man; Hogg held Scott in something like adoration, and applied to him for advice.

In his *Domestic Manners and Private Life of Sir Walter Scott*, published after Scott's death, Hogg casts light upon the quality of their friendship. It was Scott, Hogg says, who

---

[56] James Anthony Froude, *Thomas Carlyle : A History of the first forty Years of his Life 1795-1835* (henceforth cited as Froude, *Thomas Carlyle*), New York 1882, "Extracts from Note Book," II. 89.

[57] George Virtue, *The Wilkie Gallery*, London and New York n.d.

[58] *Noctes*, III. p. 311.

insured his entry into "genteel society" (this contradicts Gillies' claim).[59] And Scott guided him in his literary career. "But he would never bring me forward in any way by the shortest literary remark in any periodical—never would review any of my works, although he once promised to do it."[60]

The literary guidance Scott gave was mainly practical criticism, and Hogg often benefited from it. "I was indebted to him," Hogg says, "for the most happy and splendid piece of humorous ballad poetry which I ever wrote." The piece in question was "The Witch of Fife." In the early versions Hogg had let the old man in the ballad be burned at the stake. "What had the poor old carl done to deserve such a fate?" Scott protested. "Only taken a drappy o' drink too much, at another man's expense . . . you *must* bring off the old man, by some means or other." Which Hogg did, to the vast improvement of the poem. "I never adopted a suggestion of his, either in prose or verse," Hogg says, "which did not improve the subject."[61]

That is Hogg's opinion. Certainly, Scott's example had a great effect upon his writings. It was his work in gathering ballads for Scott's *Minstrelsy of the Scottish Border* that led Hogg to write his own ballads. It was through Scott's efforts that *The Mountain Bard* found a publisher. Scott's success in the narrative poem encouraged Hogg to try his hand at the same medium, and *The Queen's Wake*, the turning-point of his career, was the result.

But, on the whole, Hogg's reliance upon Scott's judgment was a misfortune. For he was led to imitate Scott, and his real talent lay in another direction entirely. From time to time Hogg caught glimpses of the truth. There was sometimes an insensibility in Scott, an authority running counter to Hogg's simple but earnest desires, against which he revolted. At the end of *The Queen's Wake* he protests that Scott has actually tried to discourage him from writing verse:

> O could the bard I loved so long,
> Reprove my fond aspiring song?

---

[59] *Domestic Manners*, p. 106 ; Gillies, *Memoirs of a Literary Veteran*, II. 130.
[60] *Op. cit.*, p. 106.   [61] *Op. cit.*, pp. 116-17.

Or could his tongue of candour say,
That I should throw my harp away?
Just when her notes began with skill
To sound beneath the southern hill,
And twine around my bosom's core,
How could we part for evermore?
'Twas kindness all,—I cannot blame,—
For bootless is the minstrel flame;
But sure a bard might well have known
Another's feelings by his own![62]

The incident referred to is that which Hogg describes in prose in the *Domestic Manners*. Scott undertook to engage Hogg to the post of chief shepherd to Lord Porchester, on condition that he put his "poetical talent under lock and key for ever." Hogg "spurned the terms and refused to implement the bargain."[63] It was well that he did so, for Porchester would have gained an unreliable shepherd, and we would have lost an author.

Upon publication of his novel, *The Brownie of Bodsbeck*, Hogg found himself in direct opposition to Scott, and for once he stood on his hind legs and fought back. By his account, Hogg had written *The Brownie* before Scott's *Old Mortality* appeared, but it was not published until after Scott's novel. It was consequently thought to be an imitation. Had it happened the other way round, Hogg says, Scott might have been thought to have imitated him.[64] As Scott also had made use of John Balfour of Burleigh as a character, Hogg had to revise *The Brownie*, substituting John Brown of Caldwell for John Balfour, "to the detriment of [his] story."[65] He called upon Scott on the pretence of asking his advice, but actually to get his opinion of *The Brownie of Bodsbeck*. He found Scott in no genial mood:

His shaggy eye-brows were hanging very low down, a bad prelude, which I knew too well. "I have read through your new work, Mr. Hogg," said he, "and must tell you downright plainly, as I always do, that I like it very ill—very ill indeed."[66]

[62] *Works*, II. 58.   [63] *Domestic Manners*, p. 104.
[64] "Autobiography," p. 456.   [65] *Ibid.*
               [66] *Domestic Manners*, pp. 86-7.

It was, Scott said, "a false and unfair picture of the times and the existing characters." To this Hogg answered that it was the picture he had been bred up in the belief of ever since he was born; all the incidents, he could prove from history, were true. His tale had been written not as a counterpoise to *Old Mortality*; it was written before. Scott let this pass, but reiterated his objection:

> "With the exception of Old Nanny, the crop-eared Covenanter, who is by far the best character you ever drew in your life, I dislike the tale exceedingly, and assure you it is a distorted, a prejudiced, and untrue picture of the Royal party."[67]

"It is a devilish deal truer than yours though," Hogg fired back, "and on that ground I make my appeal to my country."[68]

Scott, who had a portrait of Claverhouse hanging on his wall, was not likely to be pleased by Hogg's description of "Clavers" as a kind of hell-hound, savaging the Covenanters. Hogg's was a popular view; Scott's was Tory, coloured by his own romantic interpretations of history. Hogg's sense of history was located, so to speak, in his viscera; he was closer than Scott to the currents of feeling that make the true history of a people. And it would have been better for him in the long run, had he trusted his instincts, his grasp of tradition; he might have written more in the vein of the *Justified Sinner*, and not have wasted his time in imitating Scott. Miss Batho's comment is just: "Hogg is at his best in prose, as in poetry, when he is not trying to follow Scott too closely."[69] Fortunately, Hogg was not always imitating or being influenced by Sir Walter. His narrative poems and "Jacobite" tales modelled on Scott's are only a part of his production.

On one occasion his dependence on Scott's help brought him acute disappointment. At least, this is Hogg's version of the story—though Strout finds it inconsistent with the evidence.[70] In the "Autobiography" Hogg says that Scott's refusal to furnish even one verse for *The Poetic Mirror* compelled him to abandon his original plans for that work. Hogg left

---

[67] *Domestic Manners*, p. 88   [68] *Ibid.*
[69] Batho, p. 113.
[70] Strout, pp. 112-13. Strout's version is given below, p. 97.

Scott "in high dudgeon, sent him a very abusive letter, and would not speak to him for many a day."[71]   This was the year during which they did not meet; but, Hogg relates, on hearing that he was ill, Scott made frequent inquiries about his health, and told Grieve that he would bear the cost of the best medical care for Hogg.   "Poor Hogg!" he said, "I would not for all that I am worth in the world that anything serious should befall him."[72]

Scott's *Journal* bears witness to Hogg's struggles and Scott's admiration of his talent:

> [1826] February 15.   Poor James Hogg, the Ettrick Shepherd, came to advise with me about his affairs—he is sinking under the times ; having no assistance to give him, my advice, I fear will be of little service. . . .
>
> [1827] February 3.   There is nought but care on every hand. James Hogg writes that he is to lose his farm, on which he laid out, or rather threw away, the profit of all his publications.
>
> May 11.   Hogg called this morning to converse about trying to get him on the pecuniary list of the Royal Literary Society.   Certainly he deserves it, if genius and necessity could do so.   But I do not belong to the Society, nor do I therefore propose to enter it as a coadjutor. . . .[73]

This strange and interesting friendship between men so dissimilar in their talents was terminated by Scott's death. As Hogg describes it, the last meeting was a moving farewell. They met at the Gordon Arms and walked down the valley of the Yarrow.   Scott, his leg now almost entirely crippled, leaned upon Hogg's shoulder; he said that he had never leaned on a firmer or surer.   They talked of things "past, present and to come."   Hogg sadly observed that Scott's memory and "onward calculation" were impaired; he often changed the subject abruptly and he never laughed.   Yet still he was concerned with Hogg's welfare.   He told him that the young Duke of Buccleuch had been prejudiced against him by the lies of a game-keeper.   Hogg replied that the Duke would not

---

[71] "Autobiography," p. 453.   [72] *Ibid.*, p. 457.
[73] *The Journal of Sir Walter Scott*, edd. J. G. Tait and W. H. Parker, pp. 106, 314-15, 346.

bear animosity and the game-keeper would go to Hell. "You are still the old man, Hogg," Scott said gruffly, "careless and improvident as ever." He advised Hogg against his cherished plan of putting out an edition of his prose in twenty volumes. Things, he said were going "straight down-hill to destruction and ruin," literature in particular. On parting from him later that day Scott let fall an expression of affection, or of his interest in Hogg, that Hogg could never afterwards recollect.[74]

In one of the connected "Reminiscences" that extend the "Autobiography," Hogg says:

> There are not above five people in the world, who, I think, know Sir Walter better, or understand his character better than I do ; and if I outlive him, which is likely, as I am five months and ten days younger, I shall draw a mental portrait of him, the likeness of which to the original shall not be disputed.[75]

He kept his word, and in the summer of 1834 published *The Domestic Manners and Private Life of Sir Walter Scott.*

Even before publication the memoir had caused lively apprehension in certain quarters. Hogg was notoriously indiscreet; or, to put it another way, he did not observe the conventions of polite Edinburgh society. And what did Lockhart, gingerly turning the pages of the manuscript, discover? Together with a great deal of self-congratulation— which might be expected of the Shepherd—there were remarks which appalled and then infuriated John Gibson Lockhart, himself engaged in writing the official, monumental biography of Sir Walter Scott.

There were hints that Scott had plagiarised; it was said that Scott was jealous of his reputation. But there was more:

> The only foible I ever could discover in the character of Sir Walter, was a too strong leaning to the aristocracy of the country. His devotion for titled rank was prodigious, and in such an illustrious character, altogether out of place. It amounted almost to adoration. . . .[76]

---

[74] *Domestic Manners*, pp. 132-5.   [75] "Autobiography," p. 463.
[76] *Domestic Manners*, p. 71.

Hogg followed this with instances and examples. But the crowning offence, the most horrible indiscretion, was offered by Hogg's playful speculations as to the ancestry of Lady Scott:

> Who was Lady Scott originally ? I really wish anybody would tell me, for surely somebody must know. There is a veil of mystery hung over that dear lady's birth and parentage, which I have been unable to see through or lift up. . . . I have . . . a few cogent reasons for believing that the present Sir Walter's grandfather was a nobleman of very high rank.[77]

The passage is footnoted in the book, and the footnote may have been in the manuscript for Lockhart, lowering his gaze, to read and digest:

> This impression, strange to say, was encouraged by Sir Walter. Falconbridge was contented to be a king's bastard. The anxiety to be connected with nobility by a wife's illegitimacy, is a step beyond this, in aristocratical devotion.[78]

Lockhart handed the manuscript back to the man who had brought it. Hogg got wind of the fact that he had been less than pleased, and, in an effort to propitiate him, removed some of the objectionable parts. But the passages quoted above remained in the published book, and Lockhart was not placated. In the last volume of his life of Scott he wrote: "James Hogg, the Ettrick Shepherd, must also be mentioned. He died on the 21st of November, 1835; but it had been better for his fame had his end been of earlier date, for he did not follow his best benefactor until he had insulted his dust.[79]

In return, Mrs Garden, in her life of Hogg, retaliated against Lockhart. "When," she wrote, "all self-defence on Hogg's part had become impossible, then it was that the ungenerous pen of J. G. Lockhart assailed the now silent poet of Ettrick. Without any apparent cause Scott's son-in-law became not only the enemy but the virulent detractor of Hogg's good name."[80]

But the dust had not yet settled. Andrew Lang, in his biography of Lockhart, retaliated against Mrs Garden.

[77] *Domestic Manners*, p. 94.　　　　　[78] *Ibid.*
[79] Lockhart, *The Life of Sir Walter Scott*, VII. 419.　　　[80] Garden, pp. 288-9.

"Lockhart," he said, "was always serving, or trying to serve, Hogg; in the Memorials of the Shepherd, by his daughter Mrs Garden, Lockhart's kindness meets with its usual reward."[81] The comment casts doubt upon Lang's thoroughness; for no-one who read Lockhart's life of Scott could fail to find, beside innocuous passages, certain remarks about Hogg—that on his death is the most memorable—which are derogatory.

It may be that Hogg in his *Domestic Manners* overstepped the bounds of decorum. Yet the liveliness of the memoir and Hogg's affection for his subject outweigh his indiscretions. Besides, Scott himself could always forgive Hogg's lapses. This, I believe, rather than the book itself, was the cause of Lockhart's anger.

As Carswell says, Hogg's powers "seemed to grow with the years and reached their acme when he was on the verge of old age."[82] He still had superb physical vigour, and by the evidence of his writings, was mentally vigorous to the last. Every year he presided at the St Ronan's Border Games and "exerted himself lustily in the field." He was captain of a club of Bowmen of the Border, who wore doublets of Lincoln green and broad blue bonnets. They managed the Games, which included archery, leaping, racing, wrestling, stone-heaving, and hammer-throwing. Hogg himself "seldom failed to carry off some of the prizes, to the astonishment of his vanquished juniors." After the games they flocked to the Castle of Traquair, "*bon-vivants* of Edinburgh" mingling with the gentry and yeomanry of Tweeddale, and Hogg took the presidential chair. Among the guests might be Sir Walter Scott, Professor Wilson, Sir Adam Ferguson, and "Peter Robinson." It was the grandest evening of his year.[83]

But ordinary life continued to harass him. At the end of his lease on Mount Benger he found that, livestock of all kinds having declined one half in value, the farming venture had left him "once more without a sixpence in the world."[84]

---

[81] Andrew Lang, *The Life and Letters of John Gibson Lockhart*, London 1897, II. p. 14.
[82] Carswell, p. 204.   [83] Lockhart, *Life of Sir Walter Scott*, v. 317.
[84] "Autobiography," p. 459.

Retired to the cottage at Altrive, he cast about for ways of making money. A collected edition of his works might be the answer, something like the edition of the Waverley Novels. He began negotiations with a London bookseller, James Cochrane, and, having come to terms, went to London to arrange for the publication.

He arrived there on 1 Jan. 1832. The visit was a triumphal progress; Hogg was lionised. Many had read his works; many more had become familiar with "a phantom bearing his name" in the *Noctes Ambrosianae*.[85] They wished to see the Shepherd in his plaid and blue bonnet, to hear him let himself go in Broad Scots. The Shepherd did not disappoint them, though, in Douglas' phrase, "Time had smoothed the ruggedness of his manners since his early Edinburgh days."[86] Thomas Carlyle in his description of the visit says that Hogg behaved "easily and well," that he was charming, cheerful, mirthful, and musical, and speculates that he "is a real product of nature, and able to speak naturally, which not one in a thousand is."[87] Perhaps Hogg was helped by remembering his wife's parting advice: "Leave before you are threadbare. I do not exactly mean your coat, but leave the Londoners something to guess at."[88]

Descriptions of Hogg's London progress may seem exaggerated, now that he is forgotten, but the list of those who received him includes, among others, the Duke of Sussex, MacLeod of MacLeod, and Lord Saltoun; among celebrities, John Galt, George Cruikshank, and Neil Gow; among clubs and societies, the Beef Steak, the Literary, and the Highland.[89] He might be poor, but he was indubitably famous.

He was gladdened, but not overwhelmed, by these honours. He was now past sixty years old and had often been disappointed. Writing to his wife ten days after his arrival in London, he complains of the celebrations which prevent his getting home till three in the morning. "I cannot describe to you," he adds, "how cheerless and desolate I feel so far separated from my family. If it were not absolutely necessary to

---

[85] The phrase is Thomson's—"Life of the Ettrick Shepherd," in *Works*, II. liii.
[86] Douglas, p. 113. [87] Froude, *Thomas Carlyle*, II. 189.
[88] Mrs Hogg [to James Hogg, 22 Jan. 1832], in Garden, p. 250.
[89] Garden, *Memorials*, pp. 246-7, 260-1 ; Douglas, p. 111.

make a struggle in order to better our fortunes a little, I could not bear it."[90] Seeing the piles of dead larks in the markets of London distressed him deeply. He remembered that, in his young days, when he read in Bruce's *Travels* that the larks sang the same notes in Abyssinia that they did in Scotland, he had thought Abyssinia must be "a tolerable country after a'."[91]

The climax of his visit was a dinner at the Free Masons' Hall, on 25 January, celebrating Burns' birthday. Hogg was the guest of honour, two of Burns' sons were present, and General Sir John Malcolm presided over a gathering of two hundred, including nobles, M.P.s, and leaders of science and literature. After dinner, Hogg brewed punch in Burns' punch-bowl, which had been brought from Paisley. He received a great ovation.[92] In the following three days, he had three hundred invitations to dinner.

Soon afterwards, the publisher Cochrane went into bankruptcy. Only one volume of the *Altrive Tales*, which were to start the collected edition, appeared. The edition was sunk, and Hogg's hopes with it. On his return to Scotland he attended another congratulatory dinner, at Peebles, presided over by Wilson. In replying to the toast to his health, Hogg said that he had sought Fame in the mountains and the city, but only now, seeing so many notable men gathered together on his account, did he feel that he had found her.[93] But that year and the next, he published no new books.

He continued to write for the magazines. And perhaps there was an untapped source of income in America. He had heard that his "brethren beyond the Atlantic" were friends and admirers; thinking his pieces might "prop . . . their infant periodicals," he sent them off. But he never could learn what became of them.[94] To Dr Shelton Mackenzie, who had requested contributions for American magazines, Hogg wrote:

. . . there are nine or ten vols. of mine, which have been out of print these twenty years. We have a new set of readers

---

[90] James Hogg [to Mrs Hogg, 10 Jan. 1832], in Garden, pp. 247-8.
[91] Thomson, "Life of the Ettrick Shepherd," *Works*, ii. liii.
[92] *Ibid.* Also Douglas, p. 112.   [93] Douglas, p. 114.
[94] Hogg [to Dr Mackenzie, Altrive Lake, 5 Sep. 1833], in "Life of the Ettrick Shepherd," *Noctes Ambrosianae*, iv. xx.

D

altogether, since that period. Why may not your friends copy a tale out of these, every month, and just say, "By the Ettrick Shepherd," without saying how acquired ? Every one of them will pass for originals.[95]

In 1834, he published *A Series of Lay Sermons on Good Principles and Good Breeding*, which sold well, and in the same year, the *Domestic Manners*. He made a collection of his unpublished prose stories, *Tales of the Wars of Montrose*, and they were published, in April 1835, by Cochrane—who had resumed business. The sale promised to be brisk.

In this month he received a letter from Sir Robert Peel, the Prime Minister, offering him financial aid. Hogg accepted it, alluding playfully to his "particular facility in accepting of money," and saying that he had been "always poor and always most happy."[96]

For some time he had been suffering from an illness diagnosed as jaundice. In August he went to the moors about Birkhill, to shoot. The exercise seemed to cause an improvement; but then he became worse, and at the end of October, took to his bed. His disease showed symptoms of an acute, progressive infection of the liver. On the 17th of November he became speechless, and at noon on the 21st he died.

He was buried in Ettrick Churchyard, beside Will o' Phaup, a short walk from the place where he was born.[97]

[95] Hogg [to Dr Mackenzie, Altrive Lake, 5 Sep. 1833], in "Life of the Ettrick Shepherd," *Noctes Ambrosianae*, iv. xx.

[96] Douglas, pp. 114-5.

[97] "The Ettrick Shepherd at his death had little or no property to leave"— Thomson, *Works*, II. lv. Mrs Hogg struggled to care for their five small children (a son, James, and four daughters). In 1853 an annual royal pension was settled upon the widow. And in 1860 a public monument to Hogg was inaugurated; it stands between the Loch of the Lowes and the Loch of St Mary. Hogg's widow survived him thirty-five years.

PART II

POEMS

"I have verse the natural gate, and ither folk
by inoculation."

"Katie Cheyne"

II

Ballads and Songs

Hogg was apprenticed in the ballad. His mother, his uncle, and some of his neighbours—"a crazy old man and a woman deranged in her mind," he mentions in one letter—sang old Scottish ballads for their amusement.[1] His first attempts as a poet were "songs and ballads made up for the lasses to sing in chorus,"[2] and in *Scottish Pastorals* he published a ranting ballad of sword-play, "The Death of Sir Niel Stuart and Donald M'Vane, Esq." Later, his collaboration in gathering ballads for Scott's *Minstrelsy of the Scottish Border* turned him to writing his own in earnest, putting "traditionary stories" into metre "by chanting them to certain old tunes."[3]

The ballads that Hogg collected almost escape definition. "That ballads are *narrative songs*," says S. B. Hustvedt, "is generally agreed."[4] Whether they were originally created by individuals or by a community, the ballads, in being orally transmitted, became communal works. It was the community which finally made them what they were. To the original fragments of narrative song—some of which are shrouded in antiquity—adhere portions of Celtic and Scandinavian superstition and medieval romance. Also, the ballads embody myths that are found in general folklore. The history of ballad-collecting and classification is, understandably, complex. To Percy, ballads were rude survivals of the past, interesting as evidence of old customs and beliefs, but having small merit as poetry; the editor was therefore free to "improve" the texts, making them "fit for the perusal of cultivated

---

[1] See Carruthers, *Abbotsford Notanda*," Letter from Hogg to William Laidlaw, pp. 115-17, *passim.*

[2] "Autobiography," p. 443.　　　　　　　[3] *Ibid.*, p. 446.

[4] Sigurd Bernhard Hustvedt, *Ballad Books and Ballad Men*, Cambridge (Mass.) 1930, p. 20.

readers." Ritson, on the other hand, held that the received texts were not to be tampered with.[5]

In his *Minstrelsy* Scott "improved" the texts a great deal, in the manner of Percy. But Hogg, in supplying texts for Scott, seems to have made a real effort to take down the ballads as he heard them. He was, says Miss Batho, "a bad editor but an excellent 'source' for a collector or editor. . . . What is noteworthy is . . . Hogg's honesty in putting down what he heard, however unintelligible to him, and his frankness in declaring his own work."[6] Yet, "Auld Maitland," which Scott heard recited by Margaret Laidlaw, "The Lament of the Border Widow," and parts of "Otterburn," have been suspected to be forgeries by Hogg.[7] And in his own editing of *The Jacobite Relics*, Hogg altered texts and inserted his own pieces; when a reviewer pointed to his own "Donald Macgillavry" as an example of the authentic note, he was delighted.[8]

With Hogg's "imitations" we are on different and surer ground. These are original works with interpolated borrowings which Hogg is willing, even eager, to admit. *The Mountain Bard* is sprinkled with footnotes. "Sir David Graeme," Hogg informs the reader, is an attempt to complete the tale of "The Twa Corbies," published in the *Minstrelsy*.[9] The opening lines:

> The dow flew east, the dow flew west,
> The dow flew far ayont the fell . . .

are conscientiously footnoted:

> I borrowed the above line from a beautiful old rhyme which I have often heard my mother repeat, but of which she knew no tradition ; and from this introduction the part of the dove naturally arose. The rhyme runs thus :
>
> > "The heron flew east, the heron flew west,
> > The heron flew to the fair forest. . . ."[10]

---

[5] Hustvedt, pp. 23-4.

[6] Batho, pp. 43, 182. See also, pp. 18-43, *passim*, and pp. 169-82, *passim*.

[7] *Idem.*, p. 21.   [8] *Idem.*, pp. 38-9.   [9] *Works*, ii. 62.

[10] *Ibid.* The impression these lines made on Hogg is shown by his use of them—this time without acknowledgment of the source—in "The Bridal of Palmood" (*Tales*, ii. 62-3). Also, the scene described in the song is rendered in "The Brownie of Bodsbeck" (*Tales*, i. 155-66).

Several similar footnotes describe the traditions from which the ballads in *The Mountain Bard* are derived, round out the stories, and give alternative versions.

Hogg's ballad imitations comprise the greater part of *The Mountain Bard*; there are ten in all. In *The Forest Minstrel*, at least four pieces, "Auld Ettrick John," "Willie Wastle," "Auld John Borthwick," and "Honest Duncan," may be classed as ballads. It is not always easy to decide what is a ballad, and what a song, but, on the whole, the difference is that the ballad tells a story; the song usually does not.

The ballad form used by Hogg is the conventional quatrain, sometimes with a strict alternative rhyme (*a, b, a, b,*) sometimes with only one pair of rhymes (*a, b, c, b*):

> "Whoever fights my noble son
> May foin the best he can ;
> Whoever braves Wat Hamilton,
> Shall know he braves a man."[11]

> "Holla ! quhat's that ?" cryit blynde Robene,
> "Is there anie here to telle ?"
> "It is the bulle," quod the littil boi
> "You haif charmit him down to helle."[12]

There may be internal rhyme:

> "Come let us fly to Westmoreland,
> For here you cannot stay ;
> Short be thy shrift, our steeds are swift,
> And well I know the way."[13]

Within the same ballad there may be a mixture of rhyme-schemes: some stanzas rhyming alternately, others having only one pair of ryhmes; some lines rhyming internally, others not, as in the old ballads.

The lines most frequently used are the tetrameter and the trimeter. The iamb is ubiquitous, but Hogg is also fond of galloping anapaests:

> O wha hasna heard o' the bauld Juden Murray,
> The lord o' the Elibank castle sae high. . . .?[14]

---

[11] "Earl Walter," in *Works*, ii. 29.   [12] "The Powris of Moseke," *op. cit.*, ii. 320.
[13] " Lord Derwent," *op. cit.*, ii. 85.   [14] "The Fray of Elibank," *op. cit.*, ii. 70.

He also uses the trochee on occasion; in fact, he tries his hand at all the standard meters.

His language varies from one ballad to another—and also, unfortunately, sometimes it varies within the same piece. A ballad may be in archaic, ballad English:

> "O why look ye so pale, my lord ?
> And why look ye so wan ?
>   And why stand mounted at your gate
> So early in the dawn ?"[15]

contemporary, literary English:

> Hynde could not hunt, she could not play,
>   She could not revel in the ring ;
> She could not fast, she could not pray,
>   Nor yet disclose her languishing.[16]

archaic, ballad Scots:

> "Ye lee, ye lee, ye ill womyne,
> Se loud as I heir ye lee !
> For the ᵃwarst-faurd wyfe on the shoris of Fyfe   ᵃ *worst-favoured*
> Is cumlye comparit wi' thee."[17]

or in the vernacular:

> Sandy was a lad o' vigour,
>   Lithe an' tight o' ᵃlith an' limb :   ᵃ *joint*
> For a stout an' manly figure,
>   Few could ding or equal him.[18]

"May of the Moril Glen," beginning in archaic ballad English, soon moves into a mixture of archaic Scots and the vernacular:

> I will tell you of ane wondrous tale,
>   As ever was told by man,
> Or ever was sung by minstrel meet
>   Since this base world began:—
>
> It is of ane May, and ane lovely May,
>   That dwelt in the Moril Glen,
> The fairest flower of mortal frame,
>   But a devil amongst the men ;

---

[15] "Lord Derwent," *op. cit.*, II. 84.   [16] "Queen Hynde, *op. cit.*, II. 196."
[17] "The Witch of Fife," *op. cit.*, II. 14.   [18] "Sandy Tod," *op. cit.*, II. 14.

For nine of them sticket themselves for love,
 And ten ^alouped in the main,   *^a jumped*
And seven-and-thirty brake their hearts,
 And never loved women again.

For ^ailk ane ^btrowit she was in love,   *^a each   ^b believed*
 And ran ^awodde for a while—   *^a mad*
There was ^asiccan language in every look,   *^a such a*
 And a ^aspeire in every smile. . . .[19]   *^a question*

In later stanzas of this poem there are lapses into contemporary, literary English:

 The hawk that on her bridle arm
  Outspread his pinions blue,
 To keep him steady on the perch
  As his loved mistress flew.[20]

 The uncertainty of Hogg's use of language stems from a greater uncertainty; indeed, it points to his main weakness as a poet—he does not know for whom he is writing. Should he write in Scots, or in English, or in a mixture of Scots and English? Should he write for the English-speaking Union, and the approval of Tory Edinburgh, or for his own common people?

 He might have written in vernacular Scots. In Hogg's favourite poem, "Tam o' Shanter," and more consistently in other poems, Burns had shown how the thing might be done:

 Ah, Tam ! Ah, Tam ! thou'll get thy fairin !
 In Hell they'll roast thee like a herrin ![21]

 We twa hae paidl'd i' the burn,
  Frae morning sun till dine;
 But seas between us braid hae roar'd
  Sin' auld lang syne.[22]

---

 [19] *Works*, II. 100. In prose, also, he sometimes slips from one style into another. See below, pp. 124-125.
 [20] *Op. cit.*, II. 101.
 [21] Robert Burns, *The Poetry of Robert Burns*, ed. W. E. Henley and T. F. Henderson, Edinburgh 1896, I. 286.
 [22] Burns, *op. cit.*, III. 148.

On the other side was the prestige of English. When Burns was a child, he was schooled out of Masson's *Collection of Prose and Verse*, which contained extracts from the eighteenth-century poets, including Thomson, Gray, and Shenstone; passages from Shakespeare, Milton, and Dryden; prose selections from Addison, and from the *Letters Moral and Entertaining* of Elizabeth Rowe.[23] What Crawford says of the Ayrshire peasantry is applicable also to the inhabitants of Ettrick: they were not unfamiliar with abstract English diction and classical figures of speech.[24] We have Hogg's account of his own familiarity with the Bible and theological tracts—though, to be sure, they were read with Scottish inflexions. Then the weight of the Union was thrown behind English. As time passed, English gained and Scots lost. When Walter Scott wrote his long poems in English, and they were famous, he scored a victory for English at the expense of Scots. He had created a fashion for Scottish scenes and characters, but he had relegated the vernacular to second place and falsified those traditions which are embodied in the vernacular.

As the culture of the Scottish people was mixed, so was their language. They were accustomed to shifting from one level of usage to another.[25] In his "Scottish" poems Hogg is making a similar compromise. The language is a mixture of Scots and English words and phrases, which may perhaps best be described as "Scots-English." Ramsay, Fergusson and, on occasion, Burns, had written in Scots-English; the style had a vogue in literary circles; as Burns said, "A small sprinkling of Scotticisms, is no objection to an English reader."[26] "Kilmeny" is an example of Hogg's poetry in Scots-English:

> But lang may her [a]minny look o'er the wa',   [a] mother
> And lang may she seek i' the greenwood shaw ;
> Lang the laird of Duneira blame,
> And lang, lang [a]greet or Kilmeny come hame ![27]   [a] weep

Though Hogg is using a good many exclusively Scots words

[23] David Daiches, *Robert Burns* (henceforth cited as Daiches), New York 1950, p. 38.
[24] Thomas Crawford, *Burns, a Study of the Poems and Songs* (henceforth cited as Crawford), Edinburgh 1960, p. 3.
[25] *Ibid.*   [26] *Ibid.*   [27] *Works*, II. 32.

here—"minny," "greet"—and Scots forms—"lang," "hame"
—they are such that most educated English readers would
have been familiar with them, or could easily have guessed
them. The tone of "Kilmeny" is charmingly "Scottish," yet
one must admit that the language seems rather facile. In
other poems where the Scots is even more diluted, what we
have is the Lowland-Scots tradition as it has degenerated in
the hands of Ramsay's imitators—a conventional, watery,
pseudo-pastoral diction.

When Hogg was more ambitious, he wrote in literary
English, imitating Scott's language and attitudes. But whereas
Scott was quite at ease with English—nor was there anything
in contemporary rationalist thought that inhibited his talent—
it was not so for Hogg. Imitating Scott, writing in English,
making up romantic versions of Scottish history, and trying to
see things in the clear way that Scott did, he seems to have
taken leave of his senses, as well as his tongue. In *The Pilgrims
of the Sun* we find him retailing metaphysics in the heroic
couplets of Dryden and Pope:

> "Thus tis ordained—these grosser regions yield
> Souls, thick as blossoms of the vernal field,
> Which after death, in relative degree,
> Fairer or darker as their minds may be,
> To other worlds are led. . . ."[28]

What was the shepherd doing so far from home? It was the
literati, like the "dead lights" of his own Ettrick bogs, that led
him astray.

Daiches says of Fergusson and Burns that they "achieved
success only when they repudiated the poetic tradition of the
literati."[29] But Hogg never repudiated the tradition. Sometimes he protested against the snobbishness of the dominant
Tory clique, but he did not revolt against their literary judgment. To the contrary, he tried his best to please them, either
by writing poems in Scots-English that was "folksy" and
quaint, but not really vernacular, or by writing in literary
English.

Now, as he set about writing ballads, he could defer the

[28] *Works*, II. 135.   [29] Daiches, p. 31.

task of finding his own poetic idiom. The question was not yet urgent, for the ballads were only "imitations"—as in "The Death of Douglas," of the old ballads Hogg had taken down for the *Minstrelsy*; as in "Mess John," of the language of English ballads. In "Robin an' Nanny" he imitated Ramsay's pastorals; and as Burns has a poem to an old mare, Hogg has a ballad to "his auld dog Hector."

The ballad is one of the more difficult forms of poetry to imitate, for imitation is a sophisticated practice, and ballads are essentially naïve. (The successful literary ballads are, in fact, not imitations but original poems that do not follow antique modes closely.) The very simplicity of the form is a disadvantage, for it affords no hiding-place. A lack of narrative art, uncertainty in the use of language, vague description, and above all, insincerity, glare through the transparency of the ballad. Hogg's particular faults are too numerous to be listed; there is sometimes faulty technique, as in the language of this stanza from "Earl Walter":

> So said, so done : their helms they flung,
>> Their doublets linked and ᵃsheen;   ᵃ *shiny*
> And hauberk, armlet, cuirass, rung
>> Promiscuous on the green.[30]

And insipidity, as in "The Spirit of the Glen:"

> Then all you virgins sweet and young,
>> When the first whisperings of sin
> Begin to hanker on your minds,
>> Or steal into the soul within,
>
> Keep aye the eyes on heaven aboon,
>> Both of your body and your mind;
> For in the strength of God alone,
>> A woman's weakness strength shall find.[31]

Melodrama, action for its own sake with little or no interest in the characters involved, extends through monotonous stanzas. Hogg is weakest in his romantic manner, when

---

[30] *Works*, II. p. 30.   [31] *Op. cit.*, II. 331.

exploits of legendary names, descriptions of stage scenery, and glorification of Scotland, are substituted for dramatic action and characterisation:

> Brave Robin o' Singlee was cloven through the brain,
>   An' Kirkhope was woundit, an' young Bailleylee.
> Wi' Juden, baith Gatehope an' Plora were slain,
>   An' auld Ashiesteel gat a cut on the knee.[32]

He has little talent for romantic-historical narrative—though, led on by the example of Scott, he often attempts it. He has neither the antiquarian touch nor the artifice that is needed to produce a *Marmion*. In a letter to Lord Montagu, dated 4 Mar. 1819, Scott comments upon Hogg's lack of information:

> Hogg is here busy with his Jacobite Songs. I wish he may get handsomely through, for he is profoundly ignorant of history, and it is an awkward thing to read in order that you may write. I give him all the help I can, but he sometimes poses me. For instance he came yesterday, open mouth, enquiring what great dignified clergyman had distinguished himself at Killie-crankie—not exactly the scene where one would have expected a churchman to shine—and I found with some difficulty, that he had mistaken Major-General Canon, called, in Kennedy's Latin Song, *Canonicus Gallovidiensis*, for the canon of a cathedral. *Ex ungue leonem.*[33]

On the other hand, when Hogg is writing of the life he knows, the Scottish peasants, their customs, beliefs and superstitions, his imagination is engaged. That life is close to poverty, and the style in which he writes of it, a steady, humourous realism, renders the poverty with absolute force. Inseparable from poverty is superstition, and of this, too, he makes his tales. The harshness of necessity is relieved by sudden sorties into dreams, into a moonlit world inhabited by fairies, witches and ghosts. There, crimes and injustices are exposed by supernatural powers, riches are given to the deserving, and the wicked are punished.

He makes use of the supernatural; but does he believe in

---

[32] "The Fray of Elibank," *op. cit.*, II. 72.

[33] Letter from Sir Walter Scott—"To the Lord Montagu, Ditton Park, Windsor." "Edinburgh, 4th March, 1819"—Lockhart, *Memoir of the Life of Sir Walter Scott*, IV. 234.

it? The question cannot be easily answered, and it may be
that to attempt an answer is irrelevant—for what matters is
the effect of the work of art, not the author's private thoughts.
In general, it seems that Hogg inclined to superstition. Or,
to put it another way, he found it easier to be superstitious than
not to be. The poem "Superstition" bears witness to the
strong impression made upon his mind by superstition when
he was a child.[34] In his first book, the *Scottish Pastorals*, he
writes: .

> And in the wild and dreary waste;
>   The village fair, or noisy lawn,
> Wherever smiles the human face,
>   There spirits skim their airy round.

> A guardian friend, his fav'rite charge
>   May thus of hid events apprize,
> By great outlines, unfurl'd at large
>   In sleep, to Fancy's lidless eyes.[35]

His most original poems, "The Witch of Fife," "Kilmeny,"
"A Witch's Chant," and his most powerful prose tales, all
draw their substance from the supernatural. At times, it is
true, he may seem to be exploding superstition by offering an
ordinary explanation for strange occurrences, as in the tale
"Rob Dodds," where the "dead-lights"—that is, lights that
hang about a corpse—are proved to be only mineral vapours.[36]
But when Hogg removes an illusion he does so for the effect,
as other men to add an effect produce an illusion. There is
a mixture in Hogg's mind of superstition and incredulity, but
whenever he makes a statement of his own view it is in favour
of superstition. However, he does not often make such
statements; he prefers to leave the reader wondering. And,
indeed, this is the secret of some of his most memorable effects.[37]

"The Witch of Fife," in Hogg's opinion "the most happy
and splendid piece of humourous ballad poetry" he ever wrote,[38]
tells of witchcraft. Hogg's treatment of the subject deserves

---

[34] *Works*, II. 392-4.
[35] *Scottish Pastorals*, "A Dialogue in a Country Churchyard," p. 41.
[36] *Tales*, III. 220
[37] Hogg's use of superstition is discussed again below, pp. 157-160.
[38] *Domestic Manners*, p. 116.

our attention, for his instinctive grasp of the issue seems close to modern ideas; and here we see the advantage of his acquaintance with popular traditions.

Hogg, as his writings show, believes in the existence of a pagan cult whose devotees are called "witches." In this belief he has the facts on his side; for even if all the evidence in Scottish witch trials is ruled out, as having been obtained by torture, still there is evidence that a pagan cult lingered on throughout the Middle Ages, and after the Reformation; and indeed, remnants of it can be found as late as the eighteenth century. The religion consisted of a belief in a god incarnate in a human being or animal. This god, whom the Christian recorders of the witch-trials called the Devil, might appear to his worshippers in the guise of an animal, or dressed in black. At the "Sabbaths," men, women and children would gather to sing and dance in honour of the god, and feast, and perform the rites that promoted fertility.

After the Reformation, an act was passed ordaining the penalty of death for "any manner of witchcraft, sorcery, or necromancy," and, as Hume Brown says, "of all Acts ever sanctioned by the Scottish legislature this was the one which received the most exemplary obedience from all parties responsible for its execution."[39] Most industrious in enforcing the law were the ministers, Presbyterian and Episcopalian alike.

The Reformed Kirk projected their own feelings of guilt on to the followers of the ancient cult, denouncing them as "traffickers with the powers of darkness." But the Scottish people themselves did not regard the "witches" as an unmixed evil. Witchcraft was a source of magic, producing good effects as well as mischief. This view of the matter persisted; at the present time there is testimony to the good, as well as the evil, power of witchcraft, in a plaque that stands on the Castle Esplanade, Edinburgh, near the place where the Lady Douglas was burned as a witch. On the face of the plaque are engraved two heads: one of a good witch, the other of a bad; at the sides of the plaque are shown a "helping hand" and an "evil eye."

[39] P. Hume Brown, *History of Scotland*, Cambridge (Eng.) 1902, II. 449.

The popular view is represented by Hogg in his tale, "The Hunt of Eildon," where witches accomplish good; in his poem, "The Witch of Fife," where they are amazing, ludicrous, and entertaining, and "Superstition," where they are described with deep understanding and pity:

> Where fell the scathe ?—The beldames were amused,
> Whom eild and poverty had sorely crazed.
> What, though their feeble senses were abused
> By gleesome demon in the church-aisle raised,
> With lion tail, and eyes that baleful blazed,
> Whose bagpipe's blare made all the roof to quake !
> But ages yet unborn will stand amazed
> At thy dread power, that could the wretches make
> Believe these things all real, and swear them at the stake.[40]

It is instructive to compare this view with Scott's purely rationalist assumption that no such thing as witchcraft existed. In Hogg's words, Scott was "trying to throw cold water on the most certain, though most impalpable, phenomena of human nature."[41] In this, as in other matters, Hogg's instincts, being more deeply rooted in popular tradition than Scott's, brought him closer to the essential truth.

"The Witch of Fife" draws upon the old belief that witches ride through the air to gather with Satan. Scot's *Discovery of Witchcraft*, published in 1584, describes the superstition, to show the "lewde, unchristian practices of Witchmongers, upon aged, melancholy, ignorant, and superstitious people. . . ."[42]

> *Danens* saith, the devil oftentimes in the likenesses of a summoner, meeteth them at markets and faires, and warneth them to appear in their assemblies, at a certain hour in the night, that he may understand whom they have slaine, and how they have profited. If they be lame, he saith the devill delivereth them a staffe, to convey them thither invisibly through the air ; and that then they fall a dancing and singing of bawdy-songs, wherein he leadeth the dance himself. . . .[43]

---

[40] *Works*, II. 393. [41] *Tales*, IV. 335

[42] *Scot's Discovery of Witchcraft*, "Printed by R.C. and are to be sold by Giles Calvert, Dwelling at the Black Spread-Eagle at the West-end of Pauls, 1651." Stack #304 Sco., in the library of the American Academy in Rome, title page.

[43] *Ibid.*, p. 37.

In the course of *The Queen's Wake* the eighth bard presents "The Witch of Fife."[44] He is, Hogg tells us, from the Leven coast:

> Mounted the bard of Fife on high,
> Bushy his beard, and wild his eye :
> His cheek was furrowed by the gale,
> And his thin locks were long and pale . . .
> Some wizard of the shore he seemed,
> Who through the scenes of life had dreamed,
> Of spells that vital life benumb,
> Of formless spirits wandering dumb,
> Where aspens in the moonbeam quake,
> By mouldering pile, or mountain lake.
>
> He deemed that lays and spectres wan
> Held converse with the thoughts of man ;
> In dreams their future fates foretold,
> And spread the death-flame on the wold ;
> Or flagged at eve each restless wing
> In dells their vesper hymns to sing.
>
> Such was our bard, such were his lays. . . .

The ballad begins with a dialogue between an old man and his wife:

> "*a*Quhare haif ye been, ye ill womyne,   *a where*
>   These three lang nightis fra hame ?
> Quhat *a*garris the sweit drap fra yer brow,   *a causes . . . to*
>   Like clotis of the *a*saut sea faem ?   *a salt*
>
> "It fearis me *a*muckil ye haif seen   *a much*
>   Quhat guid man never knew ;
> It fearis me muckil ye haif been
>   Quhare the gray cock never crew.
>
> "But the spell may crack, and the brydel breck,
>   Then *a*sherpe yer *b*werde will be ;   *a sharp   b doom*
> Ye had better sleipe in yer bed at hame,
>   Wi' yer deire littil bairnis and me."—

"Sit doune, sit doune, my ^aleil auld man,   *a loyal*
 Sit doune, and listin to me ;
I'll ^agar the hayre stand on yer crown,   *a make*
 And the cauld sweit blind yer ee.

"But tell nae wordis, my guid auld man,
 Tell never word again ;
Or deire shall be yer courtisye,
 And ^adriche and ^bsair yer pain.   *a wearisome* *b sore*

"The first ^aleet night, quhan the new moon set, *a bright*
 Quhan all was ^adouffe and mirk,   *a dull*
We saddled ouir naigis wi' the moon-fern ^aleif, *a leaf*
 And rode fra Kilmerrin kirk.

"Some horses ware of the ^abrume-cow framit, *a broom-bush*
 And some of the greine bay tree ;
But mine was made of ane ^ahumloke ^bschaw, *a hemlock* *b thicket*
 And a stout stallion was he.

"We raide the ^atod doune on the hill,   *a fox*
 The martin on the ^alaw ;   *a hill*
And we huntyd the ^ahoolet out of brethe, *a owl*
 And forcit him doune to fa'."—

"Quhat guid was that, ye ill womyne ?
 Quhat guid was that to thee ?
Ye wald better haif been in yer bed at hame,
 Wi' yer deire littil bairnis and me."—

From their hunting, the wife says, the witches rode to the
"Lommond height," where they dismounted:

  "And we drank fra the hornis that never grew,
   The beer that was never brewin.

  "Then up there raise ane wee wee man,
   Fra neithe the moss-gray stane ;
  His fece was wan like the collifloure,
   For he nouthir had blude nor bane."

This creature played to them on his reed-pipe, so sweetly that the birds came close, and beasts and fishes danced to the melody; and the witches danced too, until morning.

> "Ne wonder I was a weary wycht
> Quhan I cam hame to you."

The old man reproaches her again, with his refrain:

> "Ye wald better haif bein in yer bed at hame,
> Wi' yer deire littil bairnis and me."

On the second night, says the witch-wife, they set sail on the sea in a cockle-shell:

> "And the bauld windis blew, and the ªfire-flauchtis flew,
> And the sea ran to the skie ;   ª *thunder-bolts*
> And the thunner it growlit, and the sea-dogs howlit,
> As we gaed scouryng bye."

They made for the "Norraway shore," and to Lapland, where the fairies and genii of the north "War keipyng their holiday."

> "The warlock men and the weird ªwemyng,   ª *women*
> And the fays of the wood and the steip,
> And the phantom hunteris all war there,
> And the mermaidis of the deip.

> "And they washit us all with the witch-water,
> Distillit fra the muirland dew,
> Quhill our beauty blumit like the Lapland rose,
> That wylde in the foreste grew."

Upon hearing this, the old man cries with growing indignation:

> "Ye ªlee, ye lee, ye ill womyne,   ª *lie*
> ªSe loud as I heir ye lee !   ª *so*
> For the ªwarst-faurd wyfe on the shoris of Fyfe   ª *worst-favoured*
> Is cumlye comparit wi' thee."

Then, says the wife, the mermaids sang; there was a harp on every cliff, on every tree a lyre. The witches drank:

> "Then saft in the armis of the warlock men,
> We laid us dune to sleip."

Her husband wishes she may come to a bad death, for she has

been false to God and to him. But she continues unashamed. The witches learned from fairies, she says, "And fra our master true":

> "The wordis that can beire us throu the air,
>   And lokkis and barris undo."

Last night the witches met again, and, knowing magic words that enabled them to fly, flew in the black cockle-shell over the hills and the sea, till they came to "merry Carlisle."

> "We gaed to the vault beyond the towr,
>   Quhare we enterit free as ayr ;
> And we drank, and we drank of the bishopis wyne
>   *a*Quhill we culde drynk ne mair."   *a until*

The "leil auld man," her husband, on hearing of the wine-vault, forgets his righteous indignation. His interest is thoroughly aroused:

> "*a*Gin that be true, my guid auld wife, *a if*
>   Whilk thou hast tauld to me,
> Betide my death, betide my lyfe,
>   I'll beire thee companye.

> "Neist time ye gaung to merry Carlisle
>   To drynk of the blude-reid wyne,
> Beshrew my heart, I'll fly with thee,
>   If the deil should fly behynde."

The witch-wife warns him that he little knows what dangers there are in flight. But he urges her: ". . . tell me the *word*." He will not ride her horses, nor sail the sea, but he can fly as well as she, and outdrink her. She refuses, for if she told him the world would be turned upside down; all the women would be flying, and the men after them.

Here the dialogue ends. We are told that the cunning old man bided his time, and spied on the next meeting of the witches. When they flew off in their cockle-shell, he crept out of his hole, stood in a cockle-shell, and said: "the word that I darena say." Straightway he flew after the witches and followed them into the wine-vaults of Carlisle, where he joined them in drinking, singing and dancing:

"And aye he piercit the *ᵃtither butt,   *ᵃ other (of two)*
  And he suckit, and he suckit se lang,
Quhill his een they closit, and his voice grew low,
  And his tongue wald hardly gang."

With morning, the witches had departed, but the old man still slept—and there he was found by "five rough Englishmen." To their questioning how he managed to get through the locked doors, he could only answer that he came from Fife on the wind.

"They nickit the auld man, and they prickit the auld man,
  And they yerkit his limbis with twine,
Quhill the reide blude ran in his hose and shoon,
  But some cryit it was wyne."

After this, they tied him to a bonfire, whereupon he complained

". . . *ᵃwae be to all the ill wemyng   *ᵃ woe*
  That lead puir men astray.

"Let nevir ane auld man after this
  To lawless greide inclyne ;
Let nevir ane auld man after this
  Rin post to the deil for wyne."

But, as they were burning the old man, the English saw "ane thing beth lairge and dun" swooping through the air, from the direction of Fife. It was the old man's wife, coming to see his death. She put a red cap on his head, whispered a word in his ear, and flew away. Her husband shook himself, and the bands flew off. He spoke the word, "And away to the ayr flew he." He flew with outspread arms, his feet sticking out behind, his coat flapping in the wind.

"And aye he *ᵃneicherit, and aye he flew,   *ᵃ neighed*
  For he thochte the ploy se raire ;
It was like the voice of the *ᵃgainder blue,   *ᵃ gander*
  Quhan he flees throu the ayr."

He nodded and grinned back at the Carlisle men, but "he nevir said guid-bye." So he vanished, and they still heard his laughter on the wind.

The ballad ends with an admonition:

> "May ever ilke man in the land of Fyfe
>   Read what the drinkeris ^adree ;   ^a *suffer*
> And nevir curse his puir auld wife,
>   Rychte wicked altho scho be."

Like Coleridge's "Rime of the Ancient Mariner," "The Witch of Fife" subsumes the ballad form in which it is cast. It is not an imitation, but a strikingly original poem. The tale moves with the velocity of the witches' riding, sailing and flying. The unearthly and grotesque parts are offset by the ridiculous character of the old man. It is the interruption of his low, comic humanity that makes the poem, as a whole, so credible. He denounces the witches' revels; but when wine is mentioned, he changes his tune. Pious, as long as he is not tempted, he succumbs immediately when he is. A cunning old man, as the poet says . . . his gleeful tippling in the bishop's wine-cellar, and his joy in his escape, are among Hogg's happiest creations.

The language of the poem is as fantastic as its subject. Descriptions such as this justify the use of dialect:

> . . . the ^alaibies of the auld manis cote   ^a *skirts*
>   War wauffing in the wynde.[45]

"Wauffing" is better than "flapping," for the sound and motion of broadcloth that is being drawn through the air at speed. And "waffe" or "weft," a nautical word meaning a cloth or coat suspended as a signal of distress, for its ominous connotations is appropriate in the context of this *diablerie*.

"The Witch of Fife" is not typical of Hogg's writings of the supernatural. Here an idea of witches serves as the point of departure; the rest is Hogg's fancy. His usual practice is quite different: it is to relate "uncanny" occurrences in the course of a realistic tale. The story is set in recognisable life; the supernatural is added to this. Sometimes he pretends to be only documenting a legend; a ghost, an astonishing dream, are "facts" of the legend. The effects of the mixture of the

---

[45] *Works*, II. 16.

probable and improbable is to perplex the reader, as the Scottish peasant was perplexed by these matters.

In the ballad "The Pedlar" (published in *The Mountain Bard*) it is the familiarity of its behaviour that makes the ghost real.[46] The pedlar in his supernatural role is still a pedlar; he still wears his "muckle green pack." Hogg applies the same touches to his apparitions that he applies to ordinary creatures; they walk and speak like the living, but it is dreadfully clear that they are dead. In this, as in other aspects, Hogg and Defoe are comparable. Defoe's apparition of Mrs Veal comes to her friend, Mrs Bargrave, in a gown of "scowered silk"; in the most practical manner she tells Mrs Bargrave how she wishes to dispose of her rings and pieces of gold. A practical ghost is, perhaps, the most terrifying kind.

To document "The Pedlar," Hogg prefaces the ballad with a note disclaiming his own belief in the "superstition":

> This ballad is founded on a fact, which has been magnified by popular credulity and superstition into the terrible story which follows. It is here related, according to the *best informed* old people about Ettrick, as nearly as is consistent with the method pursued in telling it. I need not inform the reader, that every part of it is believed by them to be absolute truth.[47]

The beginning is a dismal scene:

> 'Twas late, late, late on a Saturday night,
>   The moon was set an' the wind was *a*lown ;   *a gentle*
> The lazy mist *a*crap down frae the height,   *a crept*
>   An' the dim blue *a*lowe glimmered *b*laigh on the downe.
>
>   *a glow   b low*

The Lady of Thirlestane wakes with a shriek. She has dreamed that a pedlar whom she turned away from the door has been murdered; he appeared in her dream, dreadfully mangled, staring at her accusingly. Her servants reassure her that the pedlar is well; he has gone on to the mill. But the miller denies having seen him, and the pedlar has disappeared.

Then his ghost appears to the Laird of Thirlestane, carrying the "muckle green pack" on its shoulders. It shows the laird its hacked throat and, in a flash of light, vanishes into the

---

[46] *Works*, II. 64-7.   [47] *Op. cit.*, II. 64.

ground. The laird prays and faints; on coming to his senses, he returns home and tells what he has seen.

Every Saturday night thereafter, the pedlar's ghost haunts the vicinity of the mill, crying: "O Rob Riddle, hae mercy on me!" The mill is destroyed (by suspicious neighbours, it seems) and the miller is forced to escape to a far country, but the ghost continues its haunting. The lady and the terrified people do not dare venture out at night. But a minister undertakes to lay the spirit, and waits by the mill.

> Wi' a shivering groan the pedlar came on,
>   An' the muckle green pack on his shoulders had he ;
> But he nouther had flesh, blude nor bone,
>   For the moon shone through his thin bodye.

> The ducks they whackit, the dogs they yowled,
>   The herons they skraiched maist piteouslie ;
> An' the horses they snorkit for miles around,
>   While the priest an' the pedlar together might be.

The minister opens his Bible and adjures the ghost to explain its behaviour. The ghost answers that the Lady is to blame; also, it must haunt the spot unless certain crimes and villainies are revealed.

> "My body was butchered within that mill,
>   My bones lie under the inner mill-wheel,
> An' here my spirit maun wander, until
>   Some crimes an' villanies I can reveal :

> "I robbed my niece of three hundred pounds,
>   Which Providence suffered me not to enjoy ;
> For the sake of that money I gat my death's wounds ;
>   The miller me kenned, but he missed his ploy.

> "The money lies buried on Balderstone hill,
>   Beneath the mid ᵃbourack o' three times three : ᵃ *heap*
> O gie't to the owners, kind sir, an' it will
>   Bring wonderfu' comfort an' rest unto me. . . ."

Day is approaching, and the ghost vanishes, not to be seen again. A search in the mill yard turns up the pedlar's bones, and his money is found in the place the ghost described. In an aside the poet remarks that from that day to this the millers of Thirlestane have never prospered.

The tale proceeds. An old mason has kept a small bone of the pedlar's heel. The miller, now an old man but merry as millers are supposed to be, has been living in the forest of Jed. The mason travels there with his bone and finds the miller chatting among his cronies. The mason displays the bone and declares it is a wonderful curiosity. Everyone looks at it and handles it; and the miller, putting on his spectacles, desires to handle it. At his touch, the bone streams blood. Straightway the miller is accused of murder; and, being threatened with a hot iron, he confesses having killed the pedlar. He is hanged at "Jeddart" (Jedburgh).

> An' *afterwards* they in full counsel agreed,
>   That Rob Riddle he richly deserved to dee.

(This, says a footnote, refers to the old and very common proverb: "That such a one will get Jeddart justice": which is, first to hang a man, and then judge whether he was guilty or not.) The ballad concludes:

> Ca't not superstition, if reason you find it,
>   Nor laugh at a story attestit sae well. . . .

"If a person could once succeed in the genuine ballad style," Hogg thought, "his muse was adequate for any other."[48] Writing ballads may, indeed, have taught him something about rhyme and metre; but he had not developed a style of his own, nor decided what were his most profitable subjects. He never would decide these matters. When form, language and subject fused, as they did on rare occasions, his poems seemed happy accidents, or, as he would say, the result of inspiration.

As we have noted, Hogg's earliest writings were songs as well as ballads; he was encouraged to write songs by the example of Burns, and his first published song, "Donald M'Donald," gained wide popularity, though it brought him no fame. His songs appeared in *Scottish Pastorals*, *The Mountain*

[48] "Autobiography," p. 465.

Bard, The Spy, and *The Forest Minstrel,* and in periodicals and "garlands." From 1820 on, the greater part were published in *Blackwood's* and *Fraser's;* and *Songs, by the Ettrick Shepherd* (1831) presented a selection of these.

The publisher's description of *The Forest Minstrel* indicates one method used by Hogg in composing songs: they were "adapted to the most favourite Scottish airs."[49] That is, like Burns he set words to a popular tune. One result of this way of writing was that some of Hogg's songs became popular; a less fortunate result was that some were attributed to other men.[50]

The songs in his first book, *Scottish Pastorals,* borrow the manner of Allan Ramsay, treating pastoral subjects in simple stanzas and light, melodic strains. The language derives from Ramsay and his successors; it is conventional eighteenth-century Scots-English, with a sprinkle of Scotticisms:

> Don't you see yon lofty mountain,
>   Where the wanton lambies play,
> Round an' round the crystal fountain,
>   Springin' frae the sunny brae.[51]

Of the two poems in the collection that are particularly designated as "Songs," the first alone deserves the description:

> 'Twas up yon wild an' lonely glen,
> Beset w' mony lofty mountain,
>   Far frae the busy haunts o' men,
> Ae day that I gaed out a huntin' ;
>   It was a happy day to me,
> A day that fixt my rovin' fancy ;
>   For herdin' lambs on yonder ley,
> There first I saw my lovely Nancy.[52]

---

[49] *The Forest Minstrel,* Philadelphia 1816, title page.

[50] For example, in *Songs, by the Ettrick Shepherd,* Hogg says, " 'Lock the Door, Lariston' . . . was published in my own weekly paper, *The Spy,* March 30, 1811, and found its way into the London papers, and partially through Britain, as the composition of my friend Mr. Gray, now in India. I never contradicted it, thinking that any body might have known that no-one could have written the song but myself. However, it has appeared in every collection of songs with Mr. Gray's name." *Songs, by the Ettrick Shepherd,* Edinburgh, London 1831, p. 198.

[51] *Scottish Pastorals,* p. 25.   [52] *Op. cit.,* p. 56.

The story is not developed, nor are the sentiments. On the other hand, the second "Song" has, within the limits of the form, humour and complexity. It turns upon a fiction that Hogg employs elsewhere: a man may fail to recognise his mistress when she is disguised. But as Shakespeare also offends against probability in this way, perhaps we can forgive Hogg.

The song begins dramatically. We are placed straightway on an Ettrick hillside.

> O shepherd, the weather is misty and changing,
>   Will you shew me over the hills to Traquair?
> I will, gentle stranger, but where are you ranging?
>   So brisk a young gentleman walking is rare. . . .[53]

The shepherd remarks that the stranger must have left "some fair lasses a moaning," he is so handsome. The stranger replies, somewhat from the point, that if the shepherd is single he will have a fine time, for there are so many nubile girls in the region. The shepherd protests he loves only one. The stranger takes exception to this:

> For me, I'm design'd ne'er to yoke with [a]a marrow,   [a] *an equal*
>   But court ilka fair maid that comes in my way;
> This very last summer, in Ettrick and Yarrow,
>   I've lien beside twenty, who ne'er said me nay.[54]

This is bad enough, but he proceeds to specify:

> But the fondest young lassie that ever I spoke wi',
>   She lives wi' her mother, an' [a]nae mae ava,   [a] *no one else*
> Ae night I gaed to her, an', O I was lucky;
>   For that very night the auld wife was awa,
> She made up a bed, an' she bade me gang wi' her;
>   I got all I asked without e'er a frown;
> She kiss'd me an' bless'd me, an', ere I came frae her,
>   She promis'd to see me this winter in town.[55]

With an anxiety understandable enough in the circumstances, the shepherd inquires the name of this obliging young woman. "She lives upon Tyma, her name it is Jeanie," the stranger replies. The shepherd flies into a rage, for Jeanie is his girl.

[53] *Scottish Pastorals*, p. 59.
[54] *Op. cit.*, p. 60.   [55] *Ibid.*

Thereupon the stranger removes his disguise and is transformed into Jeanie herself. Having not seen him for twenty weeks, she has borrowed the clothes from a neighbour and set off to play her trick. The shepherd folds her under his plaid, declaring: "The longer I ken her I'll love her the mair."[56]

The "Song" shows Hogg's debt to ballad tradition, for it echoes, consciously or unconsciously, "The Bailiff's Daughter of Islington," a ballad printed by Percy and Ritson and, it seems, "still very much sung" in Child's day. In the ballad, the Bailiff's daughter, having been parted from her lover for seven years, disguises herself in "puggish attire" and goes to London in search of him. When they meet he asks her if she knows the Bailiff's daughter, and she replies that the Bailiff's daughter is dead. Then, he says, he will go to a far country. Thereupon she reveals her identity and promises to be his bride.[57]

Hogg's patriotic songs are the least interesting, as are all his efforts in undiluted patriotism, in verse or prose. The interest in such works must be supplied by the reader. This is not to say that Hogg could not write a rousing Scottish song. "Donald M'Donald" has a swing to it:

> My name it is Donald M'Donald,
> I live in the Hielands sae grand ;
> I hae follow'd our banner, and will do,
> Wherever my Maker has land.
> When rankit amang the blue bonnets,
> Nae danger can fear me ava ;
> I ken that my brethren around me
> Are either to conquer or fa'.
>   Brogues an' brochen an' a',
>   Brochen an' brogues an' a' ;
>   An' is nae her very weel aff,
>   Wi' her brogues an' brochen an' a' ?[58]

On the other hand, his standard patriotic song is juvenile:

> I sing of a land that was famous of yore,
> The land of Green Appin, the ward of the flood,

---

[56] *Scottish Pastorals*, p. 62.

[57] *The English and Scottish Popular Ballads*, ed. F. J. Child (henceforth cited as Child), repr. New York 1957, 5 vols. (in 3), No. 105 ; II. 426-8.

[58] *Works*, II. 283.

Where every gray cairn that broods o'er the shore,
    Marks grave of the royal, the valiant, or good. . . .[59]

At the worst, he was capable of writing stanzas such as this,
in *The Jubilee*—to be sung to the air "Miss Carmichael's
Minuet":

Who will not join the lay,
And hail the auspicious day
That first gave great George the sway
    Over our island ?
Fifty long years are gone
Since he first fill'd the throne ;
And high honours has he won
    On sea and by land. . . .[60]

Some of Hogg's songs are genteel and sentimental; others
solemnly prate about virtue; and sometimes, as in "The
Skylark," his lyrical flights are aimless:

Bird of the wilderness
Blithesome and cumberless,
Sweet be thy matin o'er moorland and lea !
Emblem of happiness,
Blest is thy dwelling-place—
Oh to abide in the desert with thee ! . . .[61]

Hogg has been compared with Burns, but only in touches
of humour and some descriptions are they at all similar.
Wilson labours the comparison in order to do justice to Hogg:

In fancy James Hogg—in spite of his name and his teeth [62]—
was not inferior to Robert Burns—and why not ? The Forest
is a better schoolroom for Fancy than ever Burns studied in ;
it overflowed with poetical traditions. . . . It is . . . where
Burns was weakest, that the Shepherd is strongest—the world
of shadows. The airy beings that to the impassioned soul of
Burns seemed cold, bloodless, unattractive, rise up lovely in
their own silent domains, before the dreaming fancy of the

---

[59] "The Stuarts of Appin," *op. cit.*, II. 415.   [60] *Op. cit.*, II. 281.
[61] *Op. cit.*, II. 411.
[62] Hogg had protruding teeth. References throughout the *Noctes*, the drawing
by Bewick, and a death-mask in the Library at Selkirk, show that he was not a
handsome man—though the portrait by Nicholson is flattering.

tender-hearted Shepherd. The still green beauty of the pastoral hills and vales where he passed all his days, inspired him with ever-brooding visions of Fairy Land, till, as he lay musing on the brae, the world of shadows seemed, in the clear depths, a softened reflection of real life, like the hills and heavens in the water of his native lake. . . .[63]

So Wilson rhapsodises, and it is easy to understand why Keats, coming upon the article, was more angered by it than he was by the *Blackwood's* review of his own *Endymion*. "The Blackwood Reviewers," he wrote in a letter to George and Georgiana Keats, "have committed themselves in a scandalous heresy— they have been putting up Hogg, the Ettrick Shepherd, against Burns: the senseless villains."[64]

Of Burns' pathos, his command of metaphor, his concentration of language, Hogg has nothing. His best songs, however, are pleasing in their own way; the fancies and the lilting music are his own. The characteristic tone is a mixture of sentiment and good humour:

> See yonder *a*pawkie shepherd   *a artful*
>   That lingers on the hill,
> His ewes are in the fauld,
>   An' his lambs are lying still ;
> Yet he *a*downa gang to bed,   *a cannot*
>   For his heart is in a flame
> To meet his bonnie lassie
>   When the kye comes hame.
>   When the kye comes hame,
>   When the kye comes hame,
>   'Tween the gloaming and the mirk,
>   When the kye comes hame. . . .[65]

Hogg's satiric vein is displayed in "The Village of Balmaquhapple" ("'Tis steep'd in iniquity up to the thrapple")[66]

---

[63] John Wilson, *The works of Professor Wilson*, ed. Professor Ferrier, Edinburgh and London 1857, IX (i), "Recreations of Christopher North," pp. 201, 202-3.
   The essay here titled "An Hour's Talk about Poetry" is revised from the essay published in *Blackwood's Edinburgh Marazine*, IV, No. 23 (Feb. 1819), pp. 521-9, under the title : "Some observations on the poetry of the agricultural and that of the pastoral districts of Scotland, illustrated by a comparative view of the genius of Burns and the Ettrick Shepherd." This was the article Keats saw.
   [64] Quoted in Strout, p. 165.   [65] *Works*, II. 413-4.
   [66] *Op. cit.*, II. 413.

and "The Lass o' Carlisle," a small masterpiece portraying the
fate of Beauty in the Scottish community—she gets "plenty
o' weans" to keep her hands and mind occupied:

> This lassie had plenty o' wooers,
>   As beauty an' wealth should hae ;
> This lassie she took her a man,
>   An' then she could get nae mae.
> This lassie had plenty o' weans,
>   That keepit her hands astir ;
> And then she dee'd and was buried,
>   An' there was an end of her. . . .[67]

Using satire seems to make Hogg self-critical, to put him on
guard against sinking. His satirical songs avoid the mawkish
sentimentality that mars his politer efforts.

In 1822 Hogg attempted to publish imitations, or rather,
new versions, of Moore's *Irish Melodies*. Hogg had his own
"Minstrel Boy":

> The minstrel boy to the glen is gone,
>   In its deepest dells you'll find him. . . .[68]

He was persuaded by Moore's publishers to withdraw the
collection, but nine years later, in *Songs, by the Ettrick Shepherd*,
he did publish these poems, with notes that argue that he, not
Moore, is the injured party. "The Maid of the Sea"

> Is one of the many songs which Moore caused me to cancel,
> for nothing I know of, but because they ran counter to his. It
> is quite natural and reasonable that an author should claim
> a copyright of a sentiment ; but it never struck me that it
> could be so exclusively his, as that another had not a right to
> contradict it.[69]

He threatens to force Moore to cancel *Lalla Rookh*, "for stealing
it wholly from the Queen's Wake." Moore "had better have
let [his] few trivial songs alone."[70]

In Miss Batho's opinion, "the Moore incident looks like
an unsuccessful joke."[71] Indeed, Hogg never was—as far as

---

[67] *Works*, II. 427.
[69] *Songs by the Ettrick Shepherd*, p. 71.
[68] *Op. cit.*, II. 411.
[70] *Ibid*.
[71] Batho, p. 154.

can be proved—dishonest. But he sometimes acted in a way that might be confused with dishonesty. It is necessary to remember that literary practices were a great deal looser in Hogg's day than they are now; that the *Blackwood's* group were given to joking in print that would not have been tolerated at a later time; and that Hogg—whose own works had been sometimes attributed to others, and to whom, in the character of the Shepherd, were attributed whole conversations he had never uttered—did not have a scrupulous idea of the rights of authorship. Moreover, he found it hard to believe that anyone could be offended with him. Writing to John Murray on 11 Aug. 1818, he says he has heard that Gifford has a "hard prejudice" against him. But he cannot believe it :

> I do not see how any man can have a prejudice against me. He may, indeed, consider me an intruder in the walks of literature, but I am only a saunterer, and malign nobody who chooses to let me pass.[72]

But in view of the Moore episode we may wonder what else Hogg borrowed. Some of his songs are strangely familiar. "Charlie is my Darling"—haven't we heard *that* before? But wasn't the wording different? Wilson broaches the question squarely:

> All great song-writers . . . have been great thieves. . . . So hath the Shepherd stolen many of the Flowers of the Forest— whose beauty had breathed there ever since Flodden's fatal overthrow ; but they had been long fading and pining away in the solitary places, wherein so many of their kind had utterly disappeared, and beneath the restoring light of his genius their bloom and their balm were for ever removed.[73]

Under the snake-oil and magic balm of Wilson's prose, the meaning is clear: Hogg took other men's songs and remade them as his own.

So he did—sometimes. But, when he borrowed, more often than not he admitted it. Certainly, he never tried to

---

[72] Smiles, II. 6.
[73] John Wilson, *The Works of Professor Wilson*, IX (i). 204-6.

deny it. Could anyone refuse him credit for "When Maggy gangs away" because, as he tells the reader, he heard a girl lilting over the first line and went away and made a song out of that?[74] And his variations on "My Love she's but a Lassie yet," as Miss Batho remarks, make it new.[75]

[74] *Songs, by the Ettrick Shepherd,* p. 77.
[75] Batho, pp. 157-8.

F

III

The Natural Gate

HIS first attempt at the long narrative poem, as we have seen, made Hogg famous. Encouraged by the success of *The Queen's Wake*, he attempted the medium again in *The Pilgrims of the Sun, Mador of the Moor*, and *Queen Hynde*. These poems were failures. His talent was not for telling a long story in verse, and if we examine *The Queen's Wake* we see that it is only the ingenious plan that enables Hogg's weaknesses in this form to be overlooked. The work succeeds, but it is not a narrative; it is a series of separate poems connected by descriptive verse, giving the appearance of a narrative.[1]

The Queen's Wake is based on the history of Queen Mary's arrival in Scotland, on 20 Aug. 1561. At Leith the Queen was met by certain nobles and by certain burgesses of Edinburgh, and escorted to the "Abbie of Holierood-house," where the Court assembled.[2] During her stay at Holyrood, in John Knox's account:

> Fyres of joy were set furth at night, and a cumpanie of maist honest men, with instruments of musick, gave ther salutation at hir chalmer windo : the melodie, as sche alledged, lyked her weill, and sche willed the sam to be continued sum nychts efter with grit diligence.[3]

The Frenchman Dufresnoy, who was in the escort, gives a less favourable account. The horses on which the queen and

---

[1] Wilson points this out : " 'The Queen's Wake' is a garland of fair forest flowers, bound with a band of rushes from the moor. It is not a poem . . . nor was it intended to be so ; you might as well call a bright bouquet of flowers a flower, which, by the by, we do in Scotland." *The Works of Professor Wilson*, IX (i), p. 202.

[2] *Works*, II. 4, n. 1. John Knox, *The History of the Reformation of Religion in Scotland*, London 1905, pp. 226-7.

[3] *Works*, II. 4, n. 1.

courtiers rode were "the little wretched hackneys of the country, and as wretchedly caparisoned; at sight of which the queen began to weep, and to compare them with the pomp and superb palfreys of France." What was worst of all, says Dufresnoy, when they had retired to rest in the Abbey:

> . . . there came under her window a crew of five or six hundred scoundrels from the city, who gave her a serenade with wretched violins and rebecks, of which there are enough in that country, and began to sing psalms so miserably mistimed and mistuned, that nothing could be worse. Alas ! what music ! and what a night's rest ![4]

On an idealisation of the event, Hogg constructs *The Queen's Wake*. In his introduction, using Scott's octosyllabic couplets, the poet announces that he has found his "mountain Lyre" again:

> I little thought that idle toy
> Should e'er become my only joy.[5]

He laments the decline of minstrelsy, which is now heard only after midnight, "When wanes the circling year away."[6] (In the early years of the nineteenth century, during the Christmas season, itinerant minstrels still performed in the streets of Edinburgh after midnight.[7]) Those wakes, he says, that are now played only by poor minstrels, first began:

> When royal MARY, blithe of mood,
> Kept holiday at Holyrood.[8]

The poet describes the Queen's progress from Leith. As she nears the Abbey, a minstrel sings to her, and she expresses her delight in the music. The Earl of Argyle tells her that this is nothing in comparison to the powers of Highland song. Arrived at Holyrood, she sends out a herald who proclaims:

> "Each Caledonian bard must seek
> Her courtly halls on Christmas week,
> That then the royal Wake may be
> Cheered by their thrilling minstrelsy.

---

[4] *Works*, II. 4, n. I.   [5] *Op. cit.*, II. 2.
[6] *Ibid*.   [7] Thomson's note, *Works*, II. 3.
[8] *Works*, II. 3.

> No ribaldry the queen must hear,
> No song unmeet for maiden's ear,
> No jest, nor adulation bland ;
> But legends of our native land ;
> And he whom most the court regards,
> High be his honours and rewards. . . .[9]

The bards prepare their songs. The time of the wake approaches:

> December came ; his aspect stern
> Glared deadly o'er the mountain cairn ;
> A polar sheet was round him flung,
> And ice-spears at his girdle hung ;
> O'er frigid field, and drifted cone,
> He strode undaunted and alone ;
> Or, throned amid the Grampians gray,
> Kept thaws and suns of heaven at bay.[10]

The bards gather at Holyrood to compete before the Queen. Their order of appearance is fixed by casting lots.

The first bard to perform is Rizzio, the Queen's secretary. His song, "Malcolm of Lorn," tells of the parting of the lovers, Ann of Glen-Ora and Malcolm; how, when she was permitted to join Malcolm, it was too late; he died of a broken heart. The song, we are told, was admired, but not liked; it was "vapid, artful, terse. . . ."[11]

The second bard, Gardyn, sings of "Young Kennedy." The hero, a savage Highlander, seduces Matilda; soon after, her father is found dead. Kennedy and Matilda are married. On the bridal night Kennedy flees naked and howling out to the moors. Matilda tells that her father's ghost has revealed that he was strangled by Kennedy, and has threatened to follow him forever. A grim phantom still wanders the gloaming.[12]

In all, seventeen bards are described by the author, among whom he portrays himself, his friend Grieve, and Allan Cunningham. The bard of Ettrick is clearly Hogg:

> Poor wight ! he never weened how hard
> For poverty to earn regard !

---

[9] *Works*, II. 5.
[11] *Op. cit.*, II. 7-9.
[10] *Op. cit.*, II. 6.
[12] *Op. cit.*, II. 10-12.

Dejection o'er his visage ran,
His coat was bare, his colour wan,
His forest doublet darned and torn,
His shepherd plaid all rent and worn . . .
The bard on Ettrick's mountain green
In nature's bosom nursed had been . . .
When o'er her mellow notes he ran,
And his wild mountain chant began,
Then first was noted in his eye
A gleam of native energy.[13]

The Ettrick bard sings of "Old David": David leads his seven sons against a den of fairies, to rescue kidnapped maidens. Since that day,

. . . fears of elf, and fairy raid
Have like a morning dream decayed.[14]

Thirteen of the bards' songs—not songs, but poems—are given in full. Hogg tells us:

. . . many a bard of name,
Who there appeared and strove for fame,
No record names, nor minstrel's tongue. . . .[15]

For this we may be thankful, for only two of the poems that are given are good: "The Witch of Fife" and "Kilmeny"— though perhaps "The Abbot M'Kinnon" also deserves to be read.

On the third night of the wake the prize is awarded. In spite of the Queen's preference for Rizzio, Gardyn—who sang "Young Kennedy"—is voted first in "the first division." Second comes the Ettrick Shepherd. Third, a nameless youth. But when it comes to judging among these contenders, a tumult breaks out. The Lord of Mar advises that they sing again and the Queen alone judge. On this, the nameless youth withdraws; Gardyn sings a love song, and the Ettrick bard, a "fairy strain." Gardyn bears away the prize, Queen Mary's harp, which—the poet tells us—"defaced of all its gems and gold," is now at Edinburgh. Seeing the shepherd's dis-appointment, the Queen offers him "a countless store" of

[13] *Works*, ii. 20-1. [14] *Op. cit.*, ii. 24.
[15] *Op. cit.*, ii. 12.

Scottish songs and a cottage. He asks for a harp instead. The
Queen has a harp "framed by wizard of the wild," of magical
power, which she awards to him. In his hands it becomes
famous. With his death it is silenced, but ages later the harp
passes to Bangour, Ramsay, Langhorn, Logan, and Walter
Scott:

> The land was charmed to list his lays ;
> It knew the harp of ancient days. . . .[16]

Scott wakes the spirits of forgotten chiefs and brings back the
fairies. Then he hands on the harp to the author of *The
Queen's Wake*. Scott, says the poet:

> Watched my first notes with curious eye,
> And wondered at my minstrelsy.[17]

Scott leaves the region; the Shepherd is now sole possessor
of the ancient harp.

A short ballad ends *The Queen's Wake*. It is winter now,
and the poet bids farewell to his harp. In the spring, he will
return to it:

> Then will I seek the aged thorn,
>   The haunted wild and fairy ring,
> Where oft thy erring numbers borne
>   Have taught the wandering winds to sing.[18]

By its structure, *The Queen's Wake* allows Hogg to display
his technique in various forms. The narrative thread, as we
have seen, consists of quick-moving octosyllabic couplets—
imitating Scott's style in *The Lay of the Last Minstrel* and *The
Lady of the Lake*. Some of the offerings of the bards—"The
Witch of Fife," "Glen-Abin," "Earl Walter," and "Mary
Scott"—are in ballad quatrains. In the other lays, Hogg
works in various metres and rhyme-schemes. But, as we have
noted, in writing verse he often lacks a sense of form and
language; he deals with his subject in jigging metre and

---

[16] *Works*, II. 58.

[17] *Ibid.* Here Hogg says that Scott attempted to discourage his early poetic
efforts. The episode is described in the *Domestic Manners*. Scott undertook to
obtain employment for him as chief shepherd to Lord Porchester, on condition
that he write no more poetry. Hogg refused. *Domestic Manners*, p. 104.

[18] *Op. cit.*, II. 59.

conventional phrases; when story and style are suited it seems
to have happened by chance.

The galloping metre and clichés of "Young Kennedy"—
sung by the prize-winning bard—combine to make the action
ridiculous:

> "The cave shall not cover, the cloud shall not hide thee ;
>   At noon I will wither thy sight with my frown :
> In gloom of the night I will lay me beside thee,
>   And pierce with this weapon thy bosom of stone."
> Fast fled the despoiler with howlings most dire,
> Fast followed the spirit with rapier of fire ;
> Away, and away, through the silent saloon,
> And away, and away, by the light of the moon.[19]

Even in the better "songs," such absurdities occur;

> No more the watch-fires gleam to the blast,
> M'Kinnon and friends arrive at last.[20]

The awarding of the prizes by Hogg invites speculation.
In rejecting Rizzio, he rejects the presumptions of authority;
the Queen cannot carry her way against the popular vote. Is
Hogg thereby revealing his own resentment of the authority
of Tory Edinburgh? When he awards the prize to the Highland
bard, and a consolatory prize to the shepherd, is he protesting
on behalf of popular Scottish poetry? It is impossible to decide
what Hogg really thinks of these matters, for the bards whom
he singles out for the awards, though they sing of Scotland,
sing in English. The only examples of native idiom in *The
Queen's Wake* are "The Witch of Fife" (a *pastiche* of archaic,
ballad Scots) and "Kilmeny" (English sprinkled with Scots,
in about the proportions that Ramsay uses in *The Gentle
Shepherd*). If Hogg prefers a Scottish song to Rizzio's, it is
Scottish only in the sense that the bard is a Highlander, and
the song describes Scottish scenes (as does Rizzio's, for that
matter). But in manner and language the prize-winning
poetry is conventionally English.

Considering the whole of *The Queen's Wake*, we see that the
two best songs are written in a mixture of English and Scots,

---

[19] "Young Kennedy," *op. cit.*, II. 12.
[20] "The Abbot M'Kinnon," *op. cit.*, II. 53.

and deal with folklore. We may therefore conclude that Hogg's strength lay in writing about folk traditions, in the vernacular. But he himself was not aware of this. If he had any dislike of the polite, literary standards then prevailing in Edinburgh, if he suspected that Scott's verse was not a perfect model, he did not express his dissatisfaction in any clear way.

In his "Autobiography" Hogg attacks "a powerful aristocracy" who think that literature is "their own peculiar right"; but he attacks them only because they resent and impede the progress of the "intruder," humble James Hogg—not because their standards are wrong.[21] To the contrary, he does his best to write for them. Still, the asperity with which Hogg rejects Rizzio's song, as artful, vapid, and somehow not "Scottish," does suggest that Hogg was not entirely at ease, in his own mind, with the literary models of the day.

We have discussed "The Witch of Fife";[22] "Kilmeny," the best known of all Hogg's poems, remains to be considered. "The poem of Kilmeny is so beautiful," says the Reverend Thomson, "that had Hogg written nothing more, it would have sufficed to place him in the front rank of our national poets."[23]

"Kilmeny" is presented by Drummond from Ern in the Highlands, a visionary bard of forbidding, wintry appearance:

> Loathed his firm soul the measured chime
> And florid films of modern rhyme :
> No other lays became his tongue
> But those his rude forefathers sung.[24]

The lay moves freely in tetrameters based on disyllabic and trisyllabic feet. The language is Scots—natural and unaffected Scots, though much diluted:

> Bonny Kilmeny gaed up the glen ;
> But it wasna to meet Duneira's men,
> Nor the rosy monk of the isle to see,
> For Kilmeny was pure as pure could be.
> It was only to hear the *Yorlin sing,   *yellow-hammer*
> And pu' the cress-flower round the spring ;

[21] "Autobiography," p. 456.   [22] See above, pp. 94-103.
[23] *Works*, II. 1.   [24] *Op. cit.*, II. 32.

The scarlet hypp and the hyndberrye,
And the nut that hung frae the hazel tree ;
For Kilmeny was pure as pure could be.
But lang may her *a*minny look o'er the wa',   *a mother*
And lang may she seek i' the greenwood shaw ;
Lang the laird of Duneira blame,
And lang, lang *a*greet or Kilmeny come hame ![25]   *a weep*

When everyone has given her up for lost and Masses have
been said for her soul, Kilmeny returns. She tells her friends
that she has been transported by spirits to "a land of light";
the spirits wished to show her to their own kind as an example
of how pure a woman might be. Then they placed her in
"the stream of life," which bore her in a whirl of glory to a
mountain; from that vantage, looking down upon Scotland,
she viewed the history of Mary, Queen of Scots, and the war
between England and France, symbolised by the struggle of a
lion and an eagle. Other scenes followed, "till . . . all was
love and harmony." She asked the spirits to let her return to
the world, to tell her friends:

> That all whose minds *a*unmeled remain   *a unstained*
> Shall bloom in beauty when time is gane.[26]

The spirits cast her into a sleep, from which she has waked after
an absence of seven years.

Kilmeny now seems a miraculous creature; she sings
"hymns of other worlds" that draw beasts and birds around
her. "It was," says the poet, "like an eve in a sinless world."
But this was only an interlude. When a month and a day
had passed, Kilmeny once more "sought the greenwood wene,"
and disappeared for ever, leaving her friends to wonder whether
she were living or dead. The poem concludes:

> It wasna her hame and she couldna remain ;
> She left this world of sorrow and pain,
> And returned to the land of thought again.[27]

Original though it seems, "Kilmeny" draws on ballad lore.
First, there is the traditional belief that "unco" folk may
bring human beings under their jurisdiction. They may do

---

[25] *Works*, II. 32.   [26] *Op. cit.*, II. 35.   [27] *Ibid.*

so by several means: by enchantment—the human being eats, drinks or speaks in the Otherworld, and is thereby enchanted; by physical contact; or through fairy gifts, music, runic charms, riddlecraft, or fairy darts.[28] As Child remarks, there is peril in dealing with "unco" folk, "be they fairies, dwarfs, water-sprites, devils, or departed spirits."[29] In the ballad cycle, "Thomas Rhymer," Thomas, having kissed the elf-queen, must go with her.[30] In "Tam Lin," Tam is abducted by the queen of fairies, but redeemed by the love of his human mistress.[31] In a footnote to "Kilmeny" Hogg mentions the "old tradition" on which the poem is founded, and relates two modern instances of abduction by fairies.[32] (He uses the theme also in "Old David," as we have seen, and in his prose tale, "Mary Burnet.") Also traditional is the place of enchantment, the "green wood" where Kilmeny falls asleep. In folklore the place of enchantment may be beneath an apple tree, at a fairy well, on an elfin hill, or in a magic wood.[33] And the spirit world of "Kilmeny," in the vagueness of its location, is traditional. L. C. Wimberly says, "The ballad geography of spiritland is decidedly puzzling. . . . Is the abode of the departed, or the land of elves and demons, associated with the forest; is it on a hill or mountain; is it subterranean, submarine, over the sea, or on an island; is it far away; is it terrestrial or celestial?"[34] Though a phrase or stanza in the ballads may enable us to answer these questions, the cosmography of the Otherworld is never clear.

This vagueness is the main fault of "Kilmeny," and tradition can hardly be pleaded as an excuse. Also, Hogg's own additions in the way of symbolism are unwieldy: the lion and eagle are types of political cartooning rather than inventions (Coleridge's albatross comes to mind) of the poetic imagination. The poem requires a suspension of thought. But, luckily, the poem is about just that—Kilmeny's suspension of thought, her trance; and for some readers, Hogg's own failure to imagine clearly has seemed part of the enchantment.

[28] Lowry Charles Wimberly, *Folklore in the English and Scottish Ballads*, Chicago 1928, pp. 275-330, *passim*.

[29] Child, No. 37 ; I. 322.

[30] *Idem.*, No. 37 ; I. 323-9.

[31] *Idem.*, No. 39 ; I. 340-54.

[32] *Works*, II. 32.

[33] Wimberly, pp. 275-330, *passim*.

[34] *Idem.*, p. 121.

However, if we compare "Kilmeny" with, for example, "Christabel," where fantastic episodes are clearly visualised and the action seems logical—as in dreams action does—"Kilmeny" is less persuasive. The real charm of the poem is in its aërial, fading music—for once Hogg has found the right form—and in the nostalgia for a world, Elfland and Eden, that is fading:

> The land of vision it would seem,
> A still, an everlasting dream.[35]

The structure of *The Queen's Wake* enabled Hogg to carry off that poem bravely. But, deceived by success, he persisted in a medium for which he was absolutely unsuited. He had written *The Queen's Wake*; the great poets of the past had written epics; the celebrated poets of his own time, Scott, Byron, and Moore, were writing long narratives. Why should he not persist? In the "Autobiography" he admits the fault of *The Pilgrims of the Sun*: ". . . it bears an impress of extravagance, and affords no relief from the story of a visionary existence."[36] But he defends his other failures. Of *Mador of the Moor* he writes: ". . . my highest and most fortunate efforts in rhyme are contained in some of the descriptions of nature in that poem."[37] Of *Queen Hynde* he says that he began it, unlike his other poems, "on a regular plan," pluming himself that it was to prove his greatest work.[38] But then the failure of his poetical drama removed his hopes of success as a poet, and he put off finishing *Queen Hynde* for several years. Scott's approval encouraged him to publish it, but "That malicious *deevil*, Jerdan, first took it up and damned it with faint praise. The rest of the reviewers followed in his wake, so that, in short, the work sold heavily and proved rather a failure."[39] He defends this, his most ambitious poem, particularly against the charge that it is inferior to *The Queen's Wake*. On one occasion, he says, he claimed that *Queen Hynde* was "the best epic poem that had ever been produced in Scotland." It is unfortunate, in his

[35] *Works*, II. 33.　　　　　[36] "Autobiography," p. 452.
[37] *Ibid.*, p. 451.　　　　　[38] *Ibid.*, p. 454.
[39] *Ibid.* Note, however, that *Blackwood's* puffed it. See *Noctes Ambrosianae*, II. 44, where North calls the poem Hogg's masterpiece, and says that "James Hogg will go down as one of the true worthies of the age."

opinion, that the plot is laid in an age so early that we have no interest in it.[40]

At this distance in time, prejudiced reviews cannot affect our judgment. On their own merits, *The Pilgrims of the Sun*, *Mador of the Moor* and *Queen Hynde* are failures, deservedly forgotten. The most apparent fault is the lack of vital form and language. This becomes a disaster when the poem extends, as does *Queen Hynde*, through 437 pages. The octosyllabic English couplets, as they trip lightly, wind the reader; the doggerel verse parodies the episodes and situations of the "epic." In *Mador of the Moor* the Spenserian stanzas move awkwardly, seeming, at best, an imitation. In *The Pilgrims of the Sun* the poet attempts to vary his technique. The first part is in ballad quatrains; the second, in unrhymed pentameters; the third, in heroic couplets—and so on. Lacking any confidence in his subject, he casts about for mechanical aids. The result of this desperate ingenuity is to dislocate the narrative. The reader is pulled this way and that; he is made all the more aware of the monotony when it is interrupted.

The uncertainty of the poet's technique is closely linked to another fault—his poor choice of subjects; and both are symptomatic of Hogg's *malaise*. It is significant of the state of Scottish culture under the Union that a writer of Hogg's undoubted genius should have wasted his time on such completely unreal subjects. Once he had permitted himself to be patronised by the Scots Tory writers, he could not help falsifying popular tradition, his own deepest inspiration, in the same way—though not, perhaps, to the same extent—as they did, and he recoiled from reality into purely romantic worlds. In *The Pilgrims of the Sun* he transports the spirit of a mildly agnostic young lady into space, instructs her in theology, history, and philosophy, and guides her on a tour of the planets. He adopts the very accents of Milton:

> Harp of Jerusalem ! how shall my hand
> Awake the hallelujahs ?—How begin
> The song that tells of light ineffable. . . .[41]

How, indeed!

---

[40] "Autobiography," p. 455.   [41] *Works*, II. 130.

In *Mador of the Moor* he imitates Scott's *Lady of the Lake*, in which are related the adventures of a king wandering in disguise. Mador the Minstrel seduces and abandons a young woman. She follows her minstrel lover to court, and discovers that he is the king, whereupon he marries her. The only vitality in this tale is shown by the heroine's parents in their peevish quarrels.

Queen Hynde is set in remote history. The young queen is hard pressed by an invader from Norway, King Eric, who is determined to marry her and appropriate Scotland. Hynde is helped by St Columba, who undertakes to bring over from Ireland the rightful heir to the Scottish throne, Prince Eiden. The form of the narrative is Scott's octosyllabic couplets. To cram his subject into the short lines, Hogg omits articles and inverts the natural order of words. On almost every page there is ridiculous verse and action. Two examples will suffice:

> Think of a lady all alone—
> The beauteous Hynde of Caledon—
> Toss'd up in air a hideous height
> On point of blood-stain'd horn to light ;
> And if to wail thou can'st delay,
> Have thou a bard's anathema ![42]

> No stately marshal was allow'd,
> Nor umpire, verging from the crowd,
> To meddle with the mortal strife ;
> Each hero fought for death or life.
> Few words on either side were spoke,
> To daunt opponent or provoke ;
> For why ? the storm so fiercely jarr'd,
> They neither could be said nor heard.
> Their weapons met with clanging blows,
> And high from helm and buckler rose.
> Mar lost his ground, as Eric press'd ;
> But calmly still the king regress'd ;
> With foe before, and foe behind,
> To quit his line he had no mind,
> And vantage of the rain and wind.[43]

---

[42] *Works*, II. 190.   [43] *Op. cit.*, II. 226.

To turn from *Queen Hynde* to the short narrative poem, "Ringan and May" is to be, once more, astonished at the distance between Hogg's worst and best.

"Ringan and May," published in *Blackwood's* in 1825 and reprinted in *A Queer Book* in 1832, has passed unnoticed, like other good poems and stories lost in the mass of Hogg's inferior writings. Yet I would place this poem above "Kilmeny" if not above "The Witch of Fife."

In a mixture of English and Scots—there is a sprinkling of Scots inflexions, but only a few distinctively Scots words and usages—a love-story is told from the viewpoint of the woman speaking. Her feelings about her lover are drawn from her reluctantly; her tongue is loosened by the passion she describes; the poem becomes lyrical, and draws back in modesty and irony, and yields again—as she herself has yielded and withdrawn:

> I heard a *ª*laverock singing with glee,   *ª lark*
> And oh but the bird sang cheerilye ;
> Then I askit at my true love Ringan,
> If he kend what the bonny bird was singing ?
>
> Now, my love Ringan is blithe and young,
> But he has a fair and flattering tongue ;
> And oh, I'm fear'd I like ower weel
> His tales of love, though kind and *ª*leal !   *ª loyal*
> So I said to him, in scornful ways,
> "You ken nae word that wee burd says !"[44]

Smiling, Ringan tells her that the bird is only singing what he himself has told her a thousand times, and translates the song: the bird is singing that his mate thinks he is the nonpareil of birds, and rhapsodising on the softness of her breast. At this, May weeps and says: "He's ane base and wicked bird."

> It's a shame to mount on his morning wing,
> At the *ª*yetts of heaven *ᵇ*sic sangs to sing ;   *ª gates   ᵇ such*
> And all to win with his amorous din,
> A sweet little virgin bird to sin. . . .[45]

---

[44] *Works*, II. 343.   [45] *Ibid.*

Then Ringan takes her in his arms. She resists him:

> For I fear'd my heart was going wrang,
> It was so moved at the laverock's sang. . . .[46]

But still the bird sings, and she asks Ringan: "What's that little deevil saying now?"

He is singing, says Ringan, that he will feed and care for his mate, and love her forever.

> Then my heart it bled with a thrilling pleasure
> When it learn'd the laverock's closing measure,
> And it rose, and rose, and would not rest,
> And would hardly bide within my breast.
> Then up I rose, and away I sprung,
> And said to my love with scornful tongue,
> That it was ane big and burning shame ;
> That he and the lark were both to blame ;
> For there were some lays so soft and bland
> That breast of maiden could not stand ;
> And if he lay in the wood his lane,
> *a*Quhill I came back to list the strain   *a till*
> Of an amorous bird amang the broom,
> Then he might lie quhill the day of doom !

> But for all the sturt and strife I made ;
> For all I did, and all I said,
> Alas ! I fear it will be lang
> Or I forget that wee burd's sang !
> And langer still or I can flee
> The lad that told that sang to me ![47]

In this poem, as in "The Adventures of Basil Lee," Hogg has rendered a woman's character with admirable realism. One phrase—"What's that little deevil saying now?"—contains more poetry than the whole of *Queen Hynde*. It is as though the admixture of colloquial Scots—slight though it is —enables Hogg to find his "natural gate." As the literary conventions are removed, his confidence in his own knowledge of human nature, and his vivacity, are renewed.

The idea of *The Poetic Mirror, or Living Bards of Britain* was suggested to Hogg, he relates in his "Autobiography," in the

---

[46] *Works*, II, 343.   [47] *Op. cit.*, II, 343-4.

following manner.[48]   He intended collecting a poem from
every living author in Britain and publishing them in a volume,
by which he might make a fortune.   He applied, either in
person or by letter, to Southey, Wilson, Wordsworth, Lloyd,
Morehead, Pringle, Paterson, and several others, all of whom
sent him "very ingenious and beautiful poems."   Wordsworth
later reclaimed his; Byron and Rogers promised, but did not
perform.   Scott absolutely refused, which was a blow, for Hogg
had counted on his support and "had never asked anything of
him in all his life that he refused."   Hogg broke with Scott—
though the rupture was only temporary.   Then he began
"with a heavy heart" to look over the pieces he had received.

> They were, indeed, all very well ; but I did not see that they
> possessed such merit as could give celebrity to any work ;[49]
> and after considering them well, I fancied that I could write
> a better poem than any that had been sent or would be sent
> to me, and this so completely in the style of each poet, that it
> should not be known but for his own production. . . . I set
> to work with great glee, as the fancy had struck me, and in a
> few days I finished my imitations of Wordsworth and Lord
> Byron. . . . The "Poetic Mirror" was completely an off-hand
> production.   I wrote it all in three weeks, except a very small
> proportion ; and in less than three months it was submitted
> to the public.[50]

The second poem, he says, "the most beautiful and ingenious piece," is not his, but Thomas Pringle's; and there is
another small secret he cannot yet reveal.   He congratulates
himself that the first edition has sold out in six weeks, and that
a second of 750 copies has since been sold.

> I do not set any particular value on any poem in the work by
> myself, except the "Gude Greye Katte," which was written as
> a caricature of "The Pilgrims of the Sun," the "Witch of
> Fife," and some others of my fairy ballads.   It is greatly

---

[48] "Autobiography," pp. 453-4, *passim*.   Gillies says that Hogg got the idea
for *The Poetic Mirror* from a "scrap-book" which lay on Gillies' table.   *Memoirs
of a Literary Veteran*, II. 185.

[49] In spite of their being "very ingenious and beautiful poems !"   This is
typical of the contradictions in the "Autobiography."

[50] "Autobiography," pp. 453-4.

superior to any of them. I have also been told that in England, one of the imitations of Wordsworth's "Excursion" has been deemed excellent.[51]

Strout questions this account of the genesis of *The Poetic Mirror* and of Scott's part in it. On 3 June 1814, Strout says, Hogg had written Byron for aid with a "poetical repository" to be published half-yearly; and on 4 June he made the same request of Southey. Hogg's abusive letter to Scott was occasioned not by Scott's refusal to support the "Repository," but "because of Scott's supposed attack on himself at the end of a criticism of a drama Hogg was attempting." Scott may have frowned on Hogg's scheme "to getting [*sic*] his poetical contemporaries to write for his benefit, but he was perfectly willing to help him with his periodical." Moreover, after the reconciliation in the spring of 1815, the relation between Hogg and Scott was most cordial. From Hogg's letters we gather that Byron's failure to send a contribution was far more important than Scott's frowning on the "joint-stock adventure in authorship" in knocking the original scheme on the head. In short, without further evidence to justify his story, Hogg's account of the genesis of *The Poetic Mirror*, as far as Scott is concerned, simply is not true.[52]

By his own account it seems that Hogg meant these poems to be taken as the work of the poets in whose style he was writing. The Advertisement to the volume carries on the subterfuge:

> The Editor claims no merit in the following work, save that of having procured from the Authors the various poems of which the volume is composed.[53]

Taking Hogg's statements at face value, Sir George Douglas expresses his opinion forcibly:

> Remarkable as is the history of its production, the new volume need scarcely detain us. All readers of the delightful *Rejected Addresses* will agree that the frank parody has its place in literature, though it is a place which ought never to be a large one. But the "poetical imitation"—a thing, at the best, of

---

[51] "Autobiography," p. 454.   [52] Strout, pp. 112-13.
[53] *Works*, II. 145.

sheer barren cleverness and the weariness bred thereof—has
no place at all. And the poems in this volume—though
innocent, of course, except as indicating some lack of respect
in the author for his calling—are simply unblushing forgeries.[54]

Here Douglas's judgment, usually acute, has deserted him.
Whatever Hogg's original intention, his performance is beyond
reproach. Though some of the poems might be read as the
works of the authors imitated, there are enough obvious
parodies in the volume to cast doubt upon the authenticity of
the "imitations." Only a very gullible reader could be
deceived.

The entertainment of the *Mirror* opens with "The Guerilla,"
a parody of Byron, presenting Juan as one of the actors in a
story told in the stanzas and rhetoric of "Childe Harold."[55]
The poem was thought by those who first heard it, Hogg
relates, to be Byron's.[56] Hogg's editor, Thomson, finds in
it "some sounding stanzas and deep feelings of misanthropical
scorn, in which the author of 'Childe Harold' might have
recognized the echoes of his own voice."[57] But, to find Byron's
true accent in these lines, one would have to be tone-deaf;
to think the tale serious, one would have to lack a sense of
humour. "The Guerilla" relates a Spanish episode. Kela,
the beloved of Alayni, is stolen away by a Frenchman.
Alayni kills his enemy and, since Kela has been stained, he kills
her too. Then he leads the guerillas against a rich convoy, and—
for he is now an absolute misogynist—plans to slaughter all the
captured women. The women are led off by the guerillas to
their beds. In the morning, they are all found decapitated,
and Alayni has fled to the mountains. He dies, we are told:

> . . . in maniac guise 'mid bloody broil,
> Laughing aloud, yet pressing to his breast
> A tiar of raven hair which every morn he kissed.[58]

There are some minds, the poet reflects, that are not framed
for happiness.

---

[54] Douglas, pp. 80-1.   [55] *Works*, II. 145-9.
[56] "Autobiography," p. 454.   [57] *Works*, II. 144.
                     [58] *Op. cit.*, II. 149.

"Wat o' the Cleuch," an imitation of Scott's narratives, is livelier than the poems in which Hogg tries to emulate them:

> Wat o' the Cleuch came down through the dale,
> In helmet and hauberk of glistening mail ;
> Full proudly he came on his berry-black steed,
> Caparisoned, belted for warrior deed.
> Oh, bold was the bearing, and brisk the career,
> And broad was the cuirass, and long was the spear,
> And tall was the plume that waved over the brow
> Of that dark reckless borderer, Wat o' the Cleuch.[59]

"Isabelle," a parody of Coleridge's "Christabel," is also a notable piece of work:

> Can there be a moon in heaven to-night,
> That the hill and the gray cloud seem so light ?
> The air is whitened by some spell,
> For there is no moon, I know it well ;
> On this third day, the sages say
> ('Tis wonderful how well they know)
> The moon is journeying far away,
> Bright somewhere in a heaven below.
>
> It is a strange and lovely night,
> A grayish pale, but not white !
> Is it rain, or is it dew,
> That falls so thick I see its hue ?
> In rays it follows, one, two, three,
> Down the air so merrily,
> Said Isabelle ; so let it be !
>
> Why does the Lady Isabelle
> Sit in the damp and dewy dell,
> Counting the racks of drizzly rain,
> And how often the rail cries over again ?
> For she's harping, harping in the brake,
> Craik, craik—Craik, craik—
> Ten times nine, and thrice eleven ;—
> That last call was an hundred and seven.

---

[59] *Works*, II. 153. An episode similar to that described in this poem is related by Hogg in his prose tale, "The Siege of Roxburgh." See *Tales*, VI. 219-33.

Craik, craik—the hour is near—
Let it come, I have no fear !
Yet it is a dreadful work, I wis,
Such doings in a night like this ![60]

But the parodies of Wordsworth are the best, infused with the "glee" Hogg says he felt when he began the *Mirror*. He had a score to settle with Wordsworth for the "triumphal arch" episode. His imitations of Scott, Coleridge and Byron are innocuous, even sympathetic; but when he imitates Wordsworth, ridicule inspires the verse. In "The Stranger: Being a further portion of the Recluse, a poem," "The Flying Tailor: Being a further extract from the Recluse, a poem," and "James Rigg: Another extract from the Recluse, a poem," Hogg presents his own *Excursion*. Wordsworth's solemnity, his tendency to present commonplace actions and thoughts as supremely important only because they refer to him, is a target for burlesque; but Hogg is also able to imitate Wordsworth's *sententia* without exaggeration, almost in Wordsworth's manner:

The horse went round
Most unrespective ; and, not satisfied
With whisking his dark tail in furious guise,
He broke on all propriety with snort
Like blustering cannon, or the noise that bursts
From heaven in thunder through the summer rain.
The boy was stunned—for on similitude
In dissimilitude, man's sole delight,
And all the sexual intercourse of things,
Do most supremely hang. The horse went round,
Jerked with his nose, and shook his harness so,
The boy waxed desperate, and oh, impious elf !
He cursed that hungry beast. The horse went round,
And round, and round. . . .[61]

A pair
Of breeches, to his philosophic eye,
Were not what unto other folks they seem,
Mere simple breeches ; but in them he saw
The symbol of the soul—mysterious, high

---

[60] *Works*, II. 175-6.   [61] "The Stranger," *op. cit.*, II. 164-5.

Hieroglyphics ! such as Egypt's priest
Adored upon the holy Pyramid,
Vainly imagined tomb of monarchs old,
But raised by wise philosophy, that sought
By darkness to illumine, and to spread
Knowledge by dim concealment—process high
Of man's imaginative, deathless soul.
Nor, haply in the abasement of the life
Which stern necessity had made his own,
Did he not recognise a genial power
Of soul-ennobling fortitude.[62]

       Something in his voice,
While thus he spake of simplest articles
Of household use, yet sunk upon my soul,
Like distant thunder from the mountain-gloom
Wakening the sleeping echoes ; so sublime
Was that old man, so plainly eloquent
His untaught tongue, though something of a lisp
(Natural defect), and a slight stutter too,
(Haply occasioned by some faint attack,
Harmless, if not renewed, of apoplex),
Rendered his utterance most peculiar ;
So that a stranger, had he heard that voice
Once only, and then travelled into lands
Beyond the ocean, had on his return,
Meet where they might, have known that curious voice
Of lisp and stutter, yet I ween withal
Graceful, and breathed from an original mind.[63]

Besides these parodies of *The Excursion* and a Words-worthian tale, "Peter of Barnet," in *The Poetic Mirror*, Hogg published, in the *Edinburgh Literary Journal*, in 1829, an "Ode to a Highland Bee" by Mr. W. W., and in 1830, "Andrew the Packman. After the manner of Wordsworth."[64] But the imitations in *The Poetic Mirror* are more telling.

It is hard to account for the high opinion Hogg had of "The Gude Greye Katt," the imitation of his own verse. The archaic language—similar to that of "The Witch of Fife" and largely his own conception—in this ballad proves nearly

---

[62] "The Flying Tailor," *op. cit.*, ii. 168-9.
[63] "James Rigg," *op. cit.*, ii. 170.
[64] Never reprinted.

impenetrable, and the tale—of witchcraft with a lame moral appended—is merely incredible. That Hogg's estimates of his own work are often mistaken, and that, on the other hand, he is a keen critic and parodist of the absurdities of other men, is not the least striking of the paradoxes with which he confronts us.

Hogg's discursive poems remain to be considered. We have noted that he is usually unable to find satisfactory subjects or forms for narrative poetry; in his discursive poetry, however, the subject is Hogg's own personality, with its queer strengths and surprises, and the language has a colloquial ease. In *The Mountain Bard*, "Farewell to Ettrick" and "The Author's Address to his auld Dog Hector" are of this kind. The "Farewell," written when Hogg was planning to move to Harris in the Hebrides, glances back at the life he has known and expresses his resolve to carry poetry into the wilderness. The refrain, in its understatement, is moving:

> Fareweel, green Ettrick, fare-thee-weel !
> I own I'm something wae to leave thee ;
> Nane kens the half o' what I feel,
> Nor half the cause I hae to grieve me ![65]

"The Author's Address to his auld Dog Hector" is also successful, striking and sustaining the characteristic tone of melancholy and humour mixed:

> To nae ªthrawn boy nor naughty wife,   ª *obstinate*
> Shall thy auld banes become a drudge ;
> At cats an' ªcallans a' thy life,   ª *boys*
> Thou ever bor'st a mortal grudge. . . .[66]

> There's nane alive will miss me mair ;
> An' though in words thou canst not wail,
> On a' the claes thy master ware,
> I ken thou'lt smell an' wag thy tail.[67]

In "Lines to Sir Walter Scott, Bart.," and "Verses Addressed to the Right Honourable Lady Anne Scott of Buccleuch" the octosyllabic couplet, misused in *Queen Hynde*, proves

[65] *Works*, II. 98.
[66] "The Author's Address to his auld Dog Hector," *op. cit.*, II. 99.
[67] *Op. cit.*, II. 100.

perfectly suited to Hogg's reminiscences and observations. As easily as into a letter he inserts episodes of his life, or his opinions; the light-moving verse creates a social ambiance in which errors of fact or differences of opinion are excused. What matters is the discourse. The quality of friendship that, as we have seen, the man had in plenty, spills into these lines:

> · I cherish still
> Mirth at the scene, and ever will,
> When o'er the fells we took our way;
> ('Tis twenty years, even to a day,
> Since we two sought the fabled urn
> Of marble blue by Rankleburn) :
> No tomb appeared ; but oft we traced
> Towns, camps, and battle-lines effaced,
> Which never were, nor could remain,
> Save in the bold enthusiast's brain :
> The same to us—it turned our lays
> To chiefs and tales of ancient days.
> One broken pot alone was found
> Deep in the rubbish under ground,
> In middle of the ancient fane—
> "A gallant helmet split in twain !"
> The truth was obvious ; but in faith
> On you all words were waste of breath ;
> You only looked demure and sly,
> And sore the brow fell o'er the eye ;
> You could not bear that you should ride
> O'er pathless waste and forest wide,
> Only to say that you had been
> *To see that nought was to be seen.*[68]

In "On the Lifting of the Banner of Buccleuch," "St Mary of the Lowes" and "The Monitors," Hogg employs a stanza that gives an effect of earnest but supple, light-moving thought. In "On the Lifting of the Banner of Buccleuch," the stanza consists of eight lines of four feet, rhyming *a b a b c d c d*; in the other poems named the rhyme is *a b a b b c b c*—an old and popular form in both Scots and English, used by Dunbar,

---

[68] "Lines to Sir Walter Scott," *op. cit.*, II. 375-6. The episode is rendered in prose in *Domestic Manners*, p. 65. See also "Verses Addressed to the Right Honourable Lady Anne Scott of Buccleuch," *Works*, II. 385-7.

three centuries before Hogg, and by Burns in "Mary Morison" and Crabbe in his "Sir Eustace Grey" and "The World of Dreams." For Hogg's reflexions the stanza, in either rhyme pattern, is a perfect vehicle—though not for other kinds of poems.[69]

"On the Lifting of the Banner of Buccleuch," written to celebrate a football game in the year of Waterloo, expresses the unity of play and duty; the same banner has been raised over fields of sport and war:

> . . . familiar to the brave,
>   'Twas thine thy gleaming moon and star
> Above their manly sports to wave
>   As free as in the field of war :
> To thee the faithful clansman's shout
>   In revel as in rage was dear ;
> The more beloved in festal rout,
>   The better fenced when foes were near.[70]

"St Mary of the Lowes" celebrates Hogg's ancestors and friends buried in the cemetery by Saint Mary's Loch.

> Here lie old Border bowmen good ;
>   Ranger and stalker sleep together
> Who for the red-deer's stately brood
>   Watch'd, in despite of want and weather,
>   Beneath the hoary hills of heather ;
> Even Scotts, and Kerrs, and Pringles, blended
>   In peaceful slumbers, rest together,
> Whose fathers there to death contended.[71]

In "The Monitors" the poet, threatened by the elements and old age, is sustained by the thought of his achievement:

> That winter wi' his joyless air,
>   An' grizzly hue, is hasting nigh,
> An' that auld age, an' carkin' care,
>   In my last stage afore me lie.

---

[69] See "On the Lifting of the Banner of Buccleuch," *Works*, II. 389-90 ; "St. Mary of the Lowes," *op. cit.*, II. 391-2 ; "The Monitors," *op. cit.*, II. 399. In "On Carmel's Brow" the stanza is used with the variation of alternating four- and three-foot lines. *Op. cit.*, II. 402.

[70] *Op. cit.*, II. 389.
                         [71] *Op. cit.*, II. 391.

Yon chill and cheerless winter sky,
Troth, but 'tis eerisome to see,
   For ah ! it points me to descry
The downfa's o' futurity.

I daurna look into the east,
   For there my morning shone sae sweet ;
An' when I turn me to the west,
   The gloaming's like to *ᵃgar me greet.*   *ᵃ make me weep*
The deadly hues o' snaw and sleet
Tell of a dreary onward path ;
   Yon new moon on her cradle sheet,
Looks like the Hainault scythe of death. . . .

And think—through ᵃpoortith's eiry breech,   *ᵃ poverty's*
   Should want approach wi' threatening brand,
I'll leave them canty sangs will reach
   From John o' Groats to Solway strand.
   Then what are houses, ᵃgoud, or land,   *ᵃ gold*
To sic an heirship left in fee ?
   An' I think mair o' auld Scotland,
Than to be fear'd for mine or me.[72]

These stanzas, in their directness of statement and felicity of phrasing, are verse of a high order. The chivalry of the clans could hardly be characterised more justly, or with greater concentration, than in the lines on "The Banner":

    The more beloved in festal rout,
      The better fenced when foes are near.

And this description from "The Monitors" does not yield to Coleridge's supernatural effects:

    Yon new moon on her cradle sheet,
    Looks like the Hainault scythe of death.

One cannot easily feel superior to the poet of "The Monitors"; at least, one can no longer consider him a simple, feckless shepherd. It is evident that his simplicity was a shield, and that, no less than Wordsworth, he was aware of the risks of poetry and had confronted the thought of "mighty poets in their misery dead."

    [72] *Works*, ii. 399.

Together with these poems we may place "Superstition,"
a meditation in Spenserian stanzas. The poem is remarkable
for Hogg's defence of "a train of airy dreams" against the
onslaughts of scepticism, and also for the sanity with which he
treats witchcraft and the deep moral insight he brings to bear
upon it. Hogg himself appears as a child both terrified and
delighted by superstition:

> And she could make the brown and careless boy
> All breathless stand, unknowing what to fear ;
> Or panting deep beneath his co'erlet lie,
> When midnight whisper stole upon his ear. . . .[73]

> But oh ! if ancient cemetery was near,
> Or cairn of harper murdered long ago,
> Or wandering pedlar for his hoarded gear,
> Of such, what glen of Scotland doth not know ?
> Or grave of suicide, upon the brow
> Of the bleak mountain, withered all and gray ;
> From these I held as from some deadly foe :
> There have I quaked by night and mused by day ;
> But chiefly where I weened the bard or warrior lay.[74]

This is informative, giving the genesis of Hogg's interest in
the supernatural; but the following stanzas render the quality
of that interest. The lines that describe the demon, in their
mixture of the terrible and the commonplace, have the effect
of his prose passages that treat of the demonic:

> If every creed has its attendant ills,
> How slight were thine !—a train of airy dreams !
> No holy awe the cynic's bosom thrills ;
> Be mine the faith diverging to extremes !
> What though, upon the moon's distempered beams,
> Erewhile thy matrons gallopped through the heaven,
> Floated like feather on the foaming streams,
> Or raised the winds by tenfold fury driven,
> Till ocean blurred the sky, and hills in twain were riven.

> Where fell the scathe ?—the beldames were amused,
> Whom eild and poverty had sorely crazed.

---

[73] *Works*, ii. 392.
[74] *Op. cit.*, ii. 392-3. In these memories there are intimations of two of
Hogg's works : "The Pedlar," and the *Justified Sinner*.

What, though their feeble senses were abused
By gleesome demon in the church-aisle raised,
With lion tail, and eyes that baleful blazed,
Whose bagpipe's blare made all the roof to quake !
But ages yet unborn will stand amazed
At thy dread power, that could the wretches make
Believe these things all real, and swear them at the stake.[75]

Unlike Scott, to whose rationalistic mind the whole matter of witchcraft was fundamentally inexplicable, Hogg sees that the "witches" believed in the reality of their visions, that they actually practiced a cult, and that this in itself did nobody much harm and may even have done its practitioners some good. But those who accused others of witchcraft did a great deal of harm. The "gleesome demon"—reminiscent of Burns' "touzie tyke, black, grim, and large !"—is less dangerous than the fanaticism of men. It is a short step from Hogg's treatment of superstition in this poem, to his arraignment of fanaticism in the *Justified Sinner*.

Though Hogg's poetry brought him a considerable reputation, few of his poems claim the attention of the modern reader, and none compare with the best of his prose. He was misled by the fashions of the day; having no definite literary standards of his own, he accepted those of polite society. It is hard to overestimate how much he lost by attending to the opinions of his more knowledgeable friends—Scott, who approved of *Queen Hynde*, and Wilson, who puffed it. Only now and then, in a handful of poems, does Hogg's native strength break through. Had he been less ambitious to please the literati, had he worked the mines of popular tradition and the vernacular, he might have written other poems of the quality of "Ringan and May," or "Kilmeny," or "The Witch of Fife." Indeed, with practice he might have done much better, developing a poetic idiom that would have been truly his own. But this is to want Hogg to have been someone else. At best, his poetry deserves the praise that Jeffrey gave it; sometimes, said Jeffrey, Hogg's fancy brought him to the borders of "a very high species of poetry."[76]

---

[75] *Works*, II. 393.   [76] *Edinburgh Review*, XXIV, No. 47, pp. 161-2.

Part III

PROSE TALES AND SKETCHES

IV

Story-Telling

IN 1817, feeling that his poetry would never succeed, Hogg determined to turn to prose.[1] Increasingly he wrote prose tales. But he had not ceased to write verse; he had ceased only to depend on it. His longest narrative poem, *Queen Hynde*, would be published in 1825, and, as Carswell remarks: "The lyrics that entitle him to his place next to Burns were written between fifty and sixty."[2]

His tales, poems, sketches and articles were published mainly in *Blackwood's Magazine*; but many also appeared in *Fraser's*, the *Scots Magazine* and the *Edinburgh Literary Journal*, with some pieces in *The Anniversary*, *The Juvenile Forget-me-not*, *The Metropolitan*, and other periodicals or annuals. Many of the pieces were never reprinted. For his writings sometimes he received liberal payment and sometimes none, "just as the editor or proprietor felt disposed."[3]

A list of the more important books published by Hogg— excluding such matter as tales published separately—between 1817 and 1835, the year of his death, gives an idea of his production:

1818
The Brownie of Bodsbeck; and other Tales (prose fiction)

1819
The Jacobite Relics of Scotland (an anthology of ballads)

1820
Winter Evening Tales (prose fiction)

1822
The Poetical Works of James Hogg
The Royal Jubilee. A Scottish Mask
The Three Perils of Man (prose fiction)

---

[1] "Autobiography," p. 454.   [2] Carswell, p. 204.
[3] "Autobiography," p. 460.

1823
The Three Perils of Woman (prose fiction)

1824
The Private Memoirs and Confessions of a Justified Sinner (prose fiction)

1825
Queen Hynde (verse)

1829
The Shepherd's Calendar (prose fiction and sketches)

1831
Songs by the Ettrick Shepherd

1832
A Queer Book (verse)
Altrive Tales (prose fiction)

1834
A Series of Lay Sermons (prose)
Tales of the Wars of Montrose (prose fiction)

Hogg's collections of tales and sketches were put together on no definite plan. In *The Shepherd's Calendar*, beside sketches, such as "Sheep" and "Prayers," that refer to pastoral life, we find a comic adventure-story, "The Marvellous Doctor," ranging as far as Spain, and tales of the supernatural, among them "The Brownie of the Black Haggs" and "Mr. Adamson of Laverhope." Nor have his editors imposed their own classifications; in the editions of Hogg's prose published after his death, the confusion is virtually unaltered. In fact, the mixture within each story precludes its being neatly classified. "The Adventures of Basil Lee" attaches to the thread of Basil's fortunes, pastoral scenes, a love-story, a war in America, supernatural occurrences on the Island of Lewis, and life in Edinburgh.

Hogg has many ways of telling a story. Sometimes he narrates in the most common technique of fiction, the simple use of the third person:

In the year 1723, Colonel Ridley returned from India, with
what, in those days, was accounted an immense fortune, and
returned to a country seat on the banks of North Tyne. . . .[4]

To add authenticity, the author himself may intrude in a story
told in the third person:

> He had received it at Dumfries, returned home, and put up
> his mare carefully in the stable, but not having courage to face
> his ruined family, he had hurried to that sequestered spot, and
> perpetrated the deed of self destruction.
>   The only thing more that I have to add is, that the Lord-
> President, having made the remark that he paid more regard
> to that poor woman, Isabella Hyslop's evidence, than to all
> the rest elicited at Dumfries, the gainers of the great plea
> became sensible that it was principally in consequence of her
> candour and invincible veracity that they were successful, and
> sent her a present of twenty pounds. She was living comfort-
> ably at Knoweback when I saw her, a contented and happy
> old maiden.[5]

He frequently pretends, as in "Tibby Hyslop's Dream,"
to be only editing traditional material. The long tale, "The
Siege of Roxburgh," is taken from the manuscript of an "old
Curate who had spent the latter part of his life in the village
of Mireton, and was given to the present Editor by one of
those tenants."[6] Not uncommonly he brackets his tale, and
sometimes he interrupts it, with editorial comments. These
may set the stage or point a moral, or they may explain the
difficulty he is having in telling a story. Some of these passages
are conventional moralisings that retard the action or destroy
the illusion, but others are informative and amusing. The
introduction to "Window Wat's Courtship," which speaks of
the confusion wrought by country beauties among their
swains, and the unexpected common sense of these girls
when they come to marry, is one of Hogg's most entertaining
essays.[7]
  A story may be related in the first person in the autobiographical manner. Such is the method of "The Adventures

---

[4] "The Long Pack," in *Tales*, III. 183.
[5] "Tibby Hyslop's Dream," *op. cit.*, IV 28.
[6] *Op. cit.*, VI. 68.   [7] *Op. cit.*, IV. 74-5.

of Basil Lee" and "The Adventures of Captain John Lochy," reminiscent of *Robinson Crusoe*, *Gulliver's Travels*, and other tales of the picaresque and marvellous:

> I was third son to a respectable farmer in the upper parts of Berwickshire, who occupied an extensive tract of land, partly arable and partly pasture. . . .[8]

"The Life of an Edinburgh Baillie" is in this manner, and so is the middle part of the *Justified Sinner*. The advantages of the method are considerable; the author allows the protagonist to describe the action only as he sees it, and the reader to observe other dimensions of meaning of which the protagonist is not aware. The protagonist is delineated by himself against the background of a fate he cannot perceive, and has the reality of human vanity and ignorance. An interesting variation of this technique is found in "The Cameronian Preacher's Tale," which is launched in arresting rhetoric straight at the reader. Only at the end are we informed that this tale was "the last sermon of the good John Farley," a preacher well known to the author.[9]

As Hogg in certain tales told in the third person pretends to be editing received or traditional material, so also he acts as "editor" of tales in the autobiographical manner. "An Edinburgh Baillie" is supposedly reconstructed from a memoir;[10] in the *Justified Sinner* an "Editor's Narrative" prepares the way for Robert Colwan's confessions and terminates the story. Similar to these are stories related in a monologue, opening with a conversation between the storyteller and another person, who then becomes a passive listener. "An Old Soldier's Tale" and "Tibby Johnston's Wraith" are of this kind.

A more awkward technique is that of relating the story in dialogue. "Katie Cheyne" carries it off well, for there the Scots conversation is humorous and lively, but the effect is usually that of stage dialogue without a stage, an action, or a point of view. At the worst, as at the beginning of "Welldean Hall," the reader feels excluded from the talk. The situation,

---

[8] "The Adventures of Basil Lee," *op. cit.*, III. 51.
[9] *Op. cit.*, II. 354.   [10] *Op. cit.*, V. 210-11.

which at the start of a story should be shown as rapidly as possible, is obscured in wandering remarks.[11]

There are also various modifications of methods already described. Thus, in "The Marvellous Doctor" the story is told by one person to another in the author's presence; in "Julia M'Kenzie" the story has been told to the author who now edits and relates it. Also, there is the tale within a tale; the story of the ghost of Molly Grieve is related by a character, Barnaby, in the course of "The Wool-Gatherer."[12]

The matter of Hogg's stories largely determines his success in narration; in verse, as we have seen, the contrary is true: it is the form that makes or spoils the poem. In the tales, when he is dealing with pastoral scenes and characters, or with what he calls "superstition," or is relating a realistic adventure story, the plot seems plausible, and the action carries the reader with it. The *Justified Sinner*, "The Cameronian Preacher's Tale" and "The Brownie of the Black Haggs" are ingeniously plotted. Other tales that are not well made still hold the reader's interest by their liveliness; the adventures of Basil Lee, though episodic, draw us on, and the Edinburgh Baillie himself commands our attention, though his story ambles. On the other hand, when—as in verse—Hogg is composing a romance in the fashion of Scott, or is parroting the sentimentalities of the age, the plot involves itself in confusion and the action wanders, bogs down and struggles to move.

In the *Domestic Manners* Hogg records a conversation with Scott which reveals his own awareness of his failings. Scott is speaking of the character of "old Peter Chisolme" in *The Three Perils of Man*:

> "Ah, man, what you might have made of that with a little more refinement, care, and patience ! But it is always the same with you, just hurrying on from one vagary to another, without consistency or proper arrangement."

Hogg protests:

> "Dear Mr Scott, a man canna do the thing that he canna do."
>
> "Yes, but you *can* do it. Witness your poems, where the

---

[11] *Tales*, ii. 190-5.   [12] *Op. cit.*, i. 201-4.

arrangements are all perfect and complete ; but in your prose tales, you seem to write merely by random, without once considering what you are going to write about."

"You are not often wrong, Mr. Scott, and you were never righter in your life than you are now, for when I write the first line of a tale or novel, I know not what the second is to be, and it is the same way in every sentence throughout. When my tale is traditionary, the work is easy, as I then see my way before me, though the tradition be ever so short, but in all my prose works of imagination, knowing little of the world, I sail on without star or compass."

"I am sorry to say, that this is too often apparent."[13]

The valuable part of this conversation is Hogg's differentiation between his "traditionary" tales and the rest. By "tradition- ary" he means that material which he has received by word of mouth, or which he has gathered from the lore of the region. He has a natural affinity for such subject-matter: legends of the Covenanters, who used to hold their conventicles in the Ettrick hills; legends of ghosts and fairies; stories of uncanny dreams and apparitions, of which every peasant community has a store. Indeed, as he says, when he writes of these matters the tale moves easily. On the other hand, when he has to "get up" his material from history, as in the tales of the Stuart court, or when he has to create a genteel milieu, as in *The Three Perils of Woman*, he simply does not know how to go about it.

His most serious fault is makeshift plotting. Frequently he seems to be making up a story as he goes along; indeed, he assures us that his "invariable practice in writing prose" is to write out his thoughts as he finds them.[14] As a result, several of his tales are merely episodes strung together. In the his- torical romances, in particular, where there is no compensating interest in the characters, the lack of a plausible plot is the last straw. "The Bridal of Polmood," "A Tale of Good Queen Bess," and "The Hunt of Eildon," all melodramas in costume, are so confused and unmotivated as to be nearly incompre- hensible. In "The Bridal of Polmood," perhaps the worst- contrived of his tales, Hogg is not above bringing a dead man

---

[13] *Domestic Manners*, p. 80.   [14] "Autobiography," p. 443.

back to life. "Some may perhaps say," he remarks, "that this tale is ill-conceived, unnatural, and that the moral of it is not palpable. . . ."[15] Nothing, indeed, could be less natural than the episode of the shepherd, William Moray. He is to be hanged for beating and insulting King James, whom he has taken to be someone else. The King intervenes, apparently intending to behead the shepherd, but instead lays his sword on his neck and knights him. William drops dead of shock at the touch of the sword. Thereupon: "King James, who was well versed in everything relating to the human frame, was the best surgeon, and the most skilful physician in the realm, succeeded at last in restoring him to life."[16]

Hogg himself is aware of his poor plotting in "The Bridal of Polmood," for he offers the apology that he has not produced "merely the creation of his own fancy," but transmitted the traditions of his country, and so has been obliged to "conform to the incidents as handed down to him."[17] Elsewhere he remarks on the difficulty of relating matters in their correct order:

> It is a difficult matter to tell a story as it should be told ; for, after the party separates, it is necessary to fly always from one to another, to bring them forward to the same notch of time.[18]

Instances of Hogg's poor plotting abound, but one further example will suffice. "Ewan M'Gabhar" presents a confusion of sequence not at all mitigated by the author's editorial intrusions. We are told that Ewan is carried by clansmen into the country of a great chief, Colin Gillespick. Then the chief goes to war. In Hogg's own words:

> A great and bloody war now commenced between Colin Moore and the king of the country that should have been Ewan's own, of which he knew nothing. Lord Downan was joined with Colin Moore in this great enterprise, which they hoped to accomplish easily. . . .[19]

". . . the country that should have been Ewan's own, of which he knew nothing . . ."—the reader, also, knows nothing of

---

[15] *Tales*, II. 122.　　　　　　[16] *Op. cit.*, II. 60.
[17] *Op. cit.*, II. 122.　　　　　[18] "Welldean Hall," *op. cit.*, II. 242.
　　　　　　[19] *Op. cit.*, I. 348.

this; it is only later that the plot reveals Ewan's claim to the throne.

However, when he is passionately interested in an idea, as in the *Justified Sinner*, or a character, as in the "Edinburgh Baillie," Hogg can contrive a plot. He can even make the improbable seem quite acceptable. In the humorous "Trials of Temper" he leads the reader through a maze of mixed identities, puzzling but not confusing him. In "Basil Lee," an episode that is improbable—Basil's not recognising his own mistress—is still acceptable, and indeed, highly effective, for the action is in keeping with the characterisations. Wishing to be rid of Clifford, Basil pays his court to an American beauty. He is glad when Clifford tells him that she is planning to be married, and consents to attend the wedding as her brother. At the wedding, he discovers that Clifford is his *inamorata*. The deception is attributable to Basil's vanity and serves to point it up.[20]

Hogg's careless plotting entails a number of other faults. He runs hither and thither like a dog that has lost the scent. He adds necessary information as an afterthought, in the wrong place:

> I forgot to mention before, that old Beattie lived at Nether Cassway with his family ; and his eldest son Thomas at Over Cassway, having, on his father's entering into a second marriage, been put in possession of that castle and these lands. Francis, of course, lived in his father's house when in Scotland ; and it was thus that his brother knew nothing of his frequent visits to Ellen Scott.[21]

Or he may simply side-step a difficulty. In "The Adventures of Colonel Peter Aston," when the hero releases the clansman Grant, an enemy of his people, he makes no explanation to them for the reappearance of Grant at large.[22] Or, being hard pressed, Hogg may use again an episode he has treated in another tale. In "The Brownie of Bodsbeck," the scene glimpsed through a window, of the heroine and the Brownie doing something sinister to a corpse, is nearly identical with

---

a scene in "A Tale of Pentland," in which the escaping Covenanter, Haliday, arriving at Johnstone's house, looks through a window and sees Johnstone's daughter and her lover apparently cutting the throat of a cavalier.[23] The explanations of these incidents are, also, much the same. Similarly, one mystery supplies Hogg for both "Ewan M'Gabhar" and "The Wool-Gatherer"; the apparently unmarried heroine is accompanied by a child that seems her own; later we discover she is of high birth and is merely caring for her sister's child.

Hogg is always willing to digress, to be diverted from his story in order to tell another story or furnish local colour. In "The Wool-Gatherer," when Lindsey and Barnaby meet, instead of giving their conversation about Jane, who is uppermost in their minds and the reader's, Hogg gives the details of their fishing, and moreover, underlines his preference for this way of telling—or rather, not telling—his story: ". . . their converse became very interesting to both parties, but we cannot interrupt the description of such a favourite rural sport just now."[24]

Here, too, we may note the effect of Hogg's digressions. As we have said, some of these are entertaining in themselves; but others are merely distracting.

> Carmichael . . . continued his flight with all expedition till he was out of danger of being overtaken. The spot which the baron chose for a hiding-place is well known, and is still pointed out by the shepherds and farmers of *the Muir* ; for so that district is called.[25]

> This distinction pleased Elizabeth more than any thing she had yet seen or heard about her intended husband, and she began to regard him as a superior character, and one whom others were likely to value. The ruling passions of her heart seem to have been hitherto levelled only to the attainment of admiration and distinction, an early foible of the sex, but though a foible, one that leads oftener to good than evil. For when a young female is placed in a circle of acquaintances who know how to estimate the qualities of the heart, the graces

---

[23] "The Brownie of Bodsbeck," *op. cit.*, I. 155-6 ; "A Tale of Pentland," *op. cit.*, I. 317-8.

[24] *Op. cit.*, I. 213.   [25] "The Bridal of Polmood," *Op. cit.*, II. 83.

of a modest deportment and endearing address, how then does this ardent and amiable desire of rendering herself agreeable stimulate to exertions in the way of goodness. But, on the contrary, when she is reared in a circle, where splendour is regarded as the badge of superiority, and title as the compendium of distinction, it is then, as in the case of the beauteous Elizabeth, that this inherent principle "leads to bewilder and dazzles to blind." The flowers of the forest and garden are not more indicative of the different soils that produce them, than the mind of a young woman is of the company she keeps.[26]

Last in this list of faults are Hogg's makeshift endings, where he does no more than wind up the action, as though action were the whole story. The effect is to reduce fiction to an anecdote, unsatisfactory even as that. The mysteries posed in "The Fords of Callum," "Adam Bell," and "A Strange Secret," are never cleared up. In "Tibby Johnston's Wraith," we are told that the coffin has been made too short for Mrs Graham, but her funeral takes place without explanation of how this problem was resolved.[27] And, then Hogg sometimes does not know where to stop. The otherwise excellent story of "Mr. Adamson of Laverhope" is marred by the tacking-on of information that has nothing to do with it. After Adamson is blasted by lightning, Hogg proceeds to tell of another death by lightning that has no bearing on the matter in hand.[28]

Hogg's prose style varies—as does that of his verse—from colloquialism to frigid artificiality. The latter is apparent in the lengthy extract we have already taken from "The Bridal of Polmood."[29] The passage is typical of Hogg's conventional moralising, a weakness to which he is prone whenever he is not on his own ground. Here, even in scenes where his own knowledge might be expected to serve him, it abandons him entirely. No one was better able than Hogg to render the dialogue of the common folk, his own people, but in "The Bridal of Polmood" even the servants talk affectedly. We are presented with this, as a specimen of the conversation of a "young serving man":

[26] *Tales*, II. 13-14.
[28] *Op. cit.*, III. 246-7.
[27] *Op. cit.*, II. 274.
[29] See above, pp. 119-120.

"Do not believe any such thing, my dear Anna ; believe me, it is nothing more than the workings of a distempered imagination. Because the late events are wrapt in mystery, the minds of people are oppressed by vague conjectures, and surmises of dark infamous deeds, and in sleep the fancy turns to these images, and is frightened by fantasies of its own creation. I would not have you, nor any woman, to believe in the existence of ghosts."[30]

With this may be contrasted Hogg's grasp of style when he is enjoying his story. In "The Adventures of Basil Lee," the old shepherd Willie Beattie tells Basil's father his opinion of his son:

"Ye'll get nae luck o' that callant, Sir," said he, "gin ye dinna haud his neb better to the grunstane. I wat weel, I hae naething to say ferrar nor what concerns the sheep ; but, I trow, gin ye dinna tie him til a job that he canna get quat o', he'll flee fra ae falderall til anither a' the days o' his life ; he'll be a plague amang the women too : an' a ' thegither ye'll mak but little mence o' him."[31]

In tales of pastoral life, the supernatural, and the picaresque, Hogg's style has a characteristic realism. Flat descriptions and flat statements of action, with the use of common speech or the vernacular, make for strong effects. The duel in "Basil Lee" is visualised so:

. . . the whole of this catastrophe, from the time that I fell on my back, was transacted in two seconds, and before our friends had time to interfere ; indeed I am never sure to this day but that they both viewed it as a piece of excellent sport. However, they now laid hold of us, and raised us up. I was choked with blood, but did not feel very much pain. All that I particularly remember was, that I was very angry with Frazer, and wanted to get at him to kill him ; and instead of being afraid of him, I would then have given all that I had in the world to have had the chance of fighting him with pistols.[32]

When this style is applied to supernatural matters, and horrors are related in ordinary words, the effect is striking. In this,

[30] *Tales*, II. 100. [31] *Op. cit.*, III. 56.
[32] *Op. cit.*, III. 74.

the style of "The Brownie of the Black Haggs" and the *Justified Sinner*, Hogg seems unique:

> The creature went away, and the moment his back was turned, the Lady fell a-screaming and struggling, like one in agony, and in spite of all the couple's exertions, she forced herself out of their hands, and ran after the retreating Merodach. When he saw better would not be, he turned upon her, and, by one blow with his stick, struck her down ; and, not content with that, continued to maltreat her in such a manner, as to all appearance would have killed twenty ordinary persons. The poor devoted dame could do nothing, but now and then utter a squeak like a half-worried cat, and writhe and grovel on the sward. . . .[33]

The realistic style may be infused with humour or satire, as in the description of Lindsey's fishing in "The Wool-Gatherer":

> He pulled out the line, and threw it in again so fast, that he appeared more like one threshing corn than angling ; he, moreover, fixed always upon the smoothest parts of the stream, where no trout in his right senses could possibly be inveigled. But the far greater part of his employment consisted in loosening the hook from different objects with which it chanced to come in contact. At one time he was to be seen stooping to the arm-pits in the middle of the water, disengaging it from some officious twig that had intercepted its progress ; at another time on the top of a tree tearing off a branch on which it had laid hold.[34]

Flashes of close observation, original metaphors and startling phrases are found throughout Hogg's prose. The Marvellous Doctor, telling of his struggle with a bull in a river, says: "I left him floating away like a huge buoy that had lost its anchor."[35] In "The Baron St Gio," "the bats came buffing out of their holes."[36] Hogg is also able to describe a complex, panoramic sweep, such as the battle in "Basil Lee," seen from Basil's shifting viewpoint, and the battle in the "Edinburgh Baillie," viewed from the fixed position of a boat anchored offshore.[37]

---

[33] "The Brownie of the Black Haggs," *op. cit.*, III, 357.
[34] *Op. cit.*, I. 180.   [35] *Op. cit.*, IV. 170.
[36] *Op. cit.*, IV. 322.   [37] *Op. cit.*, III. 82-8 ; *op. cit.*, V. 329-34.

Much of his best writing is in the Scots speech of his characters. The dialect is never too hard to understand; the reader soon gets the hang of it, and words that are not immediately understood are made clear by the context. Though in his descriptions he usually sticks to literary English, Hogg is glad of the opportunity given by dialogue to let himself go in Scots. And, sometimes, as in "Window Wat's Courtship" and "Katie Cheyne," he arranges to tell the story in dialogue. One of his characters calls English a "vile nicky-nacky language,"[38] and in several places, Hogg suggests his own preference for Scots:

> "Tell me, Croudy," said Gale, "does Mumps really run away in a panic when he perceives the king's hounds ?"
> *"Panic when he perceives the king's hounds !* Are ye gaun to keep on at bletherin' English ? Tell me, ye see—for if ye be, I'm gaun to clatter nane to ye."
> "Dear Croudy, I have often told you that there is not such a thing as English and Scotch languages ; the one is merely a modification of the other, a refinement as it were"—
> "Ay, an *exaltation* like—ation ! ation ! I'm sure nae Scot that isna a fool wad ever let that sound, *ation*, come out o' his mouth. . . ."[39]

The use of Scots strengthens his style; he casts off fashionable pieties and speaks his mind. His language, then, is vivid and humorous; sometimes, as in this passage from "Window Wat's Courtship," it is highly fanciful. The old wife wakens her daughters, the Eagle, the Snaw-fleck and the Sea-maw, with this exhortation:

> "Come, stir ye, stir ye, my bonny bairns. When the sterns o' heaven hae gane to their beds, it is time the flowers o' the yird war rising—Come, come !—No stirring yet ?—Busk ye, busk ye, like thrifty bairns, and dinna let the lads say that ye are sleepie dowdies, that lie in your beds till the sun burns holes in your coverlets. Fie, fie !—There has been a reek i' Jean Lowrie's lum this half-hour. The moor-cock has crawed, the mawkin cowered, and the whaup yammered abune the flower. Streek your young limbs—open your young een—a

---

[38] Meg in "The Wool-Gatherer," *op. cit.*, I. 228.
[39] "The Hunt of Eildon," *op. cit.*, III. 10-11.

foot on the cauld floor, and sleep will soon be aboon the cluds.—
Up, up, my winsome bairns ! ''[40]

Proverbs and sayings that have the ring of proverbs add
pungency to the spoken language: ". . . nipping and scarting
is Scots folk's wooing . . .";[41] ". . . ane's no to throw himsell
ower a linn, and trust that the Lord will kep him in a blanket."[42]
". . . the heat o' your throat will soon burn the claes aff your
back . . ." (said to an habitual drinker).[43]   In such phrases,
the morality of Scottish peasant life is more convincingly shown
than in the author's didactic statements.   Occasionally, Hogg
translates classical sayings into Scots, as in this modification
of a remark that has been attributed to the emperor Caligula:
". . . gin a' my kinsmen had but ae neck among them ye wad
chop a' off at aince."[44]

He is not always consistent in his use of dialogue; in the
historical romances in particular he may slip from Scots into
formal English.   It is a serious fault, entirely dispelling the
illusion of reality.   We have noted an example from "The
Bridal of Polmood";[45] in the same tale the shepherd William,
whose normal way of speaking is Scots dialect, delivers an
opinion of the king's faults in formal English: "It is allowed on
all hands, that James is a good-natured and merciful prince;
yet the acts of cruelty and injustice which every petty lord
and laird exercises in his own domain, are beyond all suffer-
ance."[46]   Even in the better tales, Hogg sometimes slips in this
way.   Barnaby, the shepherd of "The Wool-Gatherer," whose
normal speech is Scots, when he discourses on the *déjà vu*
assumes the style of a literary man: "I have remembered of
having seen exactly the same scene, the same faces, the same
looks, and heard the same words, though I knew all the while
that I never had seen them in reality; and that I could only
have seen them in some former vision, forgotten, or perhaps
never remembered."[47]   And in the tales told in dialogue,
Hogg sometimes slips into the style of his third-person
narratives:

[40] *Tales*, IV. 93-4.
[42] *Op. cit.*, III. 355.
[44] *Op. cit.*, VI. 24.
[46] *Op. cit.*, II. 54.
[41] *Op. cit.*, III. 354.
[43] *Op. cit.*, IV. 275.
[45] See above, p. 121.
[47] *Op. cit.*, I. 197-8.

> "By ill luck, havering Jean Jinkens came in about nine o'clock to see the mistress, and ere ever ane could prevent her, tauld that Tibby Johnston had died out on the hill the last night. . . . This intelligence threw Mrs Graham into a stupor, or rather she appeared striving to comprehend something that was beyond the grasp of her mind. . . ."[48]

This fault is as catastrophic as carelessness in plotting, for at a stroke it destroys the illusion of character.

In his dialogues in English, Hogg varies, as he does in description, from colloquialism to artificiality. In the historical and romantic tales we find his least convincing speech, for neither the action nor the relationship of the characters to the action is strongly imagined. The apparition of the armoured spectre of the late Laird of Welldean in "Welldean Hall," a "tremendous and hellish figure," draws from one of the observers the unlikely exclamation: ". . . who is this we have got here?"[49] But when he has a mind to, Hogg can render English to perfection and in several varieties. The *Justified Sinner* offers plain English, English touched with Scots, and English with Biblical overtones, as well as dialogue in Scots. The Devil in this tale speaks out of Scripture, and Robert Colwan has a ready command of Puritan cant.

In style as well as subject, the *Justified Sinner* and other of Hogg's writings remind us that a large part of his education was through hearing the Bible read aloud. "No person whom I have been acquainted with knew it so well," said his brother William.[50] Many passages, particularly in his tales of the supernatural, echo the syntax and vocabulary of the King James version:

> This was a potion so bitter that I could not swallow it, nevertheless I was compelled to do it, and then I lifted up my voice and wept.[51]

> But many were wounded, bruised, and imprisoned, and much commotion prevailed in the city.[52]

---

[48] "Tibby Johnson's Wraith," *op. cit.*, II. 272-3.
[49] *Op. cit.*, II. 205.   [50] Garden, p. 13.
[51] "An Edinburgh Baillie," in *Tales*, v. 233.
[52] *Justified Sinner*, p. 137.

In such passages we hear the accents of Scripture, and in certain of Hogg's more imaginative descriptions we glimpse the visions of the prophets. But even where the influence of the Bible is not emphatic, it still shapes his style. The realism characteristic of his writings is a kind of Puritanism, a reduction to essentials; fine writing and the fine sentiments that go with it are cast aside as insincere.

V

Ordinary Lives and Extraordinary Adventures

> We lived, as it were, inmates of the
> cloud and the storm.
>
> *"Storms"*[1]

ETTRICK is a pastoral landscape. The bare, rolling hills are spotted with herds of sheep and cattle, seemingly motionless, attended by herdsmen and their dogs. In summer the hills are bright with heather and wild flowers. Though the Forest for the most part is barren of trees— "forest" originally meant, not a growth of trees, but a hunting chase—here and there stand "solitary single trees, ancient yew or sycamore, black in the distance, but when near, how gloriously green. Tall, delicately feathered ash . . . birch in early spring . . . oak, yellow in the suns of June."[2] In winter, rain and mist creep over the hills, and sometimes they are swept by storms. Storms, Hogg writes, are the landmarks of the shepherd's life. When the drifts continue for days, animals and men struggle to survive. Some storms are calamitous; thousands of sheep are lost; at peril of their lives the shepherds labour through snow to find and dig out the buried sheep; they construct ramparts of dead bodies to protect the remnant. In one storm no less than seventeen shepherds have been known to perish in attempting to save their flocks.[3]

The land has stamped its extremes of harshness and tranquility upon the character of its inhabitants. The hills of summer inspire the shepherd to be happy; winter storms

[1] *Tales*, II. p. 128.

[2] *Noctes*, III. 261-3. North's description. The coppices and single trees that sometimes break the smoothness of the Ettrick hills are, for the most part, of later growth ; indeed, there are more trees in the Forest now than there were when Hogg was a boy. In 1811 Sir Walter Scott set about planting trees at Abbotsford and persuaded his neighbour, Scott of Gala, to do the same, and the fashion spread.

[3] "Storms," in *Tales*, II. 124-49.

remind him of the thunder of Judgement Day. His mind is divided between the authority of the Kirk and remnants of superstition. In the flash of the storm, ghosts and devils are seen to stand; in the recesses of the Forest fairies are reputed to dwell. As the "light of the gospel" advances, the fairies retire.[4] The "banditti" who have hidden in the mountains are exposed or compelled to take decent occupations. Ghosts are more rare, and with the coming of Progress the Devil has moved to Glasgow, where he sets up a factory and encourages the vices of the poor.[5]

Kirk, estate and farm are the chief institutions of the country. The farm may be owned by the estate (as Hogg's own farm at Mount Benger was owned by Buccleuch) and worked by a tenant; or the farmer may be his own master. The farm employs shepherds, a class of men that predominates in Hogg's fiction. Of all Protestants, he says, these are the most devout. They get all the learning the parish schools afford, and are thoroughly acquainted with the Scriptures and "theological works"—usually better acquainted than their masters. They are respectable; otherwise they would not be employed, for the sheep require constant attention, caution, and decision. Besides, the shepherd owns part of the stock, and this encourages him to be industrious. Also, as he is "conversant with the Almighty in his works," the shepherd cannot fail to be impressed with "the presence of an eternal God, of an omniscient eye, and an almighty arm."[6]

Inseparable from the shepherd is his dog, a creature on which the industry of sheep-farming is virtually dependent. "A single shepherd and his dog," Hogg writes, "will accomplish more in gathering a stock of sheep from a Highland farm, than twenty shepherds could do without dogs; and it is a fact, that, without this docile animal, the pastoral life would be a mere blank. Without the shepherd's dog, the whole of the open mountainous land in Scotland would not be worth a sixpence."[7]

[4] *Tales*, IV. 215.
[5] *Noctes*, V. 340. The Shepherd blames manufacture and commerce for the vices of the poor.
[6] "Prayers," in *Tales*, IV. 202.
[7] "The Shepherd's Dog," *op. cit.*, IV. 251-2.

There are pastoral scenes in most of Hogg's writings, and some sketches and tales are entirely pastoral. The sketches "Storms," "Odd Characters," "Prayers" and "The Shepherd's Dog" contain some of his liveliest anecdotes, and the rest are only slightly less rewarding.[8] In "Odd Characters" he portrays the legendary Will o' Phaup, his grandfather. Will lived on the outskirts of the Forest, an area fit only for bandits and fairies, and had several encounters with the fairies. Some of his neighbours ascribed these meetings to the effect of brandy, but Hogg states that Will was a man of probity, and "never told that for the truth which he did not believe to be so."[9] The remark is typical of Hogg's suspension of judgment when confronted with the supernatural. Here also he implies that supernatural episodes actually occurred at an earlier time; the dispelling of "superstition" has removed an actual, substantial fairy world, and the real creatures in it.

In "Prayers" we are introduced to an even more interesting character who also lived, Adam Scott of Dalgleish. Scott was famous for his family prayers, several of which were remembered afterwards word for word. As was the way in such prayers, Scott would bring the most pressing business directly to the attention of his Maker, but his prayers were less formal than most. On the marriage of one of his sons, he was reputed to have prayed: "Thou hast added one to our family—so has been thy will; but it would never hae been mine. If it's of thee, do thou bless and prosper the connexion; but if the fool hath done it out of carnal desire, against all reason and credit, may the cauld rainy cloud of adversity settle on his habitation, till he shiver in the flame that his folly hath kindled."[10] On another occasion, as he read aloud from a chapter of the Scriptures he stopped in the middle, uttered his "hemh!" of disapproval, and said: "If it had been the Lord's will, I think they might hae left out that verse."—"It hasna been his will though." said one of the girls. "It seems sae," he conceded.[11] The story of Ruth was a great favourite with

[8] "Storms," *op. cit.*, II. 124-49 ; "Odd Characters," *op. cit.*, IV. 209-25 ; "Prayers," *op. cit.*, IV. 202-9 ; "The Shepherd's Dog," *op. cit.*, IV. 241-64 ; "Sheep," *op. cit.*, IV. 197-201 ; "A Country Funeral," *op. cit.*, III. 196-200 ; "A Shepherd's Wedding," *op. cit.*, II. 150-71 ; "Emigration," *op. cit.*, IV. 265-9.
[9] *Op. cit.*, IV. 220.   [10] *Op. cit.*, IV. 203.   [11] *Op. cit.*, IV, 206.

I

him; he often read it to his family on Sabbath evenings as "a good lesson on naturality," but he never failed to remark that it was not decent of her "to creep in beside the douss man i' the night-time when he was sleeping."[12]

Besides these and other characters drawn from life, there are characters in Hogg's fiction who seem products of the pastoral environment; we can hardly imagine them in other surroundings than Ettrick Forest. The boy, Duncan Campbell, original as he is, seems representative.[13] It is one of the triumphs of imaginative fiction that in creating the unique it creates a species: the touches that make Duncan original also limn in the background a host of similar wandering boys— shepherds by trade, if they can be said to have a trade; warm-hearted, superstitious and loyal. The tale relates how Duncan is sent away by his father and stepmother to school in Edinburgh. His playmate and constant companion is a dog, Oscar. The aunt with whom he is staying falls ill; Duncan is neglected; she dies, and coming on her body suddenly, he is so terrified that he runs away. He wanders aimlessly and meets Oscar again; the dog is now the property of a cattle-drover who mistreats him. Oscar deserts to Duncan, and together they wander through the country; the youth, beauty and destitution of the boy and his friendship for his dog arouse people's sympathy and kindness. A meeting with the ghost of a piper makes Duncan highly superstitious. At length, boy and dog are given a home by the parents of the narrator; the narrator and his sister Mary grow up with Duncan and learn how to read the Bible together. This happy situation lasts until some travelling Highland women reveal that Duncan is the Laird of Glenellich's only son and heir, and that the Laird is looking for him. Duncan sets off, leaving Mary, who loves him, broken-hearted. He arrives incognito at his father's house and finds the old man being mistreated by his wife and servants. He reveals his identity, sets his father's house to rights, and claims his inheritance. Meanwhile, the narrator's family have fallen on hard times. They are about to be sold up when Duncan reappears, marries Mary and settles their debts.

<hr/>

[12] *Tales*, IV. 209.   [13] *Op. cit.*, III. 136-59.

Not the least interesting part of this tale is the account of Duncan's boyhood together with the narrator; the idyllic pastoral scenes of Hogg's poem, "A Boy's Song," are found again in this description:

As far as I remember, we felt no privation of any kind, and would have been completely happy, if it had not been for the fear of spirits. When the conversation chanced to turn upon the Piper of Dewar, the Maid of Plora, or the Pedlar of Thirlestane Mill, often have we lain with the bed-clothes drawn over our heads till nearly suffocated. We loved the fairies and the brownies, and even felt a little partiality for the mermaids, on account of their beauty and charming songs ; but we were a little jealous of the water-kelpies, and always kept aloof from the frightsome pools. We hated the devil most heartily, although we were not much afraid of him ; but a ghost ! oh, dreadful ! the names, ghost, spirit, or apparition, sounded in our ears like the knell of destruction, and our hearts sunk within us as if pierced by the cold icy shaft of death. Duncan herded my father's cows all the summer—so did I—we could not live asunder. We grew such expert fishers, that the speckled trout, with all his art, could not elude our machinations : we forced him from his watery cove, admired the beautiful shades and purple drops that were painted on his sleek sides, and forthwith added him to our number without reluctance. We assailed the habitation of the wild bee, and rifled her of all her accumulated sweets, though not without encountering the most determined resistance.[14]

---

[14] *Tales*, III. 145. Cp. "A Boy's Song " *Works*, II. 436 :

> Where the pools are bright and deep,
> Where the gray trout lies asleep,
> Up the river and o'er the lea,
> That's the way for Billy and me.
>
> Where the blackbird sings the latest,
> Where the hawthorn blooms the sweetest,
> Where the nestlings chirp and flee,
> That's the way for Billy and me.
>
> Where the mowers mow the cleanest,
> Where the hay lies thick and greenest ;
> There to trace the homeward bee,
> That's the way for Billy and me. . . .

Like Duncan, Jasper, the young shepherd of *The Brownie of Bodsbeck*, and Barnaby, the ragged shepherd of "The Wool-Gatherer," are emanations of the pastoral scene. Both are highly superstitious. Jasper is in the habit of knitting stockings while tending his sheep; once, when his yarn unravels behind him, he looks back and thinks that the coil is a horrible serpent, probably the Brownie of Bodsbeck, and he runs till he falls exhausted.[15] Barnaby, a simple, tender-hearted fellow, tends the mysterious wool-gatherer, Jane, and finds a home for her with his parents when she is driven from her cottage. In love with Jane, he knows that she is above him; like certain peasant lovers of Thomas Hardy's tales, his lot is to serve a "superior" woman without hope of reward.[16]

Not all Hogg's pastoral characters succeed; as we have noted before, when he is contriving a far-fetched plot, his grasp of even those matters he understands is liable to be weakened. In the melodramatic ghost-story, "Welldean Hall," both the wood-forester, Gilbert, and the comical Andrew are laboriously made original; all the humour of Andrew is in his stuttering.[17]

In dealing with the pastoral, Hogg sometimes expresses a sense of duty to describe things as they are. "I hate that my characters, which are all drawn from nature, should not be properly comprehended," he states in "Welldean Hall."[18] In the sketch, "A Shepherd's Wedding," having described a shepherd's cottage or steading—a description that should be noted:

> It was situated in a little valley in the bottom of a wild glen, or *hope*, as it is there called. It stood all alone ; but besides the dwelling-house, there was a little byre that held the two cows and their young,—a good stack of hay, another of peats,—a sheep-house, and two homely gardens ; and the place had altogether something of a snug, comfortable appearance. . . .

he proceeds to remark:

> Though this is only an individual picture, I am told it may be be viewed as a general one of almost every shepherd's dwelling

---

[15] *Tales*, I, 31-2.
[16] *Op. cit.*, I. 176-240.
[17] *Op. cit.*, II. 234 ff.
[18] *Op. cit.*, II. 234.

in the south of Scotland ; and it is only such pictures that, in the course of these tales, I mean to present to the public.[19]

Of the life inside such cottages there are many scenes in the tales. Such a household is found in "Window Wat's Courtship," though it can hardly be viewed as a general picture. It consists of old Tod-Lowrie, his wife and three daughters, all named after birds: the Snaw-fleck [snow bunting], the Eagle, and the Sea-maw [seagull]. Window Wat is in love with the youngest of the three, the Snaw-fleck. His friend Jock—or Jewel—undertakes to court the Snaw-fleck for him, as Wat is unpractised in these matters; and the Snaw-fleck soon shows a preference for Jock himself. But her father insists, in accordance with the "law of Padanaram," that the girls be married in the order of their ages, the eldest first. The eldest, called the Eagle, is also fond of Jock, though she has a sharp tongue.

Jock and Wat both vie for the Snaw-fleck, and Wat even learns a part of the Bible by heart, in order to triumph in the test of reading from the Bible aloud. But Jock arranges an elopement; he sets off with the Snaw-fleck; the Eagle and Wat, seemingly resigned to the situation, accompany them as best man and bridesmaid. On the ride to Edinburgh, Wat and the Snaw-fleck on one horse are separated from Jock and the Eagle on the other. They arrive at the White Horse Inn and decide to get married—for it seems that the Snaw-fleck has really preferred Wat all along; it was only his backwardness that prevented her showing it. When Jock and the Eagle arrive, the couple are already bedded. The Eagle, with help from the landlord and minister, persuades Jock to marry her; in fact, she has brought about the scheme, "to get hold of the man with the money." In the aftermath, Jock, still disappointed, emigrates with his wife to America.[20]

The Snaw-fleck's letter to her sister, explaining why she has married Wat instead of Jock, is a masterpiece of rationalisation, written in a style perfectly in keeping with the tradition of letter-writing among those characters in British fiction who may not be described as "elegant females." This is how a

---

[19] *Tales*, II. 157. [20] *Op. cit.*, IV. 74-106.

young countrywoman explains having married another than
the man she had eloped with:

DEAR SISTER,

  This cometh to let you know that I have married Walter,
thinking you and John had turned on the height, and that he
had taken the rue ; so I thought, after leaving the country
to be married, I could never set up my face in it again, without
a husband ; for you know a woman leaving home with a man,
as we both have done, can never be received into a church or
family again, unless she be married of him ; and you must
consider of this ; for if you are comed to Edinburgh with a
man, you need never go home again. John hath used me very
bad, and made me do the thing I may rue ; but I could not
help it. I hope he will die an old bachelor, as he is, and never
taste the joys of the married state. We will remain here another
night, for some refreshment, and then I go home to his mother.
This business will make a terrible noise in the country. I
would not have gone home, and me not married, for all the
whole world."[21]

  Among Hogg's peasant characters we may note, also, the
outspoken old man, Willie Beattie, in "The Adventures of
Basil Lee," of whose forthright way of speaking we have
already given an extract.[22] Similar to Beattie is John Barnet
of the *Justified Sinner*; his dislike of canting hypocrisy, which
leads to his being dismissed from his job by the hypocrite,
Wringhim, may stand for the independence of other peasants
in the tales. The Reverend Robert Wringhim, confronting
Barnet with the report that he has said Robert Colwan is
Wringhim's natural son, threatens to take the keys of the
church from him and dismiss him from his service. John
dashes the keys down at Wringhim's feet and replies:

  ". . . I hae carried them this three and thretty year, but they
hae aye been like to burn a hole i' my pouch sin' ever they
were turned for your admittance. Take them again, an' gie
them to wha you will, and muckle gude may he get o' them.
Auld John may dee a beggar in a hay barn, or at the back of a
dike, but he sall aye be master o' his ain thoughts an' gie
them vent or no, as he likes."[23]

---

[21] *Tales*, IV. 104-5.   [22] See above, p. 121.   [23] *Justified Sinner*, pp. 97-8.

To be "master o' his ain thoughts"—that is liberty of conscience in a nutshell. Peasants are not always outspoken—they cannot afford to be; free speech is a luxury in which the wealthy are better able to indulge. But when they are forced to it, Hogg's peasants are obstinate, especially in matters of conscience. Tibby Hyslop, the simple orphan of the tale, "Tibby Hyslop's Dream," gives evidence at the trial of Mr Ferret's law-suit so relentless in its honesty that Ferret is ruined and driven to kill himself. Her simplicity astonishes the court; and it is notable that truth pays: a collection is made up for Tibby by the winning side, and, like the Biblical heroines she resembles, she prospers.[24]

The pastoral landscape included more than shepherds and country girls: there were farmers and lairds, and men with singular occupations, and others with no occupation at all. At the upper end of the scale stood the laird. A Scottish laird was usually no such grand thing as his English cousin. We need only remember the unfavourable account of Mary Stuart's progress from Leith to Edinburgh, to see that the manners of Scottish gentry could not bear comparison with the elegance of Southern courts.[25] The laird—at least the Highland variety—was descended from the chieftain, a man who had distinguished himself by force of arms and cunning rather than by courtesy. The ancestors of the Lowland laird were, in all probability, no more refined. A Scottish castle was built for military use; and if the English castle, by all accounts, was a draughty building with rush-strewn floors where the master threw bones to his dog, the Scottish castle was likely to be draughtier and less furnished. The residence of the eighteenth-century laird might be only a big, rambling house.

Such a laird as the scholarly Lindsey of "The Wool-Gatherer" would be an exception. Indeed, it is the exceptional parts of his character that make him memorable. His philosophy is that things take care of themselves. Nagged by his mother to be busy about the estate, he replies: "Our farmers are all doing well, and pay their rents regularly; and as for our farm-servants, they have each of them filled the same situations so long and so creditably, that I feel quite awkward

---

[24] *Tales,* IV. 5-28.   [25] See above, pp. 82-83.

when standing looking over them." At least, she protests, he might go fishing like other gentlemen, "or shooting moor-cocks, an' paetricks, an' black-cocks," as the other country gentlemen of his age and station do. He replies that he knows nothing about fowling, that it is a cruel practice, that the same holds true of fishing; that, in fact, he does not even like to think of oxen or sheep being killed.[26]

In Lindsey aristocratic traditions are at the last gasp; he is no better than a dilettante. This portrait is not offset in Hogg's fiction by portraits of ordinary lairds; those, like the Laird of Wineholm and the Laird of Cassway, who adorn his tales, are only part of the scenery, they are not developed in their own right as gentry. His nobles appear mostly in the tales dealing with history and legend: Montrose, Argyle, and other lords in "An Edinburgh Baillie," an aristocratic family in "A Tale of Good Queen Bess," courtiers in "The Bridal of Polmood," lords and ladies in "The Siege of Rox-burgh," a chieftain and his wife in "Julia M'Kenzie," and other figures in costume. His most convincing picture of the gentry is the Colwan family in the *Justified Sinner*; but they are not grand folk, and are not presented as such. He knew little about the aristocracy of his own day, and hardly used it for fiction. He felt freer to invent Jacobite lords and ladies, but of these, unfortunately, he had even less knowledge.

With those who were prosperous or gentlemanly but not aristocratic, again Hogg was on his own ground. Though his fate is singular, the tenant farmer, Mr Adamson of Laver-hope, who puts the screws on a debtor, and is driven to pursue an evil course and finally is blasted by lightning, represents the class of tenant-farmers whom Hogg knew.[27] Duncan Stewart, of the tale, "Katie Cheyne," stands on the line that divides the common from the genteel; it is his mother's effort to push him across the line that makes the humour of this vivacious tale. In order to extricate himself from one engage-ment and, at his mother's urging, to improve his station in life, Duncan pays court to a genteel "cousin," but is distracted by her chambermaid. Finally he decides to let "the bridal

[26] *Tales*, I. 177-9.   [27] *Op. cit.*, III. 224-47.

train ride by.''[28] Duncan, like Hogg himself, is too spirited to be contained in a social compartment.

In reading Hogg's fiction we are continually reminded of the flexibility of the society it presents.[29] Before God, in the Presbyterian congregation, all men are equal; the man today may be the master tomorrow, and riches may be brought, as they were to Tibby Hyslop, by the very virtues of poverty. In "Nancy Chisolm," we see a complete cycle of family fortunes. John Chisolm, a farmer of Moorlaggen, is reduced from his rank of gentleman by unfortunate speculations. Enraged by the presumption of a tailor in courting his daughter, Nancy, he drives her out with blows. Further misfortune is brought on Chisolm by this, his own injustice, and he is reduced to poverty. Nancy, on the other hand, rises in the world, marries her tailor, who becomes wealthy, and confronts her father and forgives him.[30] As virtue can make a poor man rich, so vice can impoverish him.

Beside characters who seem products of their environment, there are those whose intelligence and eccentricity seem to alter it. Exotics in the pastoral scene, they are among Hogg's most striking creations. Andrew Gemble, the old soldier of "An Old Soldier's Tale," the Cameronian preacher, "with his long white hair and his look, mild, eloquent, and sagacious," Old Sandie Singlebeard, the prudent benefactor of "The School of Misfortune," are Scottish types—but only because they are so original.[31] And there are some who in their own person contradict all the country virtues: the Marvellous Doctor who tells of his adventures with a love-elixir belongs on the raft with Huckleberry Finn, the King and the Duke; and the Watchmaker, who spends his days thinking up ruses to obtain drink for himself and his cronies, adds a nice touch of scarlet to the puritan flowerbed.[32]

[28] *Tales*, III. 171-82. This may be an echo of the Scots proverb : "She wadna hae the walkers, and the riders juist gaed by."

[29] The episode Hogg relates as fact, in which Will o' Phaup and his laird settled an argument with blows, after which the laird ignored the affair, must have been exceptional, but still it points to a considerable freedom—or idea of freedom. (*Op. cit.*, IV. 214.)

[30] *Op. cit.*, IV. 226-41.

[31] *Op. cit.*, III. 160-71 ; *op. cit.*, II. 339-54 ; *op. cit.*, III. 276-88.

[32] *Op. cit.*, IV. 145-73 ; *op. cit.*, IV. 273-82.

As everyone knows, prudence and thrift were traditionally engrained in Scottish life. "Ane's no to throw himsell ower a linn, and trust that the Lord will kep him in a blanket," remarks Wattie Blythe, one of Hogg's shepherds, and the speech of his other pastoral folk is salted with such maxims.[33] The old laird, Sandy Singlebeard, in "The School of Misfortune," has learned that prudence and economy are essential.[34] Confronting a nephew who needs financial help, Sandy exposes his extravagances relentlessly. His nephew has a fine horse, he observes; it must have cost eighteen pounds. Eighty-five guineas, answers the ingenuous young man; and the horse has won a great deal of valuable plate. Where is the plate now? That was before he got the horse, the nephew explains. That is a pity, says Sandy, for if he had the plate he would have something to call his own. So the interrogation proceeds. A man who is doing business, says Sandy, should not travel on a fast horse: "People, instead of giving you a good order, will come to their shop-door, and say—There goes the Flying Manufacturer!—Jock, they say a rolling stone never gathers any moss. How do you think a flying one should gather it?"[35] The young man is reduced to despair; later Sandy reveals that he means to help him, but he has wanted to "curb a little that *upsetting spirit* in him, to which every young man new to business was too much addicted."[36]

The virtues taught by Scripture were the business philosophy of the new patriarchs, the Singlebeards of Glasgow and Edinburgh. If a man is diligent in his business, the Bible tells us, he will stand before kings—and the lowly Sydeserf becomes an Edinburgh baillie. On the other side of the coin, a lack of Puritan virtue may involve a man in dangerous, sordid, and highly interesting adventures. So, Basil Lee's instability of mind brings on what, in a cautionary tale, he calls his misfortunes.

A fool can best teach a wise man wit, Basil says in the preamble, and he has written his life as a model of what is to be avoided.[37] All his misfortunes are to be traced to one great

---

[33] *Tales*, III. 355.
[34] *Op. cit.*, III. 276-88.
[35] *Op. cit.*, III. 286.
[36] *Op. cit.*, III. 287.
[37] *Op. cit.*, III. 49.

evil, "from which, if youth is not warned, their success in life will be frustrated, and their old age be without comfort and without respect."[38] This evil is *"instability of mind*—that youthful impatience, so notorious in every young and aspiring breast, which impels the possessor to fly from one study to another, and from one calling to another, without the chance of succeeding in any."[39]

The third son of a Berwickshire farmer, in his youth Basil tries his hand at carpentry, ploughing, shepherding, shop-keeping, and farming, but he is too conceited and impatient to settle to anything. He then sets up a household, lives with his housekeeper, and is exploited by his servants and riotous friends. Then, in order to shed his encumbrances, he volunteers as a soldier and sets off for the American colonies, to fight the rebels.

The adventures begin when Basil sets foot on board ship. On the way out he meets a lieutenant, Colin Frazer, accompanied by a beautiful young woman named Clifford Mackay. Basil falls in love with her and offers his friendship and protection, and these offers terminate "as all these generous and benevolent protections of the fair sex do."[40] Basil thinks he is a fine fellow to have gained the affections of such a lady in so short a time.

On arriving in America he is challenged by Frazer to a duel, and with great reluctance accepts. In the struggle he receives a light wound and wounds his opponent seriously. Then Basil is told that Clifford's brother, a man of rank, will probably want to duel with him too. He proposes honourable marriage to Clifford, and is astonished when she refuses. He learns to his humiliation that, far from being a lady, she used to be a street-walker in Inverness. After a bitter quarrel the pair come to terms and continue together with toleration and affection. Basil takes the field against the colonials, and in one battle, despite his natural cowardice, acts with a desperate ferocity that gains him the reputation of a hero.

He passes a winter in Philadelphia, and embarks on the adventure we have already described, his courtship of an

[38] *Tales*, III. 49.   [39] *Ibid.*   [40] *Op. cit.*, III. 68.

unknown American lady.[41] Having arranged to get rid of Clifford by helping her marry a rich merchant, he discovers that his American was Clifford in disguise. She has duped him, and he has lost her.

Basil sees hard war service, is taken prisoner, and released through the intercession of Clifford's husband. He sails for home, but he is shipwrecked on the Isle of Lewis in the Outer Hebrides. Here he finds a superstitious people and himself becomes fascinated with the supernatural. He sees the movement of the Great Shadow across the loch and the march of a troop of ghosts; he searches for a mermaid; he sits up at night with an old crone and sees her visited by the ghost of her dead son. Then he proceeds to Inverness, where he finds Clifford's father, the cooper Mackay, and also meets Colin Frazer, Clifford's first lover, now an emaciated cripple. Basil tells Clifford's father that she is happy and prosperous, and goes on to Edinburgh.

There he subsists on an officer's half-pay, feels his old wounds, and falls into debt. He pays court in vain to several heiresses, and at length arranges to marry an old woman with a beard. From this extremity he is rescued by the sudden appearance of Clifford. Her husband has died, leaving her affluent, and together with her small son she has come to find Basil. "She added," Basil relates, "that were I married a thousand times it could not diminish her interest in me one whit."[42] Basil breaks his engagement to the old woman and marries Clifford. At the time of this telling he has lived with her for eighteen years, and, he says, "I have always found her a kind, faithful, and good-natured companion."[43]

The warning against "instability of mind" is, of course, a device, like the label on a bottle claiming it will cure lumbago, toothache and female complaints. "The Adventures of Basil Lee," like the cautionary *Moll Flanders*, is mostly alcohol. As we have seen, some of the subscribers to *The Spy* withdrew their subscriptions after reading the first instalments of the tale.[44] No doubt, they were particularly shocked by Basil's cynical

[41] See above, p. 118. [42] *Tales*, III. 129.
[43] *Ibid.* [44] See above, pp. 29-30.

description of his affair with his housekeeper.[45] Miss Batho
finds it one of Hogg's "dullest, and . . . coarsest" tales. Tales
of seduction, she explains, grow monotonous.[46]

Though it is not delicate, "Basil Lee" is hardly a tale of
seduction. It tells a love story with psychological insights that
are rare in literature. As in *Manon Lescaut* the heroine is a
cheat, and the hero pawns his honour, but they have in their
favour an ultimate loyalty to each other. If Clifford lies to
Basil and dupes him, still these are cheats forced upon her by
circumstance, and Basil in his vanity deserves no better. But
where the true, not the social, relationship is concerned, the
meeting between man and woman, she does not deceive him.
When he offers marriage she turns him down flat, for she does
not want to have him on false pretences. When she receives
dishonourable proposals she lets him know. Only when she
is offered marriage by the rich merchant does she dupe Basil,
and he has deceived her first. Her marriage, indeed, is the
salvation of them both; it enables her at the end to carry Basil
with her out of the world of lying, fighting, gambling, and
prostitution—the world in which prodigal sons and daughters
must move—to a sphere proper to their intelligence and
affection. Clifford is Hogg's most complicated and convincing
female character, an immoral good fairy seen in flashes,
never entire. Basil's thoughts about her after he has lost her
remind us of Swann's preoccupation with Odette:

> . . . to say the truth, I had felt, ever since we parted, a hanker-
> ing affection for Clifford, such as I never had for any human
> being but herself ; yet so inconsistent were all my feelings, that
> the impression she made on my heart, when I did not know
> who she was, still remained uppermost, keeping all the
> intimacy and endearments that had passed between us in the
> shade ; and I found myself deeply interested in the old drunken
> cooper on her account.[47]

"The Adventures of Captain John Lochy," published in
the *Altrive Tales* and never reprinted, in its style and picaresque

---

[45] "It seems my bed had been better than her own, for after having spent one
night in it, she was never either to teach the road back again, nor yet to press
to it. . . . My housekeeper grew nearly double her natural thickness about the
waist." *The Spy*, No. 4, 22 September 1810, p. 26.

[46] Batho, p. 65.   [47] *Tales*, III. 124.

subject resembles "Basil Lee." Though not equal to Basil's story, Lochy's has the same freedom. The autobiographical manner seems to release Hogg, and we may regret that he did not use it more often. The hero is discovered as an infant abandoned near a river. It is suspected that he is of noble birth. He is raised by the Earl of Breadalbane, put out to nurse, and given the name John Lochy. An attempt to kidnap or kill him is foiled; for his protection he is removed to Inverness and given another name. Arriving at manhood, Lochy is revealed as an ingenious but shifty fellow, not unlike Basil Lee. He serves as a soldier in Flanders under the Duke of Marlborough—of whom he has no high opinion. He provokes a drunken fencing-master into a duel and kills him merely to show his prowess. He serves in Russia with Charles of Sweden, whom he considers a fortunate madman. He fights in Scotland, first on the Jacobite side, then in the army of Argyle. In the course of his travels he attaches to himself a rascal named Finlay, whose one virtue is loyalty. He also falls in with a Russian prince, Iset, and a beautiful Jewess named Araby. Araby follows Lochy and the prince in boy's dress; Lochy, thinking she loves him, is somewhat disappointed to find that, instead, it is the Russian of whom she is enamoured. The most important (or disastrous) act that Lochy performs is to kill, purely by chance, a man who is necessary to the Jacobite cause.

The most memorable scenes of the novel do not serve to advance the plot, in so far as there is a plot. The sequel to the duel with the fencing-master is unnecessary, but we would not willingly forego it. When Lochy undertakes another duel, his antagonist reveals himself, in a dreadful moment, as the dead fencing-master. Lochy's half-hearted fascination with Araby is less interesting than his affair with a smuggler's wife, which occupies only a corner of the tale. She is a Jacobite sympathiser; when Lochy seeks refuge in her house she protects him and entertains him vivaciously. He falls in love with her, nursing the hope that her smuggler husband will be killed on one of his expeditions. When he hears that she is a widow he goes to claim her hand, but she sends him packing, for in her eyes he is a traitor, having transferred his allegiance to Argyle.

These Scottish women, Lochy reflects, are more fanatical in their politics than the men.

We do not see the end of Lochys' adventures, but we are told that, in answer to an advertisement enquiring about him, it was said that he was the son of the Honourable James Campbell of Argyle and Lady Mary Wharton, brother to the Duke of Argyle, and heir to large estates. His claim to the inheritance was the cause of attempts to do away with him.[48]

The clans were never loath to drop their plowshares, draw their claymores, and follow the bagpipes. To farmers who had faced biting poverty, India and Jamaica were attractive. And tales of adventure gave them other, less perilous escapes; the ballads, with their profusion of bloody feuds, battles and romantic loves—besides fairies, witches and ghosts—distracted poor folk from the sound of the wind howling outside. Hogg follows tradition in spinning yarns that simply entertain. In his Arabian Nights, accident alters circumstances; men travel to faraway places where customs are turned topsy-turvy; and chance, like the fairies, puts gold in empty pockets. Touches of tongue-in-cheek humour and fact are mixed with romance to give an air of verisimilitude.

As we read "The Surpassing Adventures of Allan Gordon," the reminiscences of a tailor who has been shipwrecked at the North Pole, we are reminded of *Robinson Crusoe*. Hogg is more humorous and fantastic than Defoe, and less convincing. Defoe would not have let Crusoe keep himself alive for weeks, as Allan Gordon does, by imbibing spirits through a tube. And when Allan adopts a female polar bear cub and raises her to be his playmate and friend, we enter the realm of Baron Munchausen. Nancy—that is the name Allan gives his bear—protects him from her own voracious kind. When they fall in with Eskimos, Allan's mastery over such a provider of fish wins him an important place in the tribe. But then he decides to take a human wife. To accomplish this, he has to wait till Nancy falls into her long winter sleep, for she is acutely jealous. On waking, Nancy finds she has been replaced in her master's bosom. She is inconsolable; then she disappears. Allan has reason to regret her absence, for it has entailed the

[48] "The Adventures of Captain John Lochy," *Altrive Tales*, pp. 1-142.

loss of his status in the community; besides, he misses her affection. "I found," he says, "that I had actually been happier traversing the frozen ocean on my iceberg, with one faithful and obliging animal for my companion, than I was now with an amiable wife."[49] The Eskimos are attacked by bears, and are being massacred, when one of the beasts carries Allan away. It is Nancy. She sees to it that Allan has provisions, leads him to a canoe, and bids him goodbye. He travels until he meets with a ship, and returns on it to Scotland.[50]

"The Pongos: a letter from Southern Africa" is also in the humorous-fantastic vein. The tale is in the form of a letter from "Wm. Mitchell," at "Vander Creek, near Cape Town," dated 1 October 1826. The writer tells how a royal cub of the pongos—that is, orang-outangs—"their sovereign's sole heir," was shot as they were robbing the settlers' gardens. The queen his mother proving inconsolable, the old monarch stole the narrator's small son. The queen nursed him, but the pongos thought it " a great loss that they had no means of teaching their young sovereign to speak." So they stole his mother, the narrator's wife, to be his instructor. Six months after the abstraction of the mother, a daughter was born to her. The settlers managed to recover the mother and children safely, though the pongos were loath to let them go. They had been treated royally, though the pongo king's other wife had shown some symptoms of jealousy. The narrator says that he intends to emigrate, for he has a feeling that his family is scarcely safe as long as he is on any part of the coast of Africa.[51]

The tale of "The Marvellous Doctor"—whom we have seen disputing with Margaret Laidlaw—combines magic with adventure.[52] The Doctor claims to have invented a love-elixir. Once, hearing that a professor in Spain also claimed to have such a charm, he went there and overcame him in open contest before the court and people. When the professor had gone through his bag of tricks and made several ladies attach themselves to him, the doctor capped it all by making the professor

---

[49] *Tales*, I. 310.   [50] *Op. cit.*, I. 241-316.
[51] "The Pongos : a letter from Southern Africa," *Altrive Tales*, pp. 143-63.
[52] See above, p. 7.

follow him about like a lackey. On another occasion, in England, he made a countess fall in love with him by sprinkling his elixir on a scarf. But the scarf being taken by a cow, then swallowed by a bull, the doctor was pursued by these beasts and nearly gored to death. Why, he wonders, have his adventures always turned out badly? Because, says Margaret Laidlaw, he has used his knowledge to pervert, rather than to assist nature.[53]

Some of Hogg's tales are all action. In "The Long Pack" a gentleman quits his estate to spend the winter in London, leaving a girl, Alice, a boy, Edward, and an old man named Richard in charge. A pedlar comes by, carrying a long pack. Alice refuses to let him stay the night but, on his insistence, allows him to leave the pack overnight resting on two chairs in the parlour. She thinks she sees it move, and runs for help. The old man and Edward come in and look at the pack, and Edward, having his gun with him, undertakes to shoot the pack. Neither of the others prevents him; he fires; a roar comes from the bundle and blood gushes out. Edward and Alice run away, but the old man persuades them to return. They open the pack and find a dead man in it; with the body they find pistols, a cutlass, and a "silver wind-call." A plot against the house is suspected. The neighbours gather in arms and wait for the dead man's confederates. Nothing happens until Edward has the idea of blowing the silver whistle, whereupon a whistle answers and a body of horsemen appears. Fired upon, they ride away, leaving their casualties behind. Before morning they return and remove their dead. The absence of certain members of very respectable families is afterwards noted, but no one is ever apprehended for the attempt. The servants are rewarded by their master and—the author informs us—the boy Edward, after this brave beginning, has joined the army and had a long military career.[54]

As in "The Long Pack," it is the action of "Adam Scott" that makes the tale. The story is placed at the end of Queen Anne's reign. Adam Scott, on his way back from doing business in England, carrying a sum of money on him, is

<hr/>

[53] *Tales*, IV. 145-73.   [54] *Op. cit.*, III. 183-96.

K

accosted by two men who ask him to guide them into Scotland. On the journey his suspicions are aroused, and one of the men confirms them by trying to knock him down. Scott defends himself so ably that his assailants are left unconscious; thinking he has killed them, he flies from the scene. The would-be robbers recover and have a warrant issued for his arrest, claiming the money he carries is theirs. Scott is captured and brought to trial at Carlisle, where he gets rough justice from the English. Fortunately, an old woman living in Scott's house has a dream of his plight and puts his friend, Thomas Linton, on his track. Linton goes to Carlisle, pleads Scott's case, gathers evidence and establishes his innocence. His accusers are condemned.[55]

But action sometimes degenerates into a mere sequence of episodes. "The Baron St. Gio," subtitled "The Fortunes of an Adventurous Scot," in spite of the mystery and melodrama, is tedious. The hero Jasper, having witnessed a murder, is kidnapped by the murderer and shipped off to a plantation in America; he returns to track down the criminal in Italy where he is masquerading as a baron. The foreign scenes are observed by Jasper through a vague haze, and the motives of the crime are never explained.[56] Also unsatisfactory is "A Strange Secret," which relates how the son of Lady Julia is spirited away by a Catholic bishop and then recovered.[57] In "Ewan M'Gabhar," what interest derives from the description of pastoral Scotland soon yields to melodrama, the tale of a lost heir, confused wars, and unreal courts.[58]

Fiction that depends for its interest on a narrative of improbable events is likely to seem merely improbable. For one "Long Pack" in the canon of Hogg's adventure stories, there are many tales that do not succeed, and his romances, in spite of the contrivance of journeys, disguises, confrontations, battles and changes of fortune, grow wearisome. Romance, with its forced employment of fancy, eliminates his own spontaneous fancy.

[55] *Tales*, IV. 294-305.
[57] *Op. cit.*, IV. 106-45.
[56] *Op. cit.*, IV. 306-35.
[58] *Op. cit.*, IV. 333-52.

VI

The Use of Tradition

As he told Scott, Hogg was happy when he had a tradition to go by and lost when he had none.[1] The distinction is clear in his historical tales. When writing of matters familiar to him through folklore, he can embellish a plot; but when he tries to "work up" a subject taken from romantic history—as in some of his so-called Jacobite tales—he has nothing to dress the characters in but his fancy, and their actions seem melodramatic.

The Covenanters are his most convincing historical subject. Their persecutions had been witnessed by his own ancestors and were still remembered in living oral tradition. Their stubbornness, their exalted imaginations, their almost supernatural presences, struck a sympathetic awe in Hogg's mind. Would it be far-fetched to say that he saw the Covenanters as a kind of fairies? Certainly, their religion had altered Scotland as though by magic; he had only to look around him to see the effects of the Presbyterian dream; and to recreate the martyrs, he had only to clothe his neighbours in the dress of another century.

Hogg's first novel, *The Brownie of Bodsbeck*, is laid in the autumn of 1685, after the battle of Bothwell Bridge, when "the Covenanters, or the whigs, as they were then called, were proscribed, imprisoned, and at last hunted down like wild beasts."[2] As the tale opens, fugitives hiding in the mountains of Annandale, Ettrick Forest and Tweeddale are being pursued by "Clavers" (John Graham of Claverhouse, Viscount Dundee).

The shepherd, Walter Laidlaw, who rents the farm of Chapelhope from the Laird of Drummelzier, secretly gives aid and comfort to the fugitives. Meanwhile, his daughter Katherine is suspected of being in league with evil spirits—

---

[1] See above, p. 116.   [2] *Tales*, I. 12.

perhaps the Brownie of Bodsbeck, a shapeless creature that has been seen abroad and has frightened one of the shepherds, Jasper, nearly out of his wits.

Thanks to the informing of a hypocritical curate named Clerk, Clavers and his dragoons descend on Laidlaw's house. He resists their insults to his family and is carried off to prison. In his absence the curate attempts to seduce Katherine, but the Brownie intervenes and Clerk is taken away by the super-natural creature and his troop. A further mystery is suggested by the actions of the servant Nanny, whose seeming daftness is mixed with expressions of sympathy for the Covenanters.

Laidlaw is tried at Edinburgh and set free on bail, mainly because, following the advice of a friendly sergeant, Roy Macpherson, he swears in court, and his swearing convinces the judges of his innocence. "I thankit his lordship," Laidlaw afterwards comments, "but thinks I to mysel, ye're a wheen queer chaps! Ye shoot fock for praying an' reading the bible, an' whan ane curses and damns ye, ye ca' him a true honest man!"[3]   On his return home, Laidlaw is met by the Brownie and warned not to proceed. But he continues on his way and finds his daughter sitting on her bed, attended by the Brownie and his fellow creatures, holding what looks like a man's corpse across her knee. He flees from the scene and resolves to disown Katherine.

Later, when he confronts her, she persuades him to accompany her to a cave in the mountains. It is the Brownie's hiding-place, and the Brownie turns out to be John Brown, "a strenuous and desperate reformer," whose queer gait is due to a wound received at Bothwell Bridge. His attendants are other Covenanters. Brown is also the husband of the daft-seeming Nancy, and the father of the corpse that Laidlaw has seen on his daughter's bed. As for the "corpse," it was only a young man whom Katherine was tending back to health. The secret of Katherine's supernatural activities is that she has been in league with the Covenanters, who have brought their sick to her under cover of night.

These mysteries having been cleared up, father and daughter are reconciled; and, as the persecutions of the Covenanters have been relaxed, the story ends happily.[4]

[3] *Tales*, I. 147.   [4] *Op. cit.*, I. 5-175.

The Brownie of Bodsbeck was a popular novel in its day.[5] On the whole it is a rambling, dull story, though there are livelier stretches. As we have seen, Hogg claims it was marred by his changing the hero so as not to conflict with Scott's use of John Balfour in *Old Mortality*.[6] We may also remember Scott's objection to the picture of history in it.[7] But Hogg seems to have had reason for his view; the traditions in the novel were, as he claimed, those he had been bred to believe— Walter Laidlaw, who figures heroically in the tale, was one of Hogg's own ancestors.

In the *Brownie*, as he is familiar with the scene, Hogg also has the confidence to create simulacra of the life he knows at first hand. A comical shepherd, Jasper, may be transplanted from the nineteenth century to the seventeenth without a jar. Creatures of superstition may also pass freely through the barriers of time. The prayer of the shepherd, Davie Tait, which enlivens one of the duller stretches of the tale, is a counterpart of the prayers of Adam Scott of Upper Dalgleish, which were remembered in Hogg's own day.[8] The savagery of Clavers and his dragoons allows Hogg to apply his usual realism, and the hypocrisy of the curate, Clerk, excites his detestation; indeed, Clerk is a sketch for the hypocritical Wringhims of the *Justified Sinner*.

Hogg draws again from legends of the Covenanters for "A Tale of the Martyrs," "A Tale of Pentland," and "Some Remarkable Passages in the Life of an Edinburgh Baillie" (which also tells of the wars of Montrose). "A Tale of the Martyrs" is merely an anecdote testifying to the veracity of dreams.[9] "A Tale of Pentland" ravels and unravels a misunderstanding—clarifying the scene we have already mentioned, in which Gabriel Johnstone's daughter is apparently engaged in cutting a Cavalier's throat.[10] The "Edinburgh Baillie" is far better than these; indeed, it is

---

[5] In Miss Batho's opinion we may be thankful for the *Brownie* (Batho, p. 113). In the opinion of R. P. Gillies it is "a most unreadable prose work." *Memoirs of a Literary Veteran*, II. 239.

[6] "Autobiography," p. 456. And see above, p. 42.   [7] See above, p. 43.

[8] See Davie Tait's Prayer, *Tales*, I. 133-5, and the prayers of Adam Scott, *op. cit.*, IV. 202-9.

[9] *Op. cit.*, IV. 287-93.   [10] *Op. cit.*, I. 317-32.

the most interesting of Hogg's historical tales—though in the opinion of Miss Batho it "is not good."[11] However, here as elsewhere we do not share Miss Batho's taste, and we shall attempt to show reasons for our opinion.

The story is told by the Baillie himself, with interpolations by Hogg as editor of the Baillie's "memoirs." We first see Archibald Sydeserf as a harassed and bullied young man, running the commissariat at Edinburgh Castle. He is persuaded by one of the daughters—her name is Jane—of an imprisoned Catholic, Huntly, to give over some papers which make the case against her father. After this treachery, Sydeserf follows the Huntly family in a mean capacity. He loves Jane, who is far above him in rank; her brother, Lord Enzie, insults and beats the presumptuous lover. From this springs the lifelong enmity of the two men. Sydeserf comes to believe that his grievance gives him a divine sanction to destroy Enzie, and, as he foils Enzie at every turn, the lord comes to regard Sydeserf as his evil genius, and avoids him when he can.

The "memoirs" describe the main scenes of Sydeserf's role as adviser to the Covenanters, his service with Montrose, and later, when Montrose changes and fights on the Royalist side, his service against that formidable warrior. In the course of matters, Sydeserf, who has risen to power in Edinburgh as Baillie and adviser to Argyle, manages to save old Huntly again, for which he receives property in Huntly's will. This acerbates Lord Enzie—now Huntly—so that he plots to kill the Baillie; Sydeserf escapes through the intervention of a friend of the late lord. This favour, when fortune changes, the Baillie scrupulously repays.

Through such changes and political gambits the tale proceeds, to the climactic scenes in which the Baillie hunts down his old enemy, Huntly, who still manages to evade him, and to the battle in which Montrose annihilates Argyle's army. Later, we are told, Huntly is executed, and so the Baillie triumphs. Montrose is beheaded; and in his turn, Argyle, having lost favour with King Charles, is also executed. Pondering on Argyle's disgrace and the vanities of the world, the Baillie withdraws from public life, and shortly after seeing his

[11] Batho, p. 122.

old master, Argyle, decently buried, follows him to the grave. He is buried, by a strange coincidence, at the feet of his enemy, Huntly.[12]

A Puritan who believes that he is sanctioned to destroy his enemy, a poor man who rises to a position of command in the great new middle class, the Baillie is one of Hogg's memorable characters. We shall see lineaments of his psychology again in the character of the *Justified Sinner*, and the final touch of the story, his burial at the feet of the man whom he has righteously destroyed, may be compared with the fate of Robert Colwan. Sydeserf is not a hypocrite—nor, for that matter, is Colwan; his religion is all too earnest. His sense of justification leads him into a pursuit that resembles what Hogg, in another place, calls "the passion of inveterate malice."[13] The Baillie's abandonment of his trust at Edinburgh Castle, his hopeless aspiration in love, his scrupulousness in discharging his office, his loyalty to Argyle, are manifestations of a complex character that, revealed stroke by stroke, convinces us, through its very contradictions, of psychological truth.

Legends of Montrose furnish other tales. "The Adventures of Colonel Peter Aston," tells of the feud between the clansman, Nicol Grant, and Peter Aston, a soldier of Montrose. The tale bears witness to the struggles of the clans among themselves; old grievances were always disrupting their combinations. On his way to help Montrose, Peter is treacherously attacked by Grant, who is ostensibly on the same side. The plot is complicated by Peter's love for Grant's daughter, Marsali—a girl who in her savage innocence and devotion resembles Chateaubriand's Atala; like Atala she dies in the hero's arms.[14] In "Wat Pringle o' the Yair," we are given the "inside" story of the Battle of Philiphaugh, in which Montrose was routed; the hero shows the Covenanters' army a secret way by which they take Montrose from the rear. The tale is continued with uncanny episodes, ghosts, and the story of a stolen child who returns to claim his heritage.[15]

In "A Story of the Forty-Six" and "An Old Soldier's Tale," Hogg takes his narrative from a later time, the year of

---

[12] *Tales*, v. 210-338.

[13] *Op. cit.*, III. 359.

[14] *Op. cit.*, VI. 275-323.

[15] *Op. cit.*, VI. 335-60.

Culloden. These tales are only brief anecdotes. "A Story of the Forty-Six" tells of the escape of certain rebels from Cumberland's men.[16] "An Old Soldier's Tale" shows the other side of the picture, an escape of a sergeant in the Royals from a gang of Highlanders.[17] It is noteworthy that the person who listens to the old soldier's tale, "old Margaret," is sympathetic to the Highlanders; the fierce disagreements of Scottish history have been resolved in mutual toleration.

Hogg's weaknesses as a writer of romance are glaringly evident in "The Bridal of Polmood." The novel was ready for the press at the same time as *The Brownie of Bodsbeck* but Blackwood refused to publish it. Later it was published, and in his "Autobiography" the author defends it obstinately; it has been acknowledged by all who have read it, he states, as the most finished and best written tale he ever produced.[18] Hogg was as often wrong as right in his estimates of his own work, but this is perhaps his most pig-headed opinion.

"The Bridal of Polmood" is set in the early sixteenth century. Elizabeth Manners, a lady in waiting to the Queen of Scots, is wooed by the Laird of Polmood, an elderly, uncouth, fellow; she is also courted by the young Baron Carmichael and the lecherous Duke of Rothesay. As Polmood offers immediate marriage, and Elizabeth wants above all else to shine at a wedding, she accepts him, though she does not love him. This distresses her other suitors. One night there is a mix-up of lovers wandering around in the ladies' dormitory, as a result of which Carmichael is banished from the court. Polmood marries Elizabeth and takes her to his gloomy castle. Carmichael appears there as a gardener in disguise. Rothesay also appears, discovers Carmichael's disguise, and incites Polmood to insane jealousy of Carmichael. Elizabeth helps Carmichael to run away and hide. Soon after, the bodies of two noblemen are found with the heads removed; and as Polmood also has disappeared, he is thought to be one of them. Carmichael is suspected of the murders and Elizabeth turns against him. A ghost that haunts the castle in the semblance of Polmood accuses Elizabeth of murder. A mysterious monk

[16] *Tales*, IV. 282-6.   [17] *Op. cit.*, III. 160-71.
[18] "Autobiography," p. 456.

and a shepherd then appear. As the unflaggingly lecherous Rothesay presses his attentions on Elizabeth, the monk arrives on the scene, unveils himself as Polmood, and, after a struggle, hangs Rothesay. Polmood is preparing to hang Elizabeth too when the shepherd comes to the rescue; he reveals himself to be Carmichael and, in a desperate fight, kills Polmood. Elizabeth recovers her disordered wits and marries Carmichael.[19]

Similar cloak-and-dagger nonsense constitutes "The Siege of Roxburgh," which has been retained in Hogg's *Tales* as the better part of the three-volume *Perils of Man*,[20] and the "Tale of Good Queen Bess."[21] But on the other hand, "Mary Montgomery," set in the year 1641, is surprisingly successful. Perhaps the interest of the tale is due to the admixture of tradition; certainly, the heroine has a reality not generally shared by Hogg's romantic ladies. Her fortunes hold the tale together; she is a bit of a coquette, with a sense of humour, and enjoys perplexing her suitors; withal, she is chaste and devoted to her lover. In the course of her wanderings Mary falls into the hands of King Faa of the gipsies and his formidable mother; the adventure is suspenseful; in his portrayal of the gipsies Hogg achieves a rare exoticism.[22]

A letter in the manuscript collection of the National Library of Scotland throws light upon Hogg's use of traditional material. Signed "J.A.," dated 25 Oct. 1830, and addressed to the editor of *Blackwood's Magazine*, it offers possible sources used by Hogg in composing the tale, "Julia M'Kenzie," recently published in the magazine.[23] Hogg himself in the preamble says that he has had the story from "Lady Brewster . . . the sole daughter of the celebrated Ossian M'Pherson," who assured him it was literally true. And in the north of Scotland, he says, there are numerous family traditions to substantiate it.[24] In his story, set in the time of Montrose, when "the chieftainships of the Highlands came to be much

---

[19] *Tales*, II. 1-123.   [20] *Op. cit.*, VI. 67-274.
[21] *The Tales of James Hogg, the Ettrick Shepherd*, London, Glasgow 1886, I. 268-82.
[22] *Tales*, VI. 5-66.
[23] Ms. 2245, f. 159ᵛ-160ʳ, in the National Library of Scotland.
[24] *Tales*, V. 339.

disputed," he paints a picture of primitive clan morality. The chieftain M'Kenzie's wife has borne no children; two of his clansmen, fearing that on his death the clan will be taken over by the hated Nagarre, attempt to murder his wife and provide him with a fruitful mate.[25] The correspondent states that Hogg's tale, a "frightful incident of feudal barbarity," is founded on a "traditionary memorial of the ancient family of the M'Kenzies of Kintail." Hogg has concealed the names of the principals, but there can be no harm at this time in revealing them. The writer has before him "two ancient MSS . . . relating to the family in question: The oldest assigns the attempt upon the lady's life, to the dynasty . . . of Kenneth, the 4th. Chieftain; the more modern one again,—wont [sic] have it recorded, to the dispraise of the 6th. Laird."[26]

Excerpts from the old manuscripts are given. The writer has copied his extracts from not wholly legible originals, and I have copied from the writer's hand; there are undoubtedly errors in the transcriptions, but the meaning is clear:

> Mc Kennich alias M'Kenzie Laird of Kintaile—he was tonamed Kennich ni Stroine (That is to say Kenneth with the Greatnose)—he married McCaill of Lorne's Daughter. They lived a considerable tyme together childless ; But men in these dayes (of whom he was one) preferred succession and manhood to wedlock—he caused throw her under silence of night over the Bridge of Scotwall—But by providence by the Course of the River, she was cast ashore, and repenting of the deed took her to bed and finds a child hopping in her womb so afterwards they lived together contentedly all their dayes.

> The ffifth Laird of that family was called Murdoch Mackenzie of Kintaill—he was tonamed Murdoch—(a blank) (That is Murdoch of the Bridge) being in his (a blank again) when she was thrown over it. This Murdo Married . . . of Lewis his daughter. In those dayes all the Northern . . . of Scotland (the King David Bruce being prisoner—laird then) was without any law—so that the strongest assumed over the weakest.[27]

---

[25] *Tales*, v. 339-59.
[26] Ms. 2245, f. 159ᵛ-160ʳ, in the National Library of Scotland.
[27] *Ibid.*

The second ms. is then quoted:

To him succeeded his only lawfull son called Murdo-na-droit who was ye sixt Baron of Kintaile and maried Macleod of Kerish ? his daughter—he lived long and in peace and amitie with ale his Nighbours & in great favour with his prince—he was agnamed Murdo na droit by reason of some bad treatment his lady met with at ye breidge of Scotwall which happened on this occasion he having lived for many years with his Lady and getting no children, & so fearing that ye Direct lyne of his Familie might fail in his person was not a little concerned and troubled ȳvat, g^h being understood by some sicophants and flaterers y^t was about him & woud fain currie his favor, they thought y^t they could not ingratiat themselves more to him then by puting his Lady out of y^{e}way whereby he might marie an oyr, and so waited ane opportunitie to put iyr. wicked designe to Executione (some say not without his connivance) and so on a certain evening or leat at night as she was going to Achiltie where here Laird lived, these wicked fflaterers did presumtuously & barbarously cast her—ye Breidge of Scotwall, and yn. y^r conscience accuseing them for y^t horrid act they made of with ymselves, But ye wonderfull provedence of God carried ye Innocent Lady (being then young with child) notwithstanding of ye impetousness of the River safe to Shoare, and Inabled her in ye night Time to travell ye lenth of Achillie where her Husband did Impatientlee wait her Coming, yet being ye night she promised to be home and intertained her very Kindly being greatly offended at ye maltreatment she met with. The child y^t she had then in ye womb was afterwards called Alex^r and as some say was agnamed Iniwick, because by a miracle of providence Escaped yt danger and afterward befame heir to his Father and Inherited his Estate—othrs say he was called so for his uprightness.[28]

Comparing Hogg's tale with the versions provided by the letter-writer, we see something of his preferences in making a story. The main improbability of the first ms. has been removed—that after the Laird's part in plotting to murder the Lady, they were reconciled. In Hogg's tale not only is the Laird guiltless of complicity, but he is angered and grieved

[28] Ms. 2245, f. 159^v-160^r, in the National Library of Scotland.

by the suggestion that he put away his wife and marry again. He therefore makes a sympathetic hero. To him is opposed old Carnoch, a leader of the clan, in whose mind there is no doubt that "succession and manhood" are preferable to wedlock. Carnoch and his nephew attempt the murder. After the Lady is thrown from the bridge, the criminals are accused by a girl, Lady Julia's foster-sister, who prophesies—an original touch of Hogg—that a witness will appear to expose them. On a dark, stormy night the witness appears; it is Lady Julia herself. The guilty men rush out and fall to their death from the castle. Some gnawing doubts the Lady has about her husband's innocence are removed by her foster-sister's explanation. Within a year of her return the Lady gives birth; she was not, as in the other versions we have read, pregnant at the time of her fall.

The simplified character of the Laird, with no ambiguity; the prophetic power of the girl ("I have it from the country beyond the grave"); the appearance of Lady Julia after she is thought dead, with ghostly effect—these touches, characteristic of Hogg, make all the difference between the legend and his tale.

VII

" What We Believe "

I^N "The Wool-Gatherer" the shepherd Barnaby explains
what he and the other pastoral folk believe:

"We dinna believe in a' the gomral fantastic bogles and spirits
that fley light-headed fock up an' down the country, but we
believe in a' the apparitions that warn o' death, that save life,
an' that discover guilt. I'll tell ye what we believe, ye see.

"The deil an' his adgents, they fash nane but the gude fock ;
the Cameronians, an' the prayin' ministers, an' sic like. Then
the bogles, they are a better kind o' spirits, they meddle wi'
nane but the guilty; the murderer, an' the mansworn, an'
the cheater o' the widow an' fatherless, they do for *them*.
Then the fairies, they're very harmless ; they're keener o'
fun an' frolic than aught else ; but if fock neglect kirk ordi-
nances, they see after *them*. Then the brownie, he's a kind o'
half-spirit half-man ; he'll drudge an' do a' the wark about
the town for his meat, but then he'll no work but when he
likes for a' the king's dominions. That's precisely what we a'
believe here awa', auld an' young. . . ."[1]

Barnaby's systematic and precise assignment of different types
of "visitants" to different classes of people is illuminating—
it is only the "gude fock" (an ironic phrase in Scots) who are
troubled by "the deil an' his adgents." Hogg is reporting
the popular belief with authority and deep moral insight.
And what are his own beliefs? We have already touched on
this, but we may do so again in reference to his prose.

In the poem "Superstition," he addresses superstition as a
"Great Queen" and laments her passing.[2] Superstition did no
harm; on the contrary, it was the well-spring of Fancy. But now:

All these are gone—the days of vision o'er;
The bard of fancy strikes a tuneless string.

---

[1] *Tales*, I. 199-200.   [2] *Works*, II. 394.

> Oh ! if I wist to meet thee here no more,
> My muse should wander, on unwearied wing,
> To find thy dwelling by some lonely spring. . . ."[3]

Superstition, then, is a source of fiction, and Hogg draws from it an abundance of ghosts, apparitions, witches, fairies, and supernatural incident.   Whatever his own convictions are, they do not prevent his making use of superstition as though he believed in it wholeheartedly.   If a tale needs a ghost, then for the purpose of the tale ghosts exist.

But he does not have to pretend very hard.   As we examine his works we see that he himself is superstitious.   As other men have to try to believe in the supernatural, Hogg has to try not to.   Against a handful of remarks that express scepticism, we find numerous statements and incidents that demonstrate Hogg's belief in the supernatural.

One modification of this belief may be remarked—though it seems invalidated by his other writings: supernatural powers were once operative, but are no longer so.   In the sketch "Odd Characters," he says that Will o' Phaup was the last man of the region who "heard, saw, and conversed with the Fairies," and supports the claim.[4]   In the tale "Mary Burnet," he states that in the reign of James IV "fairies, brownies and witches were at the rifest in Scotland."[5]

As we have noted, sometimes Hogg destroys the supernatural effect of a tale by giving a natural explanation—the Brownie of Bodsbeck is only John Brown.   But this should not be taken to mean that Hogg is a positivist; the turnabout is merely a surprise, a fictional device like any other.   Nor should Hogg's curious interest in optical illusions be taken to indicate positivist tendencies.   In the sketch "Storms," he describes how, after a storm, he thought he saw the heavens covered with trees; but this was an illusion.[6]   In "Nature's Magic Lantern," the appearance of "a giant blackamoor, at least thirty feet high," which fills him with astonishment and terror, is ascribed to a refraction of light against a certain kind of background.[7]   And in the same sketch, a spectacle of

[3] *Works*, II. 394.   [4] *Tales*, IV. 215.
[5] *Op. cit.*, IV. 43.   [6] *Op. cit.*, II. 136-7.
[7] *Op. cit.*, IV. 352-4.

marching troops, perceived in astonishing detail, is ascribed to the same "magic lantern."[8] (A similar phenomenon is observed by Basil Lee in his stay on the Isle of Lewis—though there a natural explanation is not offered.[9]) However, the reader who concluded from these explanations that Hogg is a positivist would be hard pressed to account for the number of unexplained uncanny occurrences in his tales, and for passages such as that in "Welldean Hall" where the literal-minded Dr Leadbeater is held up to ridicule. Dr Leadbeater attempts to explain away a ghost as the workings of over-wrought fancy, "opacity" of mental vision, "discord of colours, springing from the proportions of the vibrations propagated through the fibres of the optic nerves into the brain."[10] These arguments, Hogg comments, were no doubt replete with deep philosophy, but no one could discover their relevance.

In effect, when Hogg offers an alternative, natural explanation, he doubles a mystery; the supernatural explanation then seems more probable—it is strengthened by our preference. For we prefer to be frightened. The reader may choose to think that the old man who curses Mr Adamson of Laverhope is only an old Papist beggar; he may choose to think that the servant, Merodach, in "The Brownie of the Black Haggs" is only a servant; he may think, if he wishes, that the companion of the Justified Sinner is a figment of his imagination. Or he may feel that the Papist beggar, Merodach, and Colwan's friend are *personae* of the Prince of Darkness. Hogg's refusal to state where *he* stands, his rendering of infernal operations side by side with common life and logic, are a technique, a peculiar secret of his fiction. He leaves us with a dreadful surmise. And if we believe in the powers of darkness, it is because we will so to believe.

"Why should any body despise a dream, or anything whatever in which one seriously believes?" Hogg asks in "Adam Scott."[11] There may be superior intelligences, angels, who converse with mortals for their welfare, he proposes in "Tibby Hyslop's Dream."[12] And at the beginning of "The

---

[8] *Tales*, iv. 357-8.
[9] *Op. cit.*, iii. 107-110.
[10] *Op. cit.*, ii. 198.
[11] *Op. cit.*, iv. 305.
[12] *Op. cit.*, iv. 9, 15.

Mysterious Bride" he explicitly criticises Scott's rationalistic assumptions:

> A great number of people now-a-days are beginning broadly to insinuate that there are no such things as ghosts, or spiritual beings visible to mortal sight. Even Sir Walter Scott is turned renegade, and, with his stories made up of half-and-half, like Nathaniel Gow's toddy, is trying to throw cold water on the most certain, though most impalpable, phenomena of human nature. The bodies are daft.[13]

These and other didactic statements show his adherence to superstition. But his belief or disbelief is of slight importance; what matters is the use he makes of the supernatural in his writings. Ghosts, apparitions, devils, witches and dreams, and lesser "phenomena" such as fairies, brownies and mermaids, are the material of his most powerful fiction.

"The Cameronian Preacher's Tale" is narrated as a sermon by John Farley, "a man," the author says, "whom I knew and loved. I think I see him now, with his long white hair and his look mild, eloquent, and sagacious. He was a giver of good counsel, a sayer of wise sayings, with wit at will, learning in abundance, and a gift in sarcasm which the wildest dreaded."[14]

Long ago, says the preacher, when men above the rank of peasant still carried swords, two men on Dryfe Water in Annandale were fierce competitors in business and trials of strength: Walter Johnstone, an open-hearted but proud man, and John Macmillan, a grasping man, as proud as the other. One day both men went to the fair at Longtown and, it was said, Johnstone bettered Macmillan in bargaining. That night they were seen at a public inn glaring at each other. Johnstone rode away and then Macmillan rode after him. The next morning Johnstone's horse came to the stable without its rider and splashed with blood.

Macmillan was suspected of murder but cleared in a trial for want of evidence. A year later, at the Longtown fair, Macmillan stopped at the same inn. A voice like Johnstone's was heard outside, calling to him. He went out, and was heard conversing with someone. Later, on his way home with companions, as they neared the spot where the murder was

[13] *Tales*, IV. 335.   [14] *Op. cit.*, II. 354.

thought to have happened, Macmillan's horse started and threw him, breaking his neck.

Meanwhile, as Johnstone's wealth had been lost with his body, his widow and children had been reduced to poverty. They removed to a cottage in the Dryfesdale hills. Macmillan's only daughter had married a man named Joseph Howatson. The Cameronian preacher preached a sermon on Macmillan's death, hinting broadly that it was a sign of divine retribution. Howatson, making his way home from the kirk, wished he could know the truth of the matter, for Macmillan had been kind to him. He cried aloud, "Would to God that I could know the truth . . .," whereupon the ghost of Macmillan appeared and spoke to him. Howatson fainted, but on coming to his senses he resolved to seek out the ghost again. On the next Sabbath night he returned to the same place. The wraith appeared and revealed that he, Macmillan, had killed Johnstone in a fair fight, had carried Johnstone's body on his horse to a quagmire in Crake's Moss, and there concealed it. But first he had removed Johnstone's bills and perishable property with the intention of returning them to his family. (This curious action is not explained.) The gold he had left with the dead man. The ghost instructed Howatson that these bills were at the house of Janet Mathieson in Dumfries, in a strong-box under a hearthstone in the room where Macmillan used to stay. He urged Howatson to restore these things to Johnstone's widow and to inform her where her husband's body lay. So the ghost would have "some assuagement of misery." Threatening Howatson with dreadful consequences if he did not comply, the spirit vanished.

Howatson, knowing that his communion with the ghost meant that he himself would soon die, revealed the message to the preacher. He died, and the preacher, convinced by this, proceeded to the house in Dumfries and found Johnstone's property. Then he travelled into the hills and happened by chance upon the house of Johnstone's widow. That night a "corse" light was seen in Crake's Moss, the whole morass seeming on fire. The preacher entered the morass, found the place revealed by the ghost to Howatson, and led Johnstone's widow to the body. He turned over the dead man's property

L

to the widow and rode away. Afterwards, the Cameronian preacher's visit was remembered in legend as the intervention of a good spirit.[15]

He has told this tale, says the preacher, that his children may know "there is a God who ruleth this world by wise and invisible means, and punisheth the wicked, and cheereth the humble of heart and the lowly minded."[16]

"The Cameronian Preacher's Tale," like the ballad "The Pedlar," hinges on the revelation of injustice by a supernatural agency. It offers curious superstitions. The "corse" or "dead" lights that reveal the whereabouts of a corpse, appear here as in "Rob Dodds."[17] To commune with a ghost brings death, as Howatson believes and proves. (This superstition makes the plot of "Tibby Johnston's Wraith." In "Adam Bell" it is modified: to see a wraith when the sun is up, instead of being a prelude of instant death, prognosticates very long life.)[18] We note other curiosities that are not peculiar to Hogg: the agony of Macmillan's ghost will not abate until the injustice to Johnstone's family is righted. If Howatson does not carry out the spirit's behest he will become "a world's wonder."

But the power of the tale is not in these curiosities. Rather, it is in the narrative. The "facts" of the story are related in a style of awesome gravity. Particularly effective is the scene at the inn when Macmillan hears Johnstone's voice calling to him from outside. Like other of Hogg's supernatural scenes, what then occurs is offstage, part heard and part guessed. As in the *Justified Sinner*, the powers of darkness move outside, and though the damned man may go out to speak with them, ordinary folk and the reader do not follow:[19]

> Macmillan went to the fair of Longtown, and when evening came he was seated in the little back room which I mentioned before, and in company with two men of the names of Hunter and Hope. He sat late, drank deeply, but in the midst of the carousal a knock was heard at the door, and a voice called sharply, "John Macmillan." He started up, seemed alarmed,

---

[15] *Tales*, II. 339-54.   [16] *Op. cit.*, II. 354.
[17] See "The Cameronian Preacher's Tale," *op. cit.*, II. 351-3, and "Rob Dodds," *op. cit.*, III. 219-20.
[18] *Op. cit.*, III. 133.   [19] *Justified Sinner*, pp. 203-5, 209-11.

and exclaimed, "What in Heaven's name can *he* want with
me?" and opening the door hastily, went into the garden, for
he seemed to dread another summons lest his companions
should know the voice. As soon as he was gone, one said to
the other, "If that was not the voice of Walter Johnstone, I
never heard it in my life; he is either come back in the flesh
or in the spirit, and in either way John Macmillan has good
cause to dread him." They listened—they heard Macmillan
speaking in great agitation; he was answered only by a low
sound, yet he appeared to understand what was said, for his
concluding words were, "Never! never! I shall rather submit
to His judgment who cannot err." When he returned he was
pale and shaking, and he sat down and seemed buried in
thought. He spread his palms on his knees, shook his head
often, then, starting up, said, "The judge was a fool and no
prophet—to mortal man is not given the wisdom of God—
so, neighbours, let us ride." They mounted their horses and
rode homewards into Scotland at a brisk pace.[20]

"The Brownie of the Black Haggs" is set in a time "when
the Sprots were Lairds of Wheelhope."[21] Lady Wheelhope
torments her servants. She poisons a maid and, it is suspected,
kills a boy. But the law is not exacting in this age, and she is
not arraigned. Her husband becomes paralysed by the contemplation of her wickedness.

A new servant named Merodach enters her employment.
"He had the form of a boy, but the features of one a hundred
years old."[22] Merodach frustrates the Lady at every turn;
every attempt she makes to hurt him rebounds, as he has
warned her, double on her own head. She tries to strike him
and only wounds another servant and breaks her crockery.
She tries to poison him and poisons her pet lapdog instead.
Her son and heir is found murdered in his bed and there is
no doubt the Lady has murdered him by mistake.

She is now thoroughly demented. When Merodach leaves
the Lady also disappears. There is some speculation that she
has eloped with him. Merodach turns up at the house of a
shepherd, Wattie Blyth, closely followed by the Lady. Her
behaviour is an insane compound of hatred and attachment

[20] *Tales*, II. 343-4. [21] *Ibid.*, III. 342.
[22] *Op. cit.*, III. 345.

to Merodach. Though he casts her off and beats her, she follows him, writhing and grovelling.[23]

The Lady is brought home, but escapes again, and is seen following Merodach. He is seen beating her "as a piece of excellent amusement."[24] Her body is found in the wild haggs at Crook-burn by a party of Covenanters who are hiding there. She is buried like a dog, and Merodach is never seen again. For many years after, the author relates, the countryside was in terror of the "fiendish creature" that tormented the Lady to death, "The Brownie of the Black Haggs." The tale was told to him by "an old man named Adam Halliday, whose great-grandfather, Thomas Halliday, was one of those that found the body and buried it."[25]

The brownie of this tale, like Johnstone's ghost, is concerned with justice. However, unlike the ghost, Merodach is not evidently a supernatural creature; nor is there anything supernatural in his behaviour, unless we, like the country people, wish to think there is. The tale may be read as a case of "morbid dependency," to use a term of current psychology.[26] The Lady's hatred of Merodach manifests itself as a kind of "neurotic" love is manifested, by self-abasement and absolute attachment. The country people who conclude that when Merodach and the Lady both disappear she has eloped with him, see right to the heart of the matter. He beats her and she follows him, grovelling under his blows and squeaking like a cat. The Lady is a masochist.

That is one part of the "psychology" of the story. We have seen morbid attachments described, albeit humorously, in the adventures of the Marvellous Doctor, whose magic elixir attracts a bull to him at peril of his life.[27] The Edinburgh Baillie's pursuit and destruction of Huntly and his burial at Huntly's feet, suggest a similar mixture of love and hate.[28] In the *Justified Sinner*, Robert Colwan's hatred of his brother, George, will be indistinguishable in its manifestations from a kind of love.

---

[23] See the description quoted above, p. 122.
[24] *Tales*, III. 358. [25] *Ibid.*
[26] The term is found in the writings of Karen Horney.
[27] See above, pp. 144-145. [28] See above, pp. 149-151.

But there are other aspects of psychological observation in "The Brownie of the Black Haggs" that are no less interesting. Why does the Lady torment her servants? "Inveterate malignity" possesses her.[29] She seems unable to control herself: she is compelled to be as wicked as she can; like Lady Macbeth, she must act out her thoughts to their furthest imaginable conclusions. As with Lady Macbeth (and the Justified Sinner) there is no satisfying end for her but self-destruction. Her husband, too, is a profitable study. A good-humoured, rather foolish fellow, he is compelled by his wife's actions to take thought, and before the abyss that is revealed he withdraws into dullness and lethargy.

It has been said in Hogg's praise that he "tells a 'ghost-story' as no other man has told one."[30] But to describe "The Brownie of the Black Haggs" or the *Justified Sinner* as ghost-stories would be to give a false impression of their quality. In these tales, and in other writings by Hogg, supernatural matter is only the catalyst that releases his talent. The introduction of a ghost or demon, the propounding of a mystery, serves to break down the confines of his imagination and enlarges his skill at rendering character, action and scene. His intelligence is stimulated by the addition of "some indefinite evil"; the catalyst is submerged in a bubbling of elements.[31]

There may be superior intelligences who converse with mortals for their welfare.[32] On the other hand, as in "The Brownie of the Black Haggs," there may be intelligences who converse with mortals for their destruction. Frequently in Hogg's tales supernatural operations are in the interest of justice. In "The Wife of Lochmaben" the ghost of the smith's wife reveals that she was struck down by her husband; she did not kill herself, as has been supposed. The body is exhumed and it is discovered that, indeed, she was murdered. The suspected man is driven from the country.[33] In "The Mysterious Bride" the Laird of Birkendelly becomes fascinated with a woman he meets near Birky Brow. Her name, she tells

---

[29] *Tales*, III. 347.

[30] Douglas, p. 99.

[31] *Noctes*, III. 388. The Shepherd uses the expression "some indefinite evil."

[32] As Hogg states in "Tibby Hyslop's Dream."

[33] *Tales*, II. 172-9.

him, is Jane Ogilvie. She promises to wed him, and he is
seen riding to his wedding; later, his "blackened corpse" is
found near Birky Brow. Traditions are searched and it is
found that the Laird's father and grandfather died in the
same place. An old woman tells that the first Laird of Birkendelly, before he married, was engaged to a beautiful girl named
Jane Ogilvie. It was suspected that he murdered her. She
points out the supposed grave of the girl; it is the very spot
where the Laird's corpse was found. The earth is dug up and
the bones of a young woman are discovered. The Mysterious
Bride does not appear again.[34]

Similar to this is the tale of "Mary Burnet." An "in-
cautious" young farmer, John Allanson, makes a tryst with
Mary Burnet; she does not come, and he wishes some fairy
would bring her. She comes hastening, and, after a brief
meeting, throws herself into the lake. He tries in vain to
retrieve the body; then he proceeds to Mary's home and
rouses her parents. Mary is found safe in her bed. The next
day she disappears. Allanson then plunges into wickedness.
He goes to the hiring market at Inverlawn with the purpose
of hiring a beautiful girl whom he will then seduce. He
chooses a woman, and she gives her name as Mary Burnet.
He chooses another; the same thing happens. After several
such incidents, a lady arrives in a coach; she flatters Allanson
and makes an appointment to see him at night at her home.
Allanson goes to keep this tryst and the result is as dire as that
of the Laird of Birkendelly's tryst with Jane Ogilvie. His
body is discovered fallen into a great pit where a dark stream
foams and boils. But the author, unfortunately, adds to his
tale, and Mary turns up again as a fine lady in a coach, with
two children. She visits her parents briefly and they rejoice
in her happiness, but the reader is somewhat perplexed. If
Mary is made of flesh and blood, what supernatural creature
was it that Allanson met with? Or do spirits ride in coaches
and have ordinary children?[35]

Hogg's demons are agents of justice. Merodach in "The
Brownie of the Black Haggs," Gil-Martin in the *Justified
Sinner*, and the "old Papist beggar" who curses Mr Adamson

----

[34] *Tales*, IV. 335-52.   [35] *Op. cit.*, IV. 28-53.

of Laverhope, are servants of Satan, who is himself a servant. They tempt and lure the wicked to destruction.

On the other hand, some of Hogg's tales of the supernatural only present curiosities; an apparition or ghost, a revelation in a dream, are described to astonish the reader rather than to show the workings of justice. In "Tibby Johnston's Wraith" we perceive the significance of dreams, and observe that meeting with a wraith may entail death to the beholder. As the story is told by "auld Davie Proudfoot," Tibby Johnston dreams of a wedding, and this, she believes, signifies death. She goes to town and returns, carrying gifts for her family, but dies on the road. Mrs Graham, on her way home, sees Tibby Johnston going in front of her. Tibby falls, but when Mrs Graham comes up she finds no one; on returning home she falls into a delirium and dies. There is a double funeral.[36]

In "Tibby Hyslop's Dream" we are given an instance of the powers of prophecy, such as are possessed by old folk in particular. Old Douglas Hervey, the sister of Tibby's grandmother, has a dream which she reads to mean that Tibby, who is far from home, is in danger at the hands of Mr Forret; and her warning, of course, proves true.[37] In "The Fords of Callum," a supernatural voice that resembles their daughter's calls to Wat Douglas and his wife, Janet, from outside their house, asking if Wat is at the Fords of Callum. They go there and find their daughter dead; her clothes are torn, but she shows no marks of violence. A fortnight later Wat dies. A stranger, reported to be the Duke of Q——, appears at the girl's funeral, but his part in the mystery of the tale is not made clear.[38] In the tale of "Adam Bell," Mr Bell of Annandale being away from home, his wraith appears to his housekeeper in broad daylight. He himself does not return. Sixteen years later, a man named M'Millan reveals that at about the time of Bell's disappearance he had seen two men duelling by moonlight. One of the men was killed, and as his identity was unknown, he was buried in the Greyfriars' Churchyard. From an examination of the possessions left by the dead

---

[36] *Tales*, II. 262-74.   [37] *Op. cit.*, IV. 5-28.
[38] *The Tales of James Hogg, the Ettrick Shepherd*, I. 297-300.

man, it is evident that he was Adam Bell. The mystery of his death is not solved. The supernatural matter is presented for its own sake, to arouse wonder.[39]

Like the author of "Tam o' Shanter," Hogg found humour, as well as excitement, in *diablerie*. There is a grim delight in the actions of Merodach, and Gil-Martin has a sardonic way of speaking to the Justified Sinner; but the ghost of "Welldean Hall" provides Hogg with occasions for outright farce,[40] and in "The Witches of Traquair" and "The Hunt of Eildon" witchcraft makes mischief. Colin Hyslop, hero of "The Witches of Traquair," is raised in wickedness by Rob Kirkwood, the warlock, and his Aunt Nana, "the wickedest witch in Cristendye." They turn him into a fox, a goose, and a three-legged stool, tormenting him so that he will sign a compact with Satan. From this predicament he is rescued by equally resourceful witches, but any virtue the tale has is in the wickedness.[41] The selfish shepherd Croudy, of "The Hunt of Eildon," is changed into a hog and finally into a cat.[42] Unlike ghosts and apparitions, witches are amusing; their magic is fine entertainment. Though some witches are, or think they are, servants of Satan, when he wants anything done he does not rely on these crazy beldames.

Several of Hogg's tales demonstrate the superstitions listed by Barnaby, and the reader may gather much curious, incidental information about these beliefs.[43] In "The Laird of Cassway," we note that an apparition or wraith may be sent forth from a living man; or is it a good spirit acting in his guise?[44] A wraith, says Wat Douglas, in "The Fords of Callum," is "a guardian angel that comes to gie warning o' something that's to happen to its ward."[45] Ghosts, we discover in "Welldean Hall," cannot speak to baptised Christians till they are spoken to.[46] Mermaids are not spirits, Mary Burnet's father declares with authority; the meer-maiden is a "beastly sensitive creature, with a malicious spirit within it."[47]

Such curiosities form the scenery and drapery of the tales,

---

[39] *Tales*, III. 131-6.
[40] *Op. cit.*, II, 190-262.
[41] *Op. cit.*, IV. 173-96.
[42] *Op. cit.*, III. 1-48.
[43] See above, p. 157.
[44] *Tales*, III. 318-42.
[45] *The Tales of James Hogg, the Ettrick Shepherd*, I. 298.
[46] *Tales*, II. 251.
[47] *Op. cit.*, IV. 34.

but they are not the main reason for our interest. Indeed, it is when idea and action lag that our attention is distracted to curious details. When the story is compelling the details are subsumed, becoming, as it were, normal. Sir George Douglas remarks on the *"atmosphere* of eeriness" that Hogg creates and, as an instance of his skill in creating that atmosphere, points to the wonderful game-birds of "A Strange Secret"—"falling a prey to the sportsman . . . and directing reproachful glances upon him as they fall."[48] This is a touch of fancy. But the tales that command our interest are not merely fanciful; when Hogg is possessed by a strong idea, he writes with imagination, the faculty that "forms all into one graceful and intelligent whole" and animates the parts.[49]

[48] Douglas, p. 100.

[49] ". . . Sense is the body of poetic genius, fancy its drapery, motion its life, and imagination the soul that is everywhere, and in each ; and forms all into one graceful and intelligent whole." Samuel Taylor Coleridge, *Biographia Literaria*, London and New York 1956, p. 174.

VIII

The Antinomian Devil

We have heard much of the rage of fanaticism
in former days, but nothing to this.

The Justified Sinner [1]

WHAT if a man believes that he is justified and listed
with the elect, and that no act of his own or of other
men can alter the decree? This is the question raised
in *The Private Memoirs and Confessions of a Justified Sinner*; the
answer is shown by the life of Robert Colwan. His pride and
malice are licensed by the "fanatical" doctrine of absolute
predestination. It is a difficult theme, and one we might not
have expected of the Shepherd; indeed, some readers have
attempted to deny that Hogg could have conceived and executed the novel by himself. "What made *him*," Lang asks,
"run a tilt at the extreme doctrine (the impeccability and
assured salvation of the Elect) held by his favourite Covenanters?"[2] But, as we shall demonstrate, there is overwhelming
evidence that the *Justified Sinner*, both in idea and execution,
is all Hogg's work.

In his introduction to the novel, André Gide supposes that
Robert Colwan is, unknown to himself, an "antinomian," one
of those heretics who, in about the year 1538, listened to
Johannes Agricola's teaching that, under the Gospel Dispensation, the Law might be rejected; that "good works do not
further, nor evil works hinder salvation; that the child of God
cannot sin . . . that murder, drunkenness, etc., are sins in the
wicked but not in him. . . ."[3] In a correspondence with
Gide, Dorothy Bussy advised, "You mustn't forget that this

---

[1] James Hogg, *The Private Memoirs and Confessions of a Justified Sinner*, with an
introduction by André Gide, London 1947, p. 85.

[2] *Illustrated London News*, cv, No. 2901 (24 Nov. 1894), Supplement, 12.

[3] *Justified Sinner*, "Introduction," p. xi.

work is not English but very specifically Scotch. . . . Its whole atmosphere, the very form and substance of its Puritanism, is essentially Scottish."[4] The advice was excellent, for if we make a brief excursion into Scottish church history we find that there was a violent controversy over "antinomianism" in the early years of the eighteenth century—at the time, or near it, when the action of Hogg's novel unrolls—and that the minister at Ettrick between 1707 and 1732, the Reverend Thomas Boston, was accused of holding antinomian opinions. In all probability, Hogg took his theme from local tradition.[5]

The controversy began in this fashion.[6] In 1717, a young man named William Craig was examined by the Presbytery of Auchterarder as to his fitness to preach. His answers were not satisfactory to the Presbytery; in particular, he did not show a clear understanding of, or agreement with, their statement "that it is not sound and orthodox to teach that we must forsake sin in order to our coming to Christ, and instating us in covenant with God."[7] Craig's licence to preach was withheld. He appealed to the General Assembly, laying the statement before them. The General Assembly declared their abhorrence of the statement—it seemed to imply that a man might be sinful and yet a Christian—and commanded the Presbytery of Auchterarder to explain what they meant by it. Now, Thomas Boston and James Hog of Carnock (we shall return to this name) were among those who had helped to draw up the catechism in which the condemned statement appeared. Thus, Boston and Hog were attacked as upholders of the "Auchterarder Creed," and as antinomianists.

The second phase of the antinomian controversy began with the publication by the Reverend James Hog of a new

[4] *Justified Sinner*, "Introduction," p. x.

[5] I am indebted to Professor David A. Robertson, Jr., of Columbia University, for suggesting that I look into Scottish church history for the origins of Hogg's novel, and for directing my attention toward Thomas Boston and Hog of Carnock.

[6] My summary of the Auchterarder Creed and *Marrow* controversies is based on readings in the following works : Thomas Boston, *Memoirs of the Life, Time, and Writings of the Reverend and Learned Thomas Boston*, A. M., ed. George H. Morrison, Edinburgh 1899, *passim* ; John Cunningham, *The Church History of Scotland*, Edinburgh 1882, II. pp. 247-56 ; W. M. Hetherington, *History of the Church of Scotland*, New York 1859, pp. 340-7.

[7] Hetherington, p. 340.

edition of *The Marrow of Modern Divinity*. The book had been recommended to Hog by Boston; on the advice of his friends, Hog wrote a preface for the new edition, which appeared in 1718. The work was received with "great displeasure" by the leading men of the Church, who were nearly all Neonomians or "new-law men." To disentangle the threads of theological dispute in Scotland at this period is a task beyond the scope of this study, but in general it may be said that there were two main parties confronting each other: the Neonomians, who held that the Gospel was a new Law, promising salvation upon a certain condition (faith, or faith and repentance, or faith and repentance and obedience); and, opposing them, those whom the Neonomians called Antinomians, who held that salvation was not contingent upon faith, *et cetera*, but was the effect of justification, of grace.[8]

The publication of the *Marrow* provided an opportunity for the enemies of antinomianism. In the General Assembly they managed to have the book condemned, and the "false doctrines" contained were listed under five categories—the fifth being, "That the believer is not under the law as a rule of life."[9]

We may now return to our author, leaving the Neonomians and Antinomians, like Swift's Big-Endians and Little-Endians, disputing. What has this to do with the *Justified Sinner*? First, we can hardly doubt that James Hogg was acquainted with the history of the Auchterarder Creed and *Marrow* controversies. As we have said, Boston was minister in Hogg's own Ettrick, forty years before he was born. Hogg knew about Boston: in his sketch "Odd Characters," he describes an encounter between Boston and Daft Jock Amos, in which Jock confounds "the far-famed Boston"; in the same sketch he describes Boston marrying Willie Candlem and Meggie Coltard.[10] In his tale, "The Mysterious Bride," Hogg shows an old Scotswoman reading Boston's *The Fourfold State of Man*.[11] And Hogg could hardly have failed to look into Boston's works, for, as he says, like most Scottish Presbyterians he was accustomed to reading theology.[12] Also, he must have heard

[8] Hetherington, pp. 341-2.   [9] *Idem.*, p. 345.
[10] *Tales*, IV. 220-1, 223.   [11] *Op. cit.*, IV. 346.
                    [12] "Autobiography," p. 443.

antinomianism discussed; theology was then, as it still is, one of the vital interests of ordinary Scotsmen. Therefore, Hogg obtained the subject of antinomianism from both local tradition and his own reading. He may even, though we cannot prove it, have patterned his characters on men who took part in these controversies.

Then, let us consider the Reverend James Hog of Carnock. As far as I have been able to discover, he was not related to the Hoggs of Ettrick. However, knowing our author, I surmise that Hog of Carnock's involvement in the *Marrow* controversy may have led James Hogg of Ettrick to take a particular interest in the subject of antinomianism. As we have seen, Hogg could convince himself that he was born on the same day as Burns;[13] perhaps, by a similar prompting, he felt himself personally confronted with James Hog of Carnock, an antinomian spectre bearing his name, and was obliged to exorcise it.

"That the believer is not under the law as a rule of life" would be dangerous doctrine. Though the proponents of the *Marrow* in all probability did not mean their arguments to be taken to extremes, it seems that they were, by other, weaker intellects. Burns, in "Holy Willie's Prayer," describes the antinomian type, anticipating Hogg's study.[14] Willie praises his Maker for singling him out:

> I bless and praise Thy matchless might,
> When thousands Thou has left in night,
> That I am here before Thy sight,
>   For gifts an' grace,
> A burning and a shining light
>   To a' this place.

Willie admits to being "fash'd wi' fleshly lust," but this, he surmises, is only the Lord's way of restraining his pride. Like Hogg's justified man, he is nettled by other men's pleasures and prays for their damnation. In the "Epitaph for Holy Willie" Burns puts him squarely in Hell.[15]

The *Justified Sinner* is divided into three parts. The first, the "Editor's Narrative," presents the story of Robert Colwan's life until he is in possession at Dalcastle; the second, Colwan's

---

[13] See above, p. 5, n. 7.   [14] *The Poetry of Robert Burns*, II. 25 ff.

[15] *Op. cit.*, II. 266-7.

"Memoirs," recapitulates the events of his life from his own viewpoint, and carries the tale forward to the moment of his death; the brief third part relates his death, according to "traditionary history," and describes the finding of the memoirs.

In the year 1687, the Editor relates, George Colwan succeeded to the lands of Dalcastle and Balgrennan. When considerably advanced in life, he married the "sole heiress and reputed daughter of a Baillie Orde, of Glasgow."[16] The marriage was unhappy, for Colwan was "a droll, careless chap," with little fear of God and nearly as little fear of man.[17] He tried to get along with both the Cavaliers and Reformers. His wife, on the other hand, was a Presbyterian bigot: "Hers were not the tenets of the great reformers, but theirs mightily overstrained and deformed. . . . She had imbibed her ideas from the doctrines of one flaming predestinarian divine alone."[18]

From this situation the story proceeds. The laird at his wedding dances, drinks, and sings; he salutes all the good-looking girls and asks their sweethearts to take the same freedom with his bride. But the bride herself looks on the scene with contempt; at her side sits the "predestinarian divine." When he takes his leave she entreats him often to visit her in that "heathen land of the Amorite, the Hittite, and the Girgashite."[19] Thereupon she retires to her chamber to pray. When the laird comes to bed, she adjures him to pray too. "Prayers, Mistress! he exclaims, "is this a night for prayers!"[20] She deluges him with Scripture texts until he falls asleep and snores. The Lady then slips out of the chamber. In the morning he wakes amazed to find her gone; he finds her and bears her back to his chamber with a blanket round her mouth to stop her complaints. That day the Lady returns to her father's house. But her father welcomes her roughly, and when Dalcastle arrives she is compelled to go with the heathen. The marriage continues at variance: "She *would* convert the laird in spite of his teeth: the laird would not be converted."[21]

---

[16] *Justified Sinner*, p. 3.
[18] *Ibid.*
[20] *Op. cit.*, p. 6.

[17] *Op. cit.*, p. 4.
[19] *Op. cit.*, p. 5.
[21] *Op. cit.*, p. 11.

At length, they agree to a separate establishment. The
Lady lives upstairs with her servants; the Laird downstairs
with his. And soon the Laird is being visited by a Miss Logan.
Lady Dalcastle enquires what Miss Logan's behaviour is,
and the information is such that "prayers [are] said in the
uppermost story of Dalcastle house against the Canaanitish
woman."[22] Letters are sent to the Reverend Mr Wringhim,
the Lady's counsellor, and he arrives to argue with her about
the several kinds of Faith, and also to determine what shall be
done about the Laird's iniquity. Wringhim undertakes to
confront the Laird and Miss Logan. To the Laird's description
of him as "a presumptuous, self-conceited pedagogue, a stirrer
up of strife and commotion in church, in state, in families
and communities," Wringhim replies with a rebuke, "fragments of which have been attributed to every divine of old
notoriety throughout Scotland."[23] That night Wringhim
and Lady Dalcastle sit up discussing points of theology. But
their triumph is short-lived. Five weeks later, Arabella Logan
comes to reside with the Laird as his housekeeper.

The Lady bears a son, "a healthful and happy child"
named after his father—George Dalcastle. A year later
another son is born. But the Laird does not believe that the
second child is his. He acknowledges that he is obliged to
support him, but does not acknowledge him in church. Finally
Mr Wringhim takes the Lady as sponsor for the boy, and
baptises him by the name of Robert Wringhim. (He will be
known, also, by his family name—Robert Colwan.[24]) While
George Dalcastle is brought up and educated at Dalcastle,
becoming "a generous and kind-hearted youth," Robert
Colwan, his brother, is brought up by Mr Wringhim. He is
taught to pray twice every day, and seven times on Sabbath
days; but he is only to pray for the elect, and "doom all that
are aliens from God to destruction."[25] And, as he has heard
only evil spoken of his father and brother, Robert prays for
the cutting off and damnation of "the hoary old sinner," his

---

[22] *Justified Sinner*, p. 13.   [23] *Op. cit.*, p. 16.
[24] In the early part of the novel the hero is called Robert Wringhim. Later
he assumes the name Colwan. To avoid confuson, I have called him Robert
Colwan throughout this chapter.
[25] *Justified Sinner*, pp. 18-19.

father, and for the death of "the young stem of the corrupt trunk."[26]   He is an excellent student, fond of writing on theological controversies; he has, withal, a sternness of demeanour that repels other boys.   George is behind him in scholarship, but superior in "personal prowess, form, feature, and all that constitutes gentility."[27]   The Laird has Lady Dalcastle removed to Glasgow, "all to prevent the young laird being tainted with the company of her and her second son," for he fears the effects of their principles.[28]

One effect of his wife's bigotry has been to make the Laird hostile to the Covenanters and sympathetic to the Cavaliers. He is returned a Member of Parliament at Edinburgh.   Both factions dispute vigorously during the session, and Mr Wringhim participates as a leader of the revolutionary, or Whig party.   Both George Dalcastle and Robert Colwan are also in town.   One day George is playing tennis when he perceives "a lad with black clothes, and a methodistical face, whose countenance and eye he [dislikes] exceedingly, several times in his way."[29]   This youth—he is Robert Colwan—gets in the way of the players.   The next time George plays tennis, the youth is there again.   He again disrupts the game and mocks the players.   Asked to move, he refuses, and is knocked down by George in the course of the game.   He aims a vicious kick at George, who retaliates by striking him with his racket. The youth streams blood.   George is informed by a bystander that it is his brother.   "Is this the crazy minister's son from Glasgow?"   George says, and immediately regrets his insult.[30] George offers to make amends to his brother, but Robert kicks at his proferred hand.   The strange fellow then accompanies the tennis-players to their dinner at the Black Bull. He is driven from the door and carried to the guard-house. His Whig friends are outraged by this treatment, and there ensues a riot in which a crowd storms the Black Bull—where not only the Cavaliers, but also a party of Whigs are at dinner. No one knows who has begun the fray, and it is dismissed as a ludicrous *fracas*.   But Mr Wringhim does all that he can to

---

[26] *Justified Sinner*, p. 19.   [27] *Ibid.*
[28] *Ibid.*   [29] *Op. cit.*, p. 21.

[30] *Op. cit.*, p. 23.

rouse the populace against the young Cavaliers, especially
George Dalcastle. The next day, when George and his friends
are playing cricket, Robert Colwan again appears. It is
evident to them that for some hidden purpose he is seeking
manual chastisement at their hands, and they abandon their
game.

From this time George is followed by his brother, and is
also subjected to the hisses of the populace. Even George's
friends have to avoid his company, and he is forced to stay
indoors. He decides that Colwan must be following him to
ask a reconciliation; he will speak to Colwan as a brother;
if Colwan refuses to be reconciled, the blame will be his. Early
one morning George makes an excursion to the top of Arthur's
Seat. As he sits on the edge of a precipice, enjoying the view,
he thinks of Colwan, and looks off to the right, where he
usually appears. A dreadful apparition presents itself:

> He saw, delineated in the cloud, the shoulders, arms, and
> features of a human being of the most dreadful aspect. The
> face was the face of his brother, but dilated to twenty times the
> natural size. Its dark eyes gleamed on him through the mist,
> while every furrow of its hideous brow frowned deep as the
> ravines on the brow of the hill. George started, and his hair
> stood up in bristles as he gazed on this horrible monster. He
> saw every feature and every line of the face distinctly as it
> gazed on him with an intensity that was hardly brookable.
> Its eyes were fixed on him, in the same manner as those of
> some carnivorous animal fixed on its prey ; and yet there was
> fear and trembling in these unearthly features, as plainly
> depicted as murderous malice. The giant apparition seemed
> sometimes to be cowering down as in terror, so that nothing
> but his brow and eyes were seen ; still these never turned one
> moment from their object—again it rose imperceptively up,
> and began to approach with great caution ; and, as it neared,
> the dimensions of its form lessened, still continuing, however,
> far above the natural size.[31]

Springing backward, George falls over Colwan. Colwan runs
away shouting "Murder!" George catches and seizes him;
Colwan blubbers and begs for his life. When George releases

[31] *Justified Sinner*, p. 39.

M

him and offers to be reconciled Colwan resumes his usual manner of hatred and disdain, and stalks away. On his return home George tells his father of the incident, but the old Laird makes light of it. However, the "great divine," the elder Wringhim, has a charge of assault and battery, to the intent of committing fratricide, brought against George.

The case looks hard for George at first; but when it is sifted in court, it is seen that Colwan has pursued George with some sinister design, and he is bound over with heavy penalties to keep the peace. George and his friends celebrate his victory at the Bull Black Inn and then proceed to a bagnio. There one of the party, young Drummond, being the worse for drink, quarrels with George and steps outside. Soon after there is a knock at the door and it is opened by a woman who sees a young gentleman resembling Drummond. He asks her to tell Dalcastle to speak to him outside. George steps out, saying it must be Drummond. The next morning he is found slain not far from the spot.

Suspicion fastens on Drummond, in spite of his protestations of innocence, and he is forced to fly the country. The old Laird, stricken by the loss of his beloved heir, dies within a few weeks. Robert Colwan takes possession of his estates: the investiture is celebrated "by prayer, singing of psalms, and religious disputation."[32] But Arabella Logan suspects that Lady Dalcastle and the Wringhims are at the bottom of the young laird's murder. Her suspicions are confirmed by an extraordinary sequence of events.

A woman, Bell Calvert, has been arrested for acting as the accomplice of a robber. Some of Mrs Logan's goods have been found in her possession. Mrs Calvert's daughter asks Mrs Logan to see the prisoner. In the interview, Mrs Calvert hints that she knows the true circumstances of George Dalcastle's death. She refuses to say more. At the trial, Mrs Logan does not identify the goods as hers, and the prisoner is released. A few days later she visits Mrs Logan and tells her story. She was at a house next to the inn where the young Cavaliers were gathered. She saw Drummond go out and met him and brought him to her room. He left soon, and as

[32] *Justified Sinner*, p. 52.

she was showing him downstairs another man—later her accomplice in crime—took her upstairs. From her window she then saw Drummond going away; and then two men, one in black, the other dressed like Drummond, approached. *"One of them was extremely like Drummond."*[33] The men argued; the one who resembled Drummond was urging the other to some desperate act, to be done "as God's work." She saw him knock at the door and enquire for Dalcastle; she saw Dalcastle come out. Then she saw him quarrel with Dalcastle and the duel with swords begin. When the fighters closed, the man resembling Drummond turned Dalcastle's back to the entry where the man in black had concealed himself, crying out: "Ah, hell has it! My friend, my friend!"[34] The man in black stabbed Dalcastle from behind. The woman's companion shouted out against the unfairness of the killing, and the criminals escaped.

Mrs Logan, convinced by this of Robert Colwan's guilt, persuades Mrs Calvert to go with her to Dalcastle. At a village on the way they see Colwan walking with a friend. Mrs Calvert identifies him as the man who stabbed Dalcastle. But the appearance of his friend strikes astonishment into the woman, for he is the very image of the dead man. The women proceed to the mansion. On the road they see Colwan and his friend approaching. They conceal themselves and overhear Colwan threatening the destruction of Mrs Logan. His friend shows him where Mrs Logan and Mrs Calvert are hidden and makes off. Colwan rushes upon them; in a struggle they overpower and maltreat him, and leave him tied hand and foot. The women proceed to Edinburgh. They discuss the conversation of Colwan and his friend; among other matters the friend was urging Colwan to kill his mother. They go to Sir Thomas Wallace, the Lord Justice-Clerk, and give him all the information they have. It is decided to apprehend the Laird of Dalcastle and bring him to trial. Mrs Calvert's accomplice is sent to look at the Laird; he confirms that he was the man who stabbed George Dalcastle. Officers are sent to arrest Colwan. But he is not found. His mother also cannot be found.

[33] *Justified Sinner*, p. 68.   [34] *Op. cit.*, p. 72.

"I have now," says the Editor, "the pleasure of presenting my readers with an original document of a most singular nature. . . ."[35]

The Editor's Narrative has provided one dimension of Robert Wringhim Colwan's life, up to a point. With Colwan's Memoirs the story enters another dimension. The vigorous action, related with absolute realism and touches of sardonic humour, yields to action related by Robert Colwan in a style mixed of cant, bigotry, lies, and self-deception. Again we see the episodes of the first part, but this time through the false medium of Colwan's mind. Episodes that showed him as a coward and sneak, in his account reflect glory upon him and blame upon his enemies. In the account of his interference in the tennis matches, Colwan appears as a persecuted hero.[36] The incident on the precipice has another result than that we have seen. ". . . though I do not recollect the circumstances of that deadly scuffle very minutely," Colwan says, "I know that I vanquished him so far as to force him to ask my pardon. . . ."[37] The murder of Dalcastle is reinterpreted as a fair fight between Colwan and Dalcastle.[38] Besides these episodes which we already know, we see the "justified" youth intriguing to have one of his father's servants, John Barnet, driven from his employment, and to cast disgrace upon a scholar who surpasses him.[39]

But the character of the Justified Sinner is over-shadowed by that of his friend. From the moment of his first appearance, Gil-Martin commands the story. Significantly, he appears on the day that Robert Colwan is assured of his salvation. His reverend father has wrestled with God and has at last prevailed; he assures Robert that he is now a justified person. No past transgression, nor any future act of his own, or of other men, can be instrumental in altering the decree. "All the powers of darkness," he adds, "shall never be able to pluck you again out of your Redeemer's hand. And now, my son, be strong and steadfast in the truth. Set your face against sin, and sinful men, and resist even to blood. . . ."[40]

---

[35] *Justified Sinner*, p. 85.
[37] *Op. cit.*, p. 147.
[39] *Op. cit.*, pp. 92-8, 99-101.

[36] *Op. cit.*, p. 135.
[38] *Op. cit.*, p. 155.
[40] *Op. cit.*, p. 105.

Robert weeps with joy and goes to the fields to pray. "An exaltation of spirit lifted me, as it were, far above the earth, and the sinful creatures crawling on its surface; and I deemed myself as an eagle among the children of men, soaring on high, and looking down with pity and contempt on the grovelling creatures below."[41] As he revels in his pride, Robert observes "a young man of mysterious appearance" coming towards him. As they close, he sees with astonishment that the stranger resembles him in every particular of dress and feature. Is it his guardian angel? The stranger anticipates the words Robert is about to utter, telling him that he is his brother "not according to the flesh, but in [his] belief of the same truths. . . ."[42] Robert invites him to worship with him; the stranger tells him that he has been advised of his state, and has come to be his disciple. They discuss theology:

> I asked if he believed in the eternal and irrevocable decrees of God, regarding the salvation and condemnation of all mankind? He answered that he did so ; aye, what would signify all things else to be believed, if he did not believe in that ?[43]

The stranger is even more extreme in his views than Robert, and Robert fears that their conversation is verging on blasphemy. He returns home in a state of exaltation. To doubts expressed by the Reverend Mr Wringhim and his mother that the stranger may be Satan, Robert replies that the stranger adheres to the religious principles held by the minister. Then, says the latter, he is no agent of the Wicked One.

From this time forward, the stranger is Robert's constant companion. The truth of his character is revealed to the reader; it has not been revealed to the man who tells the story. Robert Colwan is too vain, too blinded by bigotry, to suspect that he has fallen into the hands of the Devil. He has ample warnings, but prefers to give them another construction. His friend, he observes, does not pray; taxed with this, his friend has ingenious arguments against prayer.[44] What is his

[41] *Justified Sinner*, pp. 105-6.
[43] *Ibid.*
[42] *Op. cit.*, p. 107.
[44] *Op. cit.*, pp. 116-17.

friend's name? Gil-Martin, the other answers. When Robert
enquires about his parentage, he elaborates:

> "I have no parents save one, whom I do not acknowledge,"
> said he proudly. "Therefore, pray drop that subject, for it is
> a disagreeable one. I am a being of a very peculiar temper, for,
> though I have servants and subjects more than I can number,
> yet, to gratify a certain whim, I have left them, and retired
> to this city, and, for all the society it contains, you see I have
> attached myself only to you. This is a secret, and I tell you
> only in friendship, therefore pray let it remain one, and say
> not another word about the matter."[45]

Robert concludes that his friend is no other than the Czar
Peter of Russia, for he has heard that the Czar is travelling
through Europe in disguise, and thenceforward he has "great
and mighty hopes of high preferment, as a defender and
avenger of the oppressed Christian Church, under the influence
of this great potentate."[46]

Then Gil-Martin persuades Robert to his first violent act.
The preacher Mr Blanchard has warned Robert against his
friend's influence. Gil-Martin points out the evil such men
do, and offers a most ingenious argument for murder: "If the
man Blanchard is worthy, he is only changing his situation for
a better one; and, if unworthy, it is better that one fall than
that a thousand souls perish. Let us be up and doing in our
vocations. . . ."[47] They waylay Blanchard; Gil-Martin
shoots at him but, unaccountably, misses; it is Robert's shot
that kills the preacher. Escaping from the scene, Gil-Martin
assumes the appearance of a popular young preacher—he is
able to counterfeit appearances—and the preacher is arrested
and condemned.

At times Robert has doubts about the infallibility of the
elect, but his friend always manages, with argument or mockery
to remove them. It is at Gil-Martin's prompting that Robert
undertakes the destruction of his brother and father. During
this period Robert falls ill and has strange hallucinations: "I
generally conceived myself to be two people. When I lay in
bed, I deemed there were two of us in it; when I sat up I
always beheld another person . . . this occasioned a confusion

---

[45] *Justified Sinner*, p. 118.   [46] *Ibid*   [47] *Op. cit.*, p. 122.

in all my words and ideas that utterly astounded my friends.
. . ."[48] The attempt on George's life at the precipice is made
by Robert together with Gil-Martin. At the last moment
Robert is approached by a lady in white who warns him to
desist, but Gil-Martin berates him and urges him to the act.
"I will go, meanwhile," says Gil-Martin, "and amuse his sight
by some exhibition in the contrary direction. . . ."[49] The
effect of this exhibition we have seen.[50] It is Gil-Martin who
assumes the appearance of Drummond, engages George in
sword-play and holds him so that Robert may kill him from
behind.

When Robert takes possession at Dalcastle, the consequences of his acts begin to be felt. A woman accuses him of
having seduced her daughter. He denies it vehemently, and
then it is proved to him by his friend—whom Robert has come
to fear and detest—that he has for months been intoxicated
and has acted as a profligate. A lawyer arrives and informs
Robert that he has carried out his commission to dispossess
the woman and obtain her estate by a royal grant. Of these
actions, Robert knows nothing. More and more he suspects
and fears his friend. That Gil-Martin is a good Christian, he
has no doubt; but could he be a necromancer as well?[51] He
is relieved when Gil-Martin goes away. He drinks heavily
to celebrate their parting. When he wakes, a servant whom
he has never seen before, named Scrape, informs him that
Gil-Martin has been gone for months. Robert asks after his
mother. The fellow tells him that his mother has disappeared,
and "heavy accusations" are rising against him. Full of
perplexity, Robert goes outdoors; then, to his shock, he sees
Gil-Martin:

> . . . it was the air and motion of someone that I dreaded, and
> from whom I would gladly have escaped ; but this I even had
> not power to attempt. . . . It bore the figure, air, and features
> of my late brother, I thought exactly ; yet in all these there
> were traits so forbidding, so mixed with an appearance of
> misery, chagrin and despair, that I still shrunk from the
> view. . . . But, when the being spoke, both my mental and

---

[48] *Justified Sinner*, pp. 139-40.   [49] *Op. cit.*, p. 145.
[50] See description above, p. 177.   [51] *Justified Sinner*, p. 166.

bodily frame received another shock more terrible than the first, for it was the voice of the great personage I had so long denominated my friend. . . . It was his voice, but so altered —I shall never forget it till my dying day. Nay, I can scarce conceive it possible that any earthly sounds could be so discordant, so repulsive to every feeling of a human soul, as the tones of the voice that granted on my ear at that moment. They were the sounds of the pit, wheezed through a grated cranny, or seemed so to my distempered imagination.[52]

In a voice of anger Gil-Martin accuses Robert of shunning him and taxes him with ingratitude. Robert pleads with the "great and magnificent Prince" to let him go his way; he is unworthy of the sacrifices made on his behalf. "Let me plod on towards Heaven and happiness in my own way. . . ."[53] To this Gil-Martin replies:

"Sooner shall you make the mother abandon the child of her bosom ; nay, sooner cause the shadow to relinquish the substance, than separate me from your side. Our beings are amalgamated, as it were, and consociated in one, and never shall I depart from this country until I can carry you in triumph with me."[54]

The rest of Colwan's life is a warning. Once more he submits to the influence of Gil-Martin. On 1 June 1712—he has reason to remember the day—he is told that his mother's body has been found, and that the people are gathering against him and officers have been sent for. Gil-Martin changes clothes with him, and in this disguise he flees for his life. He stays at a weaver's house. His disguise is mysteriously removed and his own clothes are substituted. The weaver suspects him and falls to beating him. From this place he escapes to Edinburgh and finds work as a printer's helper. While in this employment he begins his Memoirs and engages the printer to print them.

The Memoirs are now continued in the form of a diary, with dated entries. The printer, having read Colwan's book, consigns it to the fire. To his horror, Colwan learns that a "foreigner" has been enquiring for him. In the night he hears ". . . as it were two persons at the door, contending, as I thought, about

<hr />

[52] *Justified Sinner*, pp. 170-1.   [53] *Op. cit.*, p. 171.
[54] *Op. cit.*, p. 172.

their right and interest in me."[55] Someone enters the stable and the horses break loose in terror. Colwan is seized and dragged away; he loses his senses; he wakes naked on the kitchen table.

He pursues his flight. Again he meets with Gil-Martin: "How changed was now that majestic countenance to one of haggard despair. . . ."[56] Gil-Martin commiserates with him on his plight, and follows him still. "I prayed that the Lord would hide me in the bowels of the earth or depths of the sea."[57] Robert curses the time of his first meeting with Gil-Martin, but remembers it was the time of his election and recalls the curse.

He finds a bed in an inn at Ancrum. During the night the inn is thrown into a tumult by parties contending outside. Colwan is thrust out into the street, where fiends assail him.

> I was momently surrounded by a number of hideous fiends, who gnashed on me with their teeth, and clenched their crimson paws in my face ; and at the same instant I was seized by the collar of my coat behind, by my dreaded and devoted friend, who pushed me on and, with his gilded rapier waving and brandishing around me, defended me against all their united attacks. Horrible as my assailants were in appearance (and they all had monstrous shapes) I felt that I would rather have fallen into their hands than be thus led away captive by my defender at his will and pleasure without having the right or power to say my life, or any part of my will, was my own.[58]

At last we see him, cast out from the houses of men, still followed by Gil-Martin, who has become dreadful to look upon. He determines to put an end to his existence and that of his tormentor together. As he makes the last entry in his book, he sees his companion approaching, "his stern face blackened with horrid despair."[59] He will now conceal his book, "and cursed be he who trieth to alter or amend."[60]

The Editor resumes the novel. He quotes from a letter in *Blackwood's Magazine* for August 1823, signed by James Hogg, in which Hogg describes the grave of a suicide "on the top of a wild height called Cowan's-Croft."[61] According to tradition, states the letter, a man named Cowan, who had come from

[55] *Justified Sinner*, p. 203.
[56] *Op. cit.*, p. 206.
[57] *Op. cit.*, p. 207.
[58] *Op. cit.*, p. 211.
[59] *Op. cit.*, p. 217.
[60] *Ibid.*
[61] *Op. cit.*, pp. 217 ff.

some unknown place, hanged himself there from a hay-rick.
A driver who came on the body said "*he could almost give his
oath* that he saw two people busily engaged at the hay-rick
going round it and round it, and he thought they were dressing
it."[62]   The letter describes the partial exhumation of the body
by two shepherds; it was in an excellent state of preservation.
The Editor tells how, to satisfy his curiosity, he himself has
visited the grave and has helped to dig up the parts of the body
yet undisturbed.   Among other contents of the grave was
found a manuscript inscribed "The Private Memoirs and
Confessions of a Justified Sinner: Written by Himself. *Fideli
certa merces.*"[63]   The Editor speculates on the meaning of this
strange allegory; either the author was "not only the greatest
fool, but the greatest wretch, on whom was ever stamped the
form of humanity; or . . . a religious maniac, who wrote and
wrote about a deluded creature, till he arrived at that height
of madness that he believed himself the very object whom he
had been all along describing."[64]

If we have, in this summary, dwelt upon details of action,
it is because the power of the novel derives from its action.
Only by his behaviour can we see the character of the Justified
Sinner; it is by the development of his principles in action
that he himself is developed.   Also, the supreme actor, Satan,
is not presented all at once; he is unfolded in time, in several
aspects.   He grows on us.

An intellectual problem to be explored, an ingenious plot,[65]

[62] *Justified Sinner*, p. 219.   [63] *Op. cit.*, p. 228.   [64] *Op. cit.*, pp. 229-30.
[65] Strout finds the story "badly constructed." Yet, he says, "it is sufficient
to justify his [Hogg's] boast that he had several witches among his ancestresses"
(Strout, p. 261). Strout's interest in Hogg is mainly biographical ; there is
little criticism in his book, and what there is may be judged by this specimen.
   Andrew Lang also criticises the construction.   "The arrangement of the
piece is not good, and the scissors might be freely used for the abridgement of
the whole. . . . Nearly all is loosely done, the construction is careless, but the
substance is exactly what a master of horror might desire. . . . Finish and
compression are needed, yet there is more of both than we expect from Hogg."
(*Illustrated London News*, cv, No. 2901 [24 Nov. 1894], Supplement, 12.)
   Lang's criticism that the *Justified Sinner* is "loosely done" is not supported by
a reading of the tale.   The occasional digressions seem necessary to relieve the
compacted action and to develop the characters.   Lang seems to be writing
here, as he often does, out of a preconceived idea, without examining the text
in hand.

and several notable characterisations—among them the Laird of Dalcastle and his wife, the Reverend Robert Wringhim, George Dalcastle, and the Justified Sinner—combine to make a masterpiece. But, above all, it is the supernatural part, the personification of the Devil, that we remember. T. Earle Welby says of this, Hogg's astonishing achievement: "Poe never invented anything more horrible, or with so much spiritual significance; Defoe never did anything with more convincing particularity. But one uses these names and those of Bunyan and Hawthorne, only as a sort of critical shorthand. This book has a quality Hogg's own, and a hard, dry, view-it-all-round way of dealing with horror which is quite unique."[66] The novel, says Sir George Douglas, is a "unique attempt in our literature to incarnate the Fiend amid realistic surroundings."[67]

Is the Fiend incarnate, or is he a fantasy of Colwan's mind? The question, as we ask it, is answered by the action of the novel. But it is interesting to note that Gide, in his introduction, toys with the thought that Gil-Martin is only a hallucination. "The fantastic part . . . (except in the last pages) is always psychologically explicable, without having recourse to the supernatural, as is the case too in Henry James's admirable *Turn of the Screw*."[68] Ingenious—but untrue (and untrue, also, of *The Turn of the Screw*; James insisted that it was really a ghost story). Gide has fallen into a trap that lies open for critics: ascribing one's own preferences to the author. Similarly, Wittig finds the main interest of the *Justified Sinner* in the contrast between objective and subjective reality, in the typically Scottish questioning of the reality

[66] T. Earle Welby, "Introduction," *The Private Memoirs and Confessions of a Justified Sinner*, London 1924, p. 8.

[67] Douglas, pp. 99-100.

[68] André Gide, "Introduction," *The Private Memoirs and Confessions of a Justified Sinner* (1947 ed.), p. xv. However, note Lang's comment : ". . . The Great Friend, the Mysterious Stranger, is a subjective hallucination of the Justified Sinner's. Yes, but there are circumstances which cannot be fitted into that theory, which demand an explanation rejected by common-sense and the emancipated intellect. This device of Hogg's, it may be acknowledged, is subtle, is not what we expect from the good Shepherd. Hawthorne or Poe might not have disdained this artifice, whereof the art is cunningly hidden." (*Illustrated London News*, CV, No. 2901 [24 Nov. 1894], Supplement, 12).

of outward appearances, the "schizophrenic tendencies of a nation which came to use one language to express thought, another to express feeling."[69]   But these traits do not cancel out the actual, physical presence of Hogg's Devil.   Gil-Martin is seen by several people; his appearances astonish Robert Colwan; and, above all, Hogg has no reason to deny the supernatural.   As we have seen, not only does he use the super-natural freely in his writings, but he himself inclines to be superstitious.   Though he reveals the psychology of Colwan and other characters with startlingly "modern" touches—as in the description of Colwan's illness, a kind of schizophrenia—he has no reason to pretend that the Devil is unreal.   We may prefer the Devil to be explained as an hallucination, but Hogg has no such preference.   The best of his works, and the *Justified Sinner* in particular, are an attempt to do the very opposite: to make the supernatural evident.

Hogg's Devil is summoned on to the scene; that is to say, he appears to those who are predisposed to see him.   (That the Devil appears when he is named, or even when he is unconsciously wanted, is a time-honoured belief.)   He is prompt—it may be his extraordinary promptness that has led some readers to suppose that he is only an hallucination.   But though he is summoned, when he appears he is real.   The Devil comes to the fanatical—as the shepherd Barnaby said, "The Devil an' his adgents, they fash nane but the gude fock."[70] He attaches himself to those who in their pride hold their fellow men in contempt, and are therefore already in the way of damnation.   He comes as a servant, and shows the wicked what they truly desire, and hastens to procure it.   He helps them to realise aspects of their nature that they have not suspected.   He is the reflexion of man's pride; he shows the fanatic his own features enlarged, as it were, in a mirror. But the Devil is not insubstantial.   As man's mind is real, so is the Devil's body.   It is not mistaken to surmise that Colwan "arrived at that height of madness that he believed himself the very object whom he had all along been describing," for Colwan could not separate himself from his infernal

---

[69] Kurt Wittig, *The Scottish Tradition in Literature*, Edinburgh 1958, pp. 249-50.
[70] *Tales*, I. 199-200.

twin.[71] But it would be mistaken to think that the Devil is not actual.

"It was a bold theme for an allegory," the Editor remarks. Hogg's method is, indeed, allegorical. For the nearest precedent, we must turn to *The Pilgrim's Progress*. There, too, abstractions are embodied as concrete realities. Bunyan's devil, Apollyon, though he represents the peril in which Christian stands, is no less physically conceived for all that:

> . . . clothed with scales like a Fish (and they are his pride) he had wings like a Dragon, feet like a Bear, and out of his belly came Fire and Smoke, and his mouth was as the mouth of a Lion.[72]

Apollyon, when he speaks of his rank and domains, anticipates the princely manner of Gil-Martin:

> By this [he tells Christian] I perceive thou art one of my Subjects, for all that Country is mine ; and I am the Prince and God of it. How is it then that thou hast ran away from thy King?[73]

The allegorical method, of course, goes back further than this. In *The Faerie Queene* and in Dante we find the same embodiment of the supernatural in physical terms. Spenser's figure of Despayre appears on the scene as an embodiment of Sir Trevisan's state of mind; but Despayre himself has definite features:

> His griesie lockes, long growen, and unbound,
> Disordered hong about his shoulders round,
> And hid his face ; through which his hollow eyne,
> Lookt deadly dull, and stared as astound. . . .[74]

Despayre, like the Devil whom the shepherds think must have helped Colwan to hang himself, offers Sir Trevisan:

> . . . swords, ropes, poison, fire,
> And all that might him to perdition draw. . . .[75]

---

[71] *Justified Sinner*, p. 230.
[72] John Bunyan, *The Pilgrim's Progress*, London, New York, Toronto 1952, p. 69.
[73] Bunyan, p. 1.
[74] Edmund Spenser, *The Poetical Works*, London, New York, Toronto 1947, p. 48.   [75] Spenser, p. 50.

At the end of the *Justified Sinner*, when we glimpse the figures "going round" the hanged man, we have the old medieval picture of hell-fire and physical torment. The hills have been changed; once more we are in a world where nature and the supernatural are not divided; Earth and Hell are again composed of one physical substance. Crawford reminds us that "true Calvinism did not assert the literal existence of material torments"; nevertheless, in popular belief, the figurative "gnashing of teeth, unextinguishable fire, the ever-gnawing worm" of true Calvinism were interpreted, by many of the laity and some of the clergy, as physical realities.[76] In allegory, a form of art which expresses ideas as physical realities, Hogg found a perfect method for this tale of the supernatural.

It is impossible to consider Colwan's character apart from the fanatical creed to which he subscribes. Yet it is important to see that he is not a mere embodiment of a particular doctrine; he has a life and will of his own. If it were not so, Hogg would have imagined a certain type of character only in order to damn it; he would be practising a predestinarian way of thought, and falling into the very error he means to expose. As Hogg develops the character, though Colwan is bred in the tenets of a pernicious doctrine, it is of his own free will that he carries the doctrine to extremes. He chooses to be criminal. Though it is impossible to separate the man from his creed, my own impression of Colwan is that he is a religious fanatic because he is wicked, rather than that he is wicked because he is a fanatic. That is, the *Justified Sinner* is a work of art, and not a theological argument. The novel hangs on Hogg's portrayal of Colwan's psychology; we must believe in his existence.

To see how well Hogg succeeds in the creation of this character, there is no other way than to read the novel. But, if art may be compared with actual life, Colwan's story seems all the more "authentic" when we compare it with actual cases. For example, there is Nicol Muschet, who was hanged at the Grassmarket in 1721. As Muschet's *Confession* was reprinted in Edinburgh in 1818, Hogg might have known the

[76] Crawford, pp. 27-8.

details of Muschet's crime, and read his explanation.[77] The wretched man, abetted by evil companions, particularly one called Burnbank—like Colwan, Muschet had a Friend—made several attempts to do away with his wife, by administering poison and lying in wait to "knock her on the head," and finally achieved his object by cutting her throat in the Duke's Walk. The details of the crime, as Muschet reveals them, are gripping enough, but the relevance for the reader of the *Justified Sinner* lies in his confession—so similar, in the religious overtones, to Colwan's story.

Muschet ascribes his evil-doing to the influence of the Devil. His prompter, Burnbank, seemed to him not merely an influence, but actually the Devil's emissary:

> I . . . met with James Campbell [Burnbank] . . . who was the only viceregent of the devil to prompt me up to be guilty of all the following wickedness. . . .[78]

As he confesses, Muschet always pictures his own actions as the result of the Devil's acting upon him. Everything is dramatised, externalised, and disconnected from the centre of his own being, his will. In this drama he figures as a victim— even while he is hacking at the poor woman; his conscience remains essentially unstained and redeemable. Indeed, there is a curious ambiguity in the description of the murder itself, which suggests that not he, Nicol Muschet, but the Devil, is responsible:

> . . . the devil, that cunning adversary, suggested to me, being now hardened and also desperate, by all the foresaid plots failing, that it was but a light thing whether he or I were the executioner : whereupon I yielding to the temptation, did as my indictment bears.[79]

Perhaps the most startling part of Muschet's confession is that in which he suggests that he may be one of the "chosen," and that his crime was preordained by God, even to his honour:

> . . . blessed for ever be his glorious name, who has given me an heart to accept willingly of the punishment of my sin, and

---

[77] Nicol Muschet, *The Confession, &c. of Nicol Muschet of Boghal* (henceforth cited as Muschet), Edinburgh, Glasgow, London 1818.

[78] Muschet, p. 12. [79] *Idem.*, p. 35.

to acknowledge his justice and sovereignty, yea, his infinitely good and wise dispensation in bringing me into this affliction. What shall I say of God's free grace and mercy ! . . . What matter of admiration is it that ever a holy and just God should have cast his eye in mercy upon me, the chief of sinners, who have made it my business to delight myself in the works of darkness, most part of my short life ! But very oft of the rudest pieces of clay, that most excellent potter makes vessels of honour, the more to manifest his singular power and art.[80]

O felix culpa![81] To such a conclusion the Justified Sinner might say *Amen!* And so would Holy Willie.

In his *Essays in English Literature, 1780-1860*, published in 1890, George Saintsbury offered the hypothesis that "the actual imagination" of the *Justified Sinner* was Hogg's, but the "editing, and perhaps something more than editing" was Lockhart's.[82] The hypothesis is not supported by evidence— to the contrary, all the evidence refutes it—and in the absence of proof that Hogg was not sole author of the novel that bears his name it is unfortunate that we should have to consider the hypothesis at all. However, in justice to Hogg, it is necessary to do so; for the opinion persists—at least, it is expressed as late as 1924, by Welby in his introduction to the novel, though Miss Batho, writing three years later, argues against it.

Saintsbury admits that his opinion is not founded on evidence; nevertheless, he attempts to support it with reasons. The line of argument is confused but may be summarised as follows: Hogg was always trying the supernatural, and he failed in it, except in this instance, as often as he tried it. Why should he on this particular occasion have been saved from himself; and who saved him?[83] (It is hard to resist interrupting the argument at its beginning. First, Hogg did not fail

---

[80] Muschet, p. 58.

[81] "O felix culpa, quae talem ac tantum meruit habere Redemptorem !" The *Justified Sinner* opens on vistas of theological argument, reaching back to Christian literature of the fourth century. Arthur O. Lovejoy, in his essay, "Milton and the Paradox of the Fortunate Fall," touches on antinomianism, as part of the history of the paradox.

[82] George Saintsbury, *Essays in English Literature, 1780-1860*, "Hogg," pp. 62-5. In the preface to the *Essays* Saintsbury says that this essay was first published, with other essays, in *Macmillan's Magazine* in 1889. But I have been unable to find the essay in *Macmillan's*.

[83] *Op. cit.*, pp. 62-3.

in the supernatural as often as he tried it. Second: that he had to be saved from himself—even were it true—does not prove that someone, in this instance, did save him. On the second point Saintsbury's whole hypothesis hangs.) He proceeds to point out "certain coincidences and probabilities." Lockhart's name figures in the postscript of the book. Lockhart was a literary ally of Hogg's. At one time Hogg planned that Lockhart should edit all his works. Further:

> . . . the vein of the *Confessions* is very closely akin to, if not wholly identical with, a vein which Lockhart not only worked on his own account but worked at this very same time. It was in these very years of his residence at Chiefswood that Lockhart produced the little masterpiece of "Adam Blair" (where the terrors and temptations of a convinced Presbyterian minister are dwelt upon), and "Matthew Wald," which is itself the history of a lunatic as full of horrors, and those of no very different kind, as the *Confessions* themselves.[84]

Did Hogg also write "Adam Blair" and "Matthew Wald"? The argument might be reversed.

> That editing, and perhaps something more than editing, on Lockhart's part would have been exactly the thing necessary to prune and train and direct the Shepherd's disorderly luxuriance into the methodical madness of the Justified Sinner —to give Hogg's loose though by no means vulgar style the dress of his own polished manner . . . nobody who knows the undoubted writing of the two men will deny.[85]

Moreover, Lockhart was "careless of his work" and would not have claimed a share in the *Justified Sinner*. On the other hand, Hogg would not have thought of acknowledging such editing or collaboration. Also, the theory explains why Hogg, usually vain, "set apparently little store by the book."[86]
Saintsbury concludes:

> It is only a hypothesis of course, and a hypothesis which is very unlikely ever to be proved, while in the nature of things it is even less capable of disproof. But I think there is good critical reason for it.[87]

---

[84] Saintsbury, pp. 63-4   [85] *Idem.*, p. 64.
[86] *Idem.*, p. 65.   [87] *Idem.*

N

On 24 Nov. 1894, Andrew Lang published an article entitled "Confessions of a Justified Sinner" in the *Illustrated London News*. The article was mostly critical, but in one place Lang put forward Saintsbury's hypothesis—albeit with a reservation: "So unlike Hogg is the sustained terror of the tale and the refinement of some scenes that I and others have suspected the collaboration of Lockhart. But of this there is no documentary proof."[88]

In 1895, J. Shiells & Co. published a new edition of the novel, titled, *The Suicide's Grave, being the Private Memoirs and Confessions of a Justified Sinner written by Himself.* The Publishers' Note stated: "Mr. Andrew Lang and some others incline to the opinion that the book was not wholly written by Hogg, but that J. G. Lockhart had some part in its production; for this opinion, however, there is no documentary support."[89]

This provoked a reply. On 16 Nov. 1895, in the *Athenæum*, Mrs Garden entered the fray. Under the title "The Suicide's Grave" she summarised the arguments for Hogg's exclusive authorship of the novel.[90] First she quoted the Publishers' Note, given above, altering it to read "Mr. Lang and other critics. . . ." Then she quoted Lang's opinion, as given above. "I believe," said Mrs Garden, "this opinion to be a mistaken one, and it would require very strong documentary proof to convince me that Lockhart aided in the production of this tale."[91] She proceeded to give the evidence for her belief:

> In the first place, the MS. of the work is in my possession, clearly and neatly written in my father's hand, and showing no mark whatever of having been corrected or added to by Lockhart.
>
> In the second place, this tale, under the title of "Confessions of a Fanatic," along with my father's other collected works, was corrected by himself just before his death, and was in the hands of Messrs. Blackie at the time that event occurred ; and

---

[88] Andrew Lang, "Confessions of a Justified Sinner," *Illustrated London News*, cv, No. 2901 (24 Nov. 1894), Supplement, 12.

[89] Publishers' Note, *The Suicide's Grave, being the Private Memoirs and Confessions of a Justified Sinner*, London 1895.

[90] Mrs. Garden, "The Suicide's Grave," in *The Athenæum*, No. 3551, 16 Nov. 1895, p. 681.

[91] *Ibid.*

with the exception of a few trifling alterations, the text is the same as that now given to the public.

> I am not one of the critics, but, if I were, I should say I saw the mark of Hogg's pen in every line.[92]

To this Lang answered, in a letter to the *Athenæum* of 30 Nov. 1895:

> I am unable to recover the impression that Lockhart's hand shows in Hogg's "Justified Sinner" or "Suicide's Grave." The book appeared anonymously ; Lockhart is mentioned, and Hogg is described among his *paulies* at Thirlestane Fair. Of course, in recording my first impression, that Lockhart collaborated or assisted, I meant no suggestion against the literary honesty of the Shepherd, on which see the remarks as to literary *supercheries* attributed to Lockhart at the close of the "Justified Sinner." As far as internal or external evidence goes, I am now quite of Mrs. Garden's opinion.[93]

This is a retraction, for outside of "internal or external evidence" there remains only Lang's "impression," insubstantial as a dream.

In his biography of Hogg, Sir George Douglas repeated Mrs Garden's argument and added:

> . . . though the power of developing character shown in the work under consideration is perhaps unique in Hogg's writings, most readers will be inclined to agree with his daughter when she writes that she sees the "mark of Hogg's pen in every line."[94]

And Douglas—fairly enough, for this is the kind of "impressionism" introduced by the supporters of Saintsbury's hypothesis—remarks that Lockhart was certainly a more accomplished "man-of-letters" than Hogg, but of Hogg's genius he had nothing.[95]

The history of the controversy should now be at an end, were reason decisive in such matters. But there is also Rumour

[92] Mrs. Garden, "The Suicide's Grave," in *The Athenæum*, No. 3551, 16 Nov. 1895, p. 681.

[93] Andrew Lang, "The Suicide's Grave," in *The Athenæum*, No. 3553, 30 Nov. 1895, p. 754.

[94] Douglas, p. 104. [95] *Ibid.*

painted full of tongues, and in T. Earle Welby's introduction
to the edition of the *Justified Sinner* published in 1924, we see
that rumour has outstayed argument:

> That Hogg owed something of such success to Lockhart can
> hardly be disputed ; yet it is well to remember that his,
> anyone's capital difficulty in work of this sort would be to find
> the method, and, that found, only consistency in using it would
> be necessary for such a genius as Hogg to achieve what he did
> in this wonderful book. Of the rightness of the method found
> by Hogg, or suggested to him, there cannot be the slightest
> doubt.[96]

The only critical study of Hogg's works, that by Miss Batho,
ascribes the novel entirely to Hogg; her comments, though
faint, are firm:

> . . . there is no convincing reason for depriving the Shepherd
> of the full credit for his work. He could write well, when he
> took the trouble, and for once he did write consistently. The
> *Confessions* are written in his usual style and are hardly more
> closely woven and concentrated than passages in his other
> stories. There are even some blunders in the use of words,
> which Lockhart would not have been likely to pass in revision
> . . . . [97]

The evidence for Hogg's unaided authorship of the
Justified Sinner seems conclusive. First, the major idea of the
novel, the theme of antinomianism, was available to Hogg
from Ettrick traditions. He was, as we have said, raised in
the very place where Thomas Boston, a champion of the
antinomian quarrel, had preached and written. Nor is this
novel the only work by Hogg in which the theme appears;
the Edinburgh Baillie, who thinks that he has divine sanction
to destroy his enemy, shares some characteristics of the Justified Sinner.[98] Secondary themes of the *Justified Sinner* also
appear in other works by Hogg: the idea of a demon being
inseparably attached to the protagonist is found in "The
Brownie of the Black Haggs";[99] the theme of divine

---

[96] Welby, "Introduction," *The Private Memoirs and Confessions of a Justified
Sinner* (1924 ed.), pp. 7-8.

[97] Batho, p. 123.   [98] *Tales*, v. 210-338.

[99] *Op. cit.*, III. 342-59.

retribution brought about by a supernatural agency is too common in his tales to need further comment.

As for Lockhart's editing or revising the novel, the evidence here, too, shows that the execution is Hogg's. Let us pursue the argument along the line indicated by Mrs Garden, comparing the text of the *Justified Sinner* with texts of Hogg's other works. None of the controversialists, as far as I have been able to discover, has attempted to do this.

In plot, situation, and characterisation, as well as in idea, passages in the *Justified Sinner* run parallel to passages in Hogg's other tales. Let the reader compare the actions of Reverend Robert Wringhim and Robert Colwan with the actions of the hypocritical curate, Clerk, in *The Brownie of Bodsbeck*.[1] Let him compare the actions of Gil-Martin with those of the demon Merodach, in "The Brownie of the Black Haggs";[2] and the appearances of Robert Colwan's friend with that of the old beggar in "Mr. Adamson of Laverhope."[3] As Robert Colwan's hatred of Dalcastle entails his own destruction, similarly the Edinburgh Baillie is buried at the feet of his enemy, Huntly.[4] The *diablerie* outside the stable-loft and the houses where the Justified Sinner seeks refuge recalls the scene in "The Cameronian Preacher's Tale" where Macmillan is summoned outside the inn by the wraith of Johnstone.[5]

Also, there are close resemblances of style between the *Justified Sinner* and Hogg's other tales. The matter-of-fact treatment of the supernatural, the touches of sardonic humour, and the realistic descriptions of the *Justified Sinner* are found throughout Hogg's works. There is a characteristic gaiety in his treatment of demons:

> . . . the last time she was seen alive, it was following the uncouth creature up the water of Daur, weary, wounded, and lame, while he was all the way beating her, as a piece of excellent amusement.[6]

---

[1] See "The Brownie of Bodsbeck," *op. cit.*, I. 14-15, 90-4.
[2] *Op. cit.*, III. 342-59.   [3] *Op. cit.*, III. 224-47.
[4] *Op. cit.*, V. 338.   [5] See above, pp. 162-163.
[6] "The Brownie of the Black Haggs," III. 358.

To this we may compare the infernal morris-dance, our last glimpse of Robert Colwan:

> . . . the driver said, when he first came in view, *he could almost give his oath* that he saw two people busily engaged at the hay-rick, going round it and round it, and he thought they were dressing it.[7]

Or let us recall the canting of the Edinburgh Baillie:

> I gave the young gentleman several hints to beware how he maltreated me, for that I was a dangerous personage, and never missed setting my foot on the necks of my enemies. . . .[8]

Is not this the very style of the *Justified Sinner*?

> . . . my ascendancy over my enemies was great indeed. . . .[9]

Last, let us compare the scene of the *Justified Sinner* in which George Dalcastle, on the precipice at Arthur's Seat, perceives a gigantic, demonic form glaring at him,[10] with the following passage from Hogg's sketch, "Nature's Magic Lantern":

> One morning, at the time when I was about nineteen years of age, I was ascending a hill-side towards the ewe-buchts, deeply absorbed in admiration of the halo around me, when suddenly my eyes fell upon a huge dark semblance of the human figure, which stood at a very small distance from me, and at first appeared to my affrighted imagination as the enemy of mankind. Without taking a moment to consider, I rushed from the spot, and never drew breath till I had got safe among the ewe-milkers. All that day, I felt very ill at ease ; but next morning, being obliged to go past the same spot at the same hour, I resolved to exert, if possible, a little more courage, and put the phenomenon fairly to the proof. The fog was more dense than on the preceding morning, and when the sun arose, his brilliancy and fervour were more bright above. The lovely halo was thrown around me, and at length I reached the haunted spot without diverging a step from my usual little footpath ; and at the very place there arose the same terrible apparition which had frightened me so much the morning

---

[7] *Justified Sinner*, p. 219.
[9] *Justified Sinner*, p. 139.
[8] *Tales*, v. 314.
[10] See above, p. 177.

before. It was a giant blackamoor, at least thirty feet high, and equally proportioned, and very near me. I was actually struck powerless with astonishment and terror.[11]

Can there be any doubt that this, Hogg's description of an optical illusion, is another draft of the scene at Arthur's Seat? And if Hogg could transform an experience of his own into the most striking pages of the novel, what was to prevent his doing the rest? Or must we suppose that Lockhart also wrote "Nature's Magic Lantern?" But this is absurd. What has Lockhart to do with it? No evidence, circumstantial or textual, supports the claim—which Lockhart himself never made—that he had a hand in writing the *Justified Sinner*. The credit is Hogg's alone.

[11] *Tales*, IV. 352-3.

IX

Characteristics

Be mine the faith diverging to extremes !
"Superstition"

HOGG was original. He often said he was, and others have
agreed with him—meaning, too often, that he was
merely picturesque. When he himself attempted to
define his talent, that in which his true gift lay, he was apt to
sound like a bragging ignoramus. It all comes down to this,
he tells us: poets are born, not made. One either has the gift
of "fancy," or one does not. It was thus, says the Shepherd
of the *Noctes*, that "Kilmeny" came to him: ". . . though I
wrott doon the poem on the sclate in the prime o' manhood,
anither being than mysell did in verity compose or creawte
it. . . ."[1] As for rules of art—they are likely only to do harm.
Such observations are strewn throughout the *Noctes*, and though
—as we have shown—they may not represent Hogg's actual
words, they certainly represent his opinion.[2] In *A Series of
Lay Sermons* he speaks in his own voice to the same point. Do
not trust reviewers, he advises the reader; they are tools of a
party. Consult your own taste. Great books are "the natural
expressions of men of good sense," and are not written by
following rules. "No rules ever devised by man can make a
poet. The fire and rapidity of true genius will always overstep
the cold restraints of art. . . ."[3]

Gillies describes one of the pernicious effects of Hogg's
"inspiration":

> He had taken up the absurd notion that prose should not only
> be written as fast as one can speak, but *ought not* to receive any

---

[1] *Noctes*, IV. 216-7.
[2] *E.g.*, in *Noctes*, III. 272, Hogg attacks "philosophical criticism." It is "useless."
[3] *A Series of Lay Sermons*, pp. 272-4.

emendation whatever. The result was, that in almost all his prose stories, there were good points thrown away, for want of proper management.[4]

Hogg's theory of "inspiration" is not so much a principle as it is a defence of his own sharply felt shortcomings. For in spite of his protestations, he did rely exceedingly on "rules," imitating the works of other men and blindly accepting their criteria. Thus we have the sad record of his imitations of Scott, crowned by the monstrosity, *Queen Hynde*. And Scott was not the only bad model. In his novel *The Three Perils of Woman*, Hogg composed a kind of compendium of false taste. Here, in the story of Gatty Bell and her lover M'Ion, is all the perversely genteel sentimentality of the age. When M'Ion tells Gatty that he has been informed of certain indiscreet remarks she has made, she faints:

> These reflections were not to be borne ; they deranged the regular current of the fountain of life, sending it to the extremities, and back to the heart several times, with such power and velocity, that at length it chilled and stagnated at the spring, and poor Miss Bell sank quietly into a swoon.[5]

There is an attempt to revive her by blood-letting; then, as M'Ion embraces her, the blood jets from her arm over the bedclothes. Such was Hogg's idea of the novel of manners.

To some who knew him, and others who have written about him, Hogg's originality consisted not in his works but in his person, his role as the Ettrick Shepherd. Carlyle describes Hogg as he seemed in public:

> Hogg is a little red-skinned sack of a body, with quite the common air of an Ettrick shepherd, except that he has a highish though sloping brow (among his yellow grizzled hair), and two clear little beads of blue or grey eyes that sparkle, if not with thought, yet with animation.[6]

He wonders at the Shepherd's vanity and good-nature, and remarks, "I do not well understand the man; his significance

---

[4] *Fraser's Magazine*, xx, No. 118 (Oct. 1839), pp. 422-3.

[5] *The Three Perils of Woman ; or, Love, Leasing and Jealousy*, London 1823, i. 133-4.

[6] Froude, *Thomas Carlyle*, ii. 189.

is perhaps considerable."[7]　Veitch attempts to define the significance:

> . . . when shall we see such another shepherd? There is not in all Border history a more complete type of a man of power nourished by the Border glens and streams, haughs and hills, story, ballad, and tradition, than he. There is no more complete example anywhere of the rise to intellectual eminence of a nearly entirely self-taught man.[8]

If this were all, if Hogg were only a "primitive," and an example of how talent may rise by its own exertions, he would have sunk again into total oblivion, like that other self-taught poet, Byron's Amos Cottle.

But Hogg was an original writer. When we read his tales of Scottish peasant life, or his "Basil Lee" and "Edinburgh Baillie," and above all, his tales and poems of the supernatural, we are engaged by peculiar powers. Behind the Ettrick Shepherd, whom we are likely to think that we understand very well, the poseur who spoils everything, stands the shadow of James Hogg, a strange and by no means simple figure.

There are contradictions in Hogg's mind between Puritanism and his own lively imagination. The intensity of his rendering of the demonic, his realisation of the very *physique* of evil, is characteristic of Puritanism. The Scottish Puritans have suppressed so much feeling that it has become demonic.[9] The saints, those various actors of the Christian drama, have been banished, and the stage is stripped bare. The drama itself has been reduced to theological argument. But fantasy, blocked in one direction, will issue in another. As the adornments of Heaven are removed, "Hell"—in Gil-Martin's ringing cry—"has it." Even as the preacher warns his congregation of the ubiquity of devils, his words cast an adorning glow on that side of the argument. In Hogg we note again the peculiar characteristic of Puritan literature: the detail, even the delight

---

[7] Froude, *Thomas Carlyle*, II. 189.　　　　　[8] Veitch, pp. 485-6.

[9] I have attributed the "suppression of feeling" to Scottish Puritanism. But it is arguable that the Scots became so Calvinist after the Reformation because they were already in the habit of suppressing their feelings. To maintain their independence, they had to suppress feeling and cultivate the military virtues. In *The Wallace*, when Wallace falls in love with Helen Braidfute, he tries to resist it, so as to be able to go on fighting the English.

with which it envisions evil; the faint imagining of good. Evil
is not an abstraction, but a Prince of Darkness strutting at
large. In Milton he is sublime; in Bunyan, a monster; in
Hogg, a familiar, whose passion is pushing theological doctrine
to extremes—a very Scottish Devil.

On the other hand, Hogg, like his own Basil Lee, is an
amoral creature; his high spirits are opposed to the blank
necessity of everyday life, and the "methodistical face" of
religion. Hogg's unconventional humour is one of his most
striking characteristics. Chambers, writing to Hogg about
his tale, "The Watchmaker," and protesting against the
tacked-on moral, says, "Your humourous genius is apt to make
rather a wry face when attempting anything of that kind."[10]

His unconventionality goes deeper than temperament. He
has been bred in the Forest, where folk still hanker after pagan
superstitions. He was, Gilfillan says, "born and bred, nursed
and dandled in the arms of sublime superstition."[11] J. C.
Shairp remarks that Hogg was "perhaps among the last who
had a genuine feeling and belief of these symbols."[12] As Hogg
is opposed to "methodism" in religion, so too he is against
positivism, or any other theory which, by denying the supernatural, impoverishes "fancy." If we turn to his poem "Superstition," we see just how familiar Hogg was with pagan beliefs.
He had seen them actually put into practice.

> Oh! I have seen the door most closely barred;
> The green turf fire where stuck was many a pin;
> The rhymes of incantation I have heard,
> And seen the black dish solemnly laid in
> Amid the boiling liquid— Was it sin?
> Ah! no— 'twas all in fair defence of right.[13]

To Hogg, these matters were not sinful, whatever the "gude
fock" might say. They were another kind of morality than
the Christian; a way of life rapidly becoming extinct, with
which he had deep affinities.

These divisions make Hogg shift from one way of writing

[10] W. Chambers, Ms. 2265, in National Library of Scotland, p. 220.
[11] Gilfillan, *A Gallery of Literary Portraits*, p. 349.
[12] J. C. Shairp, *On Poetic Interpretation of Nature*, Boston 1885, p. 67.
[13] *Works*, II. 393.

to another, and cause the disorder of his life. Uncertain of his beliefs—and the old superstitions are dying—he retires into a public role, playing the buffoon to civilised men. But at rare moments, in the privacy of art, he is free to be serious, and his true talent issues in extraordinary works.

Appendix A

A Chronological Description of Hogg's Tales and Sketches

Hogg's prose fiction first appears in numbers of *The Spy*, the periodical he edited in 1810 and 1811. Here are the originals of the stories—or tales, as he called them—that he later revised : "On Instability in one's Calling" (revised and reprinted as "The Adventures of Basil Lee"), "Autobiography of the Spy" ("The Love Adventures of Mr. George Cochrane"), "Story of the Ghost of Lochmaben" ("The Wife of Lochmaben"), "The Country Laird" ("The Wool-Gatherer"), "Love of Fame" ("Adam Bell"), and "Duncan Campbell."

We may pass over his unimportant writings, most of which Hogg himself excluded in planning a collected edition. The rest are an impressive quantity, increasing sharply after 1818, the year of the publication of *The Brownie of Bodsbeck*. It was at about this time, according to the "Autobiography," that he determined to rely no more upon his verse.

The year 1817 saw the publication of the sketch, "A Country Wedding," under the description, "Tales and Anecdotes of Pastoral Life." In the same year he published "The Long Pack," one of his more popular tales. In 1818 *The Brownie of Bodsbeck ; and other Tales*, in two volumes, marked his first large excursion into prose fiction. *The Brownie* is of novel length ; the "other tales" are "The Wool-Gatherer," a novelette, and "The Hunt of Eildon."

The following year marks the *début* of "The Shepherd's Calendar," a series of tales and sketches in *Blackwood's Magazine* which comprises, besides stories and anecdotes of pastoral life, legendary tales and adventures which do not directly relate to it. After the first sketch, "Storms," there were no additions until 1823 ; thereafter, Hogg published pieces with fair regularity under this running title, and in 1829 gathered them into two volumes.

In 1820 he published *Winter Evening Tales*, a collection in two volumes of the tales and sketches named above—all but those in *The Brownie of Bodsbeck*—with these notable additions : "An Old Soldier's Tale," "The Bridal of Polmood," "Cousin Mattie," "Welldean Hall," and "Tibby Johnston's Wraith." There were also other unimportant pieces that had not previously been published.

The Three Perils of Man ; or War, Women, and Witchcraft. *A Border Romance*, a novel in three volumes published in 1822, was later cut down by Hogg to the long tale, "The Siege of Roxburgh," which appears in the edition of 1837.

The Three Perils of Man was followed by *The Three Perils of Woman; or, Love, Leasing, and Jealousy. A Series of Domestic Scottish Tales*, also in three volumes (1823). The work has never been reprinted.

The Private Memoirs and Confessions of a Justified Sinner, a novel, was published anonymously in 1824. It was reprinted as *The Suicide's Grave* and acknowledged by Hogg in 1828 ; and reprinted as *The Confessions of a Fanatic*, with alterations and omissions, in the edition of 1837.

In 1827, Hogg published a short tale, "The Marvellous Doctor" ; in 1828, "Trials of Temper," and in the next year, "The Brownie of the Black Haggs," also short tales.

The Shepherd's Calendar was published in two volumes in 1829, with revisions and new tales and sketches. The contents are "Rob Dodds," "Mr. Adamson of Laverhope," "The Prodigal Son," "The School of Misfortune," "George Dobson's Expedition to Hell," "The Souters of Selkirk," "The Laird of Cassway," "Tibby Hyslop's Dream," "Window Wat's Courtship," "A Strange Secret," "The Marvellous Doctor," "The Witches of Traquair," "Sheep," "Prayers," "Odd Characters," "Nancy Chisholm," "Snow-Storms," "The Shepherd's Dog," "Mary Burnet," "The Brownie of the Black Haggs," and "The Laird of Wineholm."

Between 1829 and 1830, we note the following tales published in periodicals : "Sound Morality," "A Tale of the Martyrs," "A Story of the Forty-Six," "The Cameronian Preacher's Tale," "Some Remarkable Passages in the Remarkable Life of the Baron St Gio," "Story of Adam Scott," "A Horrible Instance of the effects of Clanship" ("Julia M'Kenzie"), "The Mysterious Bride," and "The Fords of Callum."

Altrive Tales, the first and only volume of the collected edition that failed, appeared in 1832. It contained three tales : "Adventures of Captain John Lochy," "The Pongos : a letter from Southern Africa," and "Marion's Jock," none of which have been reprinted.

The tale, "Ewan M'Gabhar," was published in the same year. And in 1835, shortly before Hogg died, he launched *Tales of the Wars of Montrose*, a collection in three volumes, containing : "Some

Remarkable Passages in the Life of an Edinburgh Baillie," "The Adventures of Colonel Peter Aston," "Julia M'Kenzie," "The Remarkable Adventures of Sir Simon Brodie," "Wat Pringle o' the Yair," and "Mary Montgomery."

The edition of his prose published in 1837, *Tales and Sketches by the Ettrick Shepherd*, contains in six volumes the works of which Hogg himself approved, with his own revisions of the text, carried out shortly before his death. *Tales and Sketches* also includes several pieces "not before printed" : "Allan Gordon," "A Tale of Pentland," "Katie Cheyne," "Emigration," "The Watchmaker," "Nature's Magic Lantern," and "Gordon the Gipsey." The only large fault of this edition is the inclusion of *The Confessions of a Fanatic*, instead of the original *Justified Sinner*. There are also several omissions ; the *Altrive Tales*, among others, are not included. But the text is reliable, and I have used it in this study.

In 1865 a new edition of Hogg's tales and sketches appeared in *The Works of the Ettrick Shepherd*, edited by the Reverend Thomas Thomson. (The reader should be on guard against this edition, for the original texts have been altered and expurgated. Nor is it, as the title suggests, a complete edition ; there has never been a complete edition of Hogg's works.) *The Tales of James Hogg, the Ettrick Shepherd*, published in 1880, follows the text of 1837.

We may note also the republication of the original text of the *Justified Sinner* in 1895, 1924, 1947, and 1959, and the republication of *The Brownie of Bodsbeck* in 1903.

Appendix B

The Pseudo-Hogg of the *Noctes Ambrosianae*

The *Noctes* are entertaining table-talk, and the reader may speculate that some of the remarks credited to his *alter ego* were actually uttered by Hogg :

On philosophy :

"I hae nae philosophy, my dear Mr. North ; but I howp I hae some religion."[1]

On education :

"Edicate a' men and women too, say I, as much as possible—but dinna expeck impossible results. If edication be confined to the mere understandin', a man may gang out o' school and institutions, and colleges, after seven years' study, far waur than a coof. For a coof generally kens, or at least suspecks that he is a coof ; but an 'Intellectual-all-in-all,' as Wordsworth weel ca's him, thinks himsell the verra perfection o' God's creters."[2]

On the "false delicate" :

"There canna, sir, be a mair fatal symptom o' the decline and corruption o' national morals than what's ca'd *squeamishness*. Human natur, I fancy, is the same in essentials in high and low degree—and I ken ae thing for a dead certainty, that there never was a lass yet in a' the Forest that was misfortunate, who had nae aye lookit as if butter would nae hae melted in her mouth ; and what was the upshot ? A skirlin' babbie at the dead hour o' night, to the astonishment o' her mither and a' her sisters. . . ."[3]

On politics :

"The great majority o' shepherds are Conservatives. They're a thinkin' people, sir, as ye ken ; and though far frae bein' inspeculative, or unwillin' to adopt new contrivances as sune's they hae got an insicht intil the principle on which they wark, yet a newfangle in their een's but a newfangle . . . they're no to be ta'en in by the nostrums o' every reformer. . . ."[4]

On public executions :

"I cannot bide away from a hangin'. . . . I wad gang a lang gait

---

[1] *Noctes*, III, 96.
[3] *Op. cit.*, III. 161.
[2] *Op. cit.*, III. 186.
[4] *Op. cit.*, V. 439.

to see a beheading. A beheading for my siller—it's clear afore ony other way."[5]

On superstition :

"I'm just excessive superstitious."[6]

Beside these random remarks, there are lengthy set pieces, such as the Shepherd's account of his romance with a Mermaid,[7] his description of a mad dog,[8] and his dream of himself as a lion,[9] which exhibit a good deal of "fancy." However, it is not Hogg's fancy. The descriptions are evidently synthetic, the work of a man imagining himself as a shepherd-poet—i.e., Professor Wilson. Hogg, with all his faults, never abuses his imagination ; he is not a writer of *tours de force*. The poetic-sentimental style of the Shepherd is exemplified by his dream of himself as a lion in a previous incarnation. Here is the lion's "honeymoon" :

SHEPHERD : We were perfectly happy, sir. Afore the hinny-moon had filled her horns, mony an antelope, and not a few monkeys, had we twa together devoored ! Oh, sirs ! but she was fleet ! and sly as swift ! She would lie couchin' in a bush till she was surrounded wi' grazin' edibles suspectin' nae harm, and ever and anon ceasin' to crap the twigs, and playin' wi' ane anither, like lambs in the Forest, where it is now my lot as a human cretur to leeve ! Then up in the air and amang them wi' a roar, smitin' them dead in dizzens wi' ae touch o' her paw, though it was safter than velvet— and singlin' out the leader by his horns, that purrin' she micht leasurely sook his bluid—nor at sic times wou'd it hae been safe even for me, her lion and her lord, to ha'e interfered wi' her repast. For in the desert, hunger and thirst are as fierce as love. As for me, in this respect, I was mair generous, and mony is the time and aft that I hae gi'en her the tid-bits o' fat frae the flank o' a deer o' my ain killin' when she had missed her aim by owrespringin't—for I never ken't her spang fa' short—without her so much as thankin' me—for she was owre prood ever to seem gratefu' for ony favor— and carried hersell, like a Beauty as she was, and a spoiled Bride. I was sometimes sair tempted to throttle her—but then, to be sure, a playfu' pat frae her paw could smooth my bristles at ony time, or mak' me lift up my mane for her delicht, that she might lie down bashfully aneath its shadow, or as if shelterin' there frae some object o' her fear, crouch pantin' amang that envelopment o' hairy clouds.

TICKLER : Whew ![10]

---

[5] *Noctes*, I. 295.
[6] *Op. cit.*, II. 244.
[7] *Op. cit.*, II. 400-2.
[8] *Op. cit.*, IV. 131-3.
[9] *Op. cit.*, V. 416-25.
[10] *Op. cit.*, V. 420-1.

O

Bibliography

Altrive Tales. London (James Cochrane) 1822.

The Brownie of Bodsbeck ; and Other Tales. 2 vols., Edinburgh (William Blackwood) and London (John Murray) 1818.

The Domestic Manners and Private Life of Sir Walter Scott. Glasgow (John Reid), Edinburgh (Oliver & Boyd), and London (Whittaker, Treacher) 1834.

Dramatic Tales. 2 vols., London (Longham, Hurst, Rees, Orme, and Brown) and Edinburgh (John Ballantyne) 1817.

The Forest Minstrel ; a Selection of Songs . . . by James Hogg . . . and Others. London (Constable) 1810. [I have not seen this edn. The description is from the "Bibliography" in Batho, *The Ettrick Shepherd*, p. 188.]

The Forest Minstrel. Philadelphia (M. Carey) 1816.

The Hunting of Badlewe. London (Henry Colburn) and Edinburgh (George Goldie) 1814.

The Jacobite Relics of Scotland. First series, Edinburgh (William Blackwood) and London (T. Cadell and W. Davies) 1819.

The Jacobite Relics of Scotland. Second series, Edinburgh (William Blackwood) and London (T. Cadell and W. Davies) 1821.

Mador of the Moor. Edinburgh (William Blackwood) and London (John Murray) 1816.

The Mountain Bard. Edinburgh (Archibald Constable) and London (John Murray) 1807. [This publication contains the *Memoir of the Life of James Hogg*, afterwards revised and published as Hogg's "Autobiography."]

The Pilgrims of the Sun. Edinburgh (William Blackwood) and London (John Murray) 1815.

The Poetic Mirror. London (Longman, Hurst, Rees, Orme, and Brown) and Edinburgh (John Ballantyne) 1816.

The Poetical Works of the Ettrick Shepherd. 5 vols., Glasgow, Edinburgh and London (Blackie) 1838-40.

The Poetical Works of James Hogg. 4 vols., Edinburgh (A. Constable) and London (Hurst, Robinson) 1822.

The Private Memoirs and Confessions of a Justified Sinner. London (Longman, Hurst, Rees, Orme, Brown, and Green) 1824. Published anonymously. Repr. as *The Suicide's Grave* and acknowledged by Hogg 1828. Repr.

with omissions and alterations, as *Confessions of a Fanatic*, in *Tales and Sketches*, 1837. See Batho, *The Ettrick Shepherd*, "Bibliography," p. 202.

The Private Memoirs and Confessions of a Justified Sinner. With intro. by T. Earle Welby. London (A. M. Philpot) 1924.

The Private Memoirs and Confessions of a Justified Sinner. With intro. by André Gide. London (Cresset Press) 1947. New York (Grove Press) 1959.

Queen Hynde. London (Longman, Hurst, Rees, Orme, Brown, and Green) and Edinburgh (William Blackwood) 1825.

The Queen's Wake. Edinburgh (G. Goldie) and London (Longman, Hurst, Rees, Orme, and Brown) 1813.

A Queer Book. Edinburgh (William Blackwood). London (T. Cadell) 1832.

The Royal Jubilee. Edinburgh (William Blackwood) and London (T. Cadell) 1822.

Scottish Pastorals, Poems, Songs, Etc. Edinburgh (J. Taylor) 1801. Copies in British Museum, National Library of Scotland, and Edinburgh University Library.

Selected Poems of James Hogg. Ed. J. W. Oliver. Edinburgh (Oliver and Boyd) 1946.

A Series of Lay Sermons on Good Principles and Good Breeding. London (J. Fraser) 1834.

The Shepherd's Calendar. 2 vols., Edinburgh (William Blackwood) and London (T. Cadell) 1829.

The Shepherd's Guide : being a practical treatise on the diseases of sheep. . . . Edinburgh (Archibald Constable) and London (John Murray) 1807.

Songs, by the Ettrick Shepherd. Edinburgh (William Blackwood) and London (T. Cadell) 1831.

The Spy. 52 numbers, Edinburgh (J. Robertson) 1810-11. Copy in the National Library of Scotland.

The Suicide's Grave, being the Private Memoirs and Confessions of a Justified Sinner. London (J. Shiels) 1895.

Tales and Sketches, by the Ettrick Shepherd. 6 vols., Glasgow, Edinburgh and London (Blackie) 1837.

The Tales of James Hogg, the Ettrick Shepherd. 2 vols., London (Hamilton, Adams) and Glasgow (T. D. Morison) 1886.

Tales of the Wars of Montrose. 3 vols., London (James Cochrane) 1835.

The Three Perils of Man ; or War, Women, and Witchcraft. 3 vols., London (Longman, Hurst, Rees, Orme, and Brown) 1822. Repr. as "The Siege of Roxburgh," in *Tales and Sketches*, 1837.

The Three Perils of Woman ; or Love, Leasing, and Jealousy. 3 vols., London (Longman, Hurst, Rees, Orme, Brown, and Green) 1823.

Winter Evening Tales. 2 vols., Edinburgh (Oliver and Boyd) and London (G. & W. B. Whittaker) 1820.

The Works of the Ettrick Shepherd. Ed. the Rev. Thomas Thomson. London. Glasgow, and Edinburgh (Blackie) 1865. Vol. II includes (pp. 441-68) the "Autobiography of the Ettrick Shepherd," and (pp. ix-lvi) Thomson's "Biographical Sketch of the Ettrick Shepherd."

II. OTHERS

ANDERSON, WILLIAM. *The Scottish Nation*, Vol. II. Edinburgh and London (A. Fullarton & Co.) 1861.

BATHO, EDITH C. *The Ettrick Shepherd.* Cambridge (University Press) 1927.

——: *Notes on the Bibliography of James Hogg, the Ettrick Shepherd.* London (Bibliographical Society, repr. from *Transactions of the Bibliographical Society*, pp. 309-26) 1935.

BOSTON, THOMAS. *Memoirs of the Life, Time and Writings of the Reverend and Learned Thomas Boston A.M.*, ed. George H. Morrison. Edinburgh and London (Oliphant, Anderson & Ferrier) 1899.

BUNYAN, JOHN. *The Pilgrim's Progress.* London, New York and Toronto Oxford (University Press) 1952.

BURNS, ROBERT: *The Poetry of Robert Burns*, edd. W. E. Henley and T. F. Henderson. 4 vols., Edinburgh (T. C. and E. C. Jack) 1896.

BROWN, P. HUME: *History of Scotland*, Vol. II. Cambridge (University Press) 1902.

CARSWELL, DONALD: *Sir Walter : A Four-part Study in Biography.* London (John Murray) 1930.

CARLYLE, THOMAS: "Extracts from Note Book," in James Anthony Froude, *Thomas Carlyle: A History of the first forty Years of his Life, 1795-1835*, Vol. II, ch. 10. New York (Scribner's) 1882.

CASH, WILLIAM J.: *The Mind of the South.* New York (Doubleday) 1954.

Chambers' Cyclopedia of English Literature, s.v. "Hogg, James," Vol. III, pp. 8, 292. London and Edinburgh (W. & R. Chambers) 1903.

CHAMBERS, ROBERT. *Life of Sir Walter Scott . . . with Abbotsford Notanda by Robert Carruthers*, ed. W. Chambers. London and Edinburgh (W. & R. Chambers) 1871.

CHAMBERS, WILLIAM: Letter to James Hogg about "The Watchmaker," dated "19 Waterloo Place, Edinburgh. May 17, 1833." N.L.S. Ms. 2245, p. 220.

——: *Memoir of Robert Chambers.* Edinburgh and London (W. & R. Chambers) 1872.

CHILD, FRANCIS JAMES: The English and Scottish Popular Ballads. 5 vols., Boston (Houghton Miffin) and London (Henry Stevens) 1884 ; repr., 5 vols. in 3, New York (Folklore Press) 1957.

214 *Bibliography*

COLERIDGE, SAMUEL TAYLOR: *Biographia Literaria.* London (J. M. Dent) and New York (E. P. Dutton) 1956.

CONSTABLE, THOMAS: *Archibald Constable and his Literary Correspondents.* 3 vols., Edinburgh (Edmonston and Douglas) 1873. Correspondence of James Hogg in Vol. II, pp. 353-63.

CRAWFORD, THOMAS: *Burns: A Study of the Poems and Songs.* Edinburgh and London (Oliver and Boyd) and Stanford (University Press) 1960.

CUNNINGHAM, JOHN: *The Church History of Scotland.* 2 vols., Edinburgh (James Thin) 1882.

DAICHES, DAVID: *Robert Burns.* New York (Rinehart) 1950.

DEFOE, DANIEL: *The Works of Daniel Defoe,* Vol. II. London (John Clements) 1841.

Dictionary of National Biography, s.v. "Hogg, James," Vol. IX, pp. 992-5.

DOUGLAS, GEORGE: *James Hogg.* Edinburgh and London (Oliphant, Anderson and Ferrier) 1899.

FROUDE: *See* CARLYLE.

GARDEN, MRS [MARY GRAY HOGG]: *Memorials of James Hogg, the Ettrick Shepherd,* ed. Mrs Garden. London (Alexander Gardner) 1885.

——: "The Suicide's Grave," letter to the *Athenæum,* No. 3551 (16 Nov. 1895), p. 681.

GIDE, ANDRÉ: Introduction to James Hogg, *The Private Memoirs and Confessions of a Justified Sinner.* London (Cresset Press) 1947.

GILFILLAN, GEORGE: "Allan Cunningham and the Rural Poets," in *A Gallery of Literary Portraits,* pp. 348-55. Edinburgh (William Tait), London (Simpkin Marshall), and Dublin (J. Cumming) 1845.

GILLIES, R. P.: *Memoirs of a Literary Veteran.* 3 vols., London (Richard Bentley) 1851.

——: "Some Recollections of James Hogg," in *Fraser's Magazine,* xx (Oct. 1839), pp. 414-30.

GORDON, MRS [MARY]: *"Christopher North," a Memoir of John Wilson.* Edinburgh (Thomas C. Jack) and London (Hamilton, Adams) 1879.

HETHERINGTON, W. M.: History of the Church of Scotland. New York (Robert Carter) 1859.

HOGG, WILLIAM DODDS: *The First Editions of the Writings of James Hogg the Ettrick Shepherd.* Repr. from the Publications of the Edinburgh Bibliographical Society, Vol. XII, Edinburgh 1924.

HUSTVEDT, SIGURD BERNHARD: *Ballad Books and Ballad Men.* Cambridge, Mass. (Harvard U. P.) 1930.

J.A.: Letter to *Blackwood's Edinburgh Magazine,* about "Julia M'Kenzie," dated "Edinr. 25th Oct. 1830." N.L.S. Ms. 2245, ff. 159^v-160^r.

JEFFREY, FRANCIS: Review of *The Queen's Wake,* in *Edinburgh Review,* xxiv, No. 47, pp. 161-2.

"A Journey through the Highlands of Scotland," with prefatory letter signed S. W., in *Scots Magazine*, LXIV (1802), pp. 813-18.

KNOX, JOHN: *The History of the Reformation in Scotland*. London (Andrew Melrose) 1905.

LANG, ANDREW: "Confessions of a Justified Sinner," in *Illustrated London News*, CV (24 Nov. 1894), Supplement, 12.

——: *The Life and Letters of John Gibson Lockhart*. 2 vols., London (John C. Nimmo) and New York (Scribner's) 1897.

——: "The Suicide's Grave," letter to the *Athenæum*, No. 3553 (30 Nov. 1895), p. 754.

LOCKHART, JOHN GIBSON: *Memoirs of the Life of Sir Walter Scott*, Bart. 7 vols., Edinburgh (Robert Cadell) and London (John Murray and Whittaker) 1837.

——: *Peter's Letters to his Kinsfolk*. 3 vols., Edinburgh (William Blackwood) and London (T. Cadell and W. Davies) 1819.

LOVEJOY, ARTHUR O.: *Essays in the History of Ideas*. New York (Putnam) 1960.

MACKENZIE, R. SHELTON: [1]"History of Blackwood's Magazine," and [2]"Life of the Ettrick Shepherd," in *Noctes Ambrosianae*, New York (W. J. Widdleton) 1863, [1]I. vii-xx and [2]IV. iii-xxii.

MOORE, THOMAS: *The Life of Lord Byron with his Letters and Journals*. London (John Murray) 1854.

MORRISON, JOHN: "Random Reminiscences of Sir Walter Scott, of the Ettrick Shepherd, Sir Henry Raeburn, &c.," in *Tait's Edinburgh Magazine*, X (Sep., Oct., and Dec. 1843), pp. 569-78, 626-8, and 780-6.

MUSCHET, NICOL: *The Confession, &c., of Nicol Muschet of Boghal*. Edinburgh, Glasgow, and London (Oliver and Boyd) 1818.

"New Publications." Notice of *Scottish Pastorals*, in *Scots Magazine*, LXIII (Feb. 1801), p. 119.

OLIPHANT, MRS M.O.W., and MRS GERALD PORTER. *Annals of a Publishing House; William Blackwood and his Sons*. 3 vols. Edinburgh and London (William Blackwood) 1897. Vol. III is by Mrs Porter.

Oxford Dictionary of the Christian Church, The. Ed. F. L. Cross. London, New York, and Toronto (Oxford U.P.) 1957.

PETRIE, CHARLES: *The Jacobite Movement. The Last Phase. 1716-1807*. London (Eyre & Spottiswoode) 1950.

SCOT, REGINALD: *Scot's Discovery of Witchcraft*. "Printed by R. C. and are to be sold by Giles Calvert, dwelling at the Black Spread-Eagle at the West-end of Pauls, 1651."

SCOTT, SIR WALTER: *The Journal of Sir Walter Scott*. Ed. J. G. Tait and W. M. Parker. Edinburgh and London (Oliver and Boyd) 1950.

——: *The Lay of the Last Minstrel*. London (Longman, Hurst, Rees, and Orme) and Edinburgh (A. Constable) 1805.

SCOTT, SIR WALTER: *Minstrelsy of the Scottish Border.* Ed. T. F. Henderson. 4 vols. Edinburgh and London (William Blackwood) and New York (Scribner's) 1902.

SHARP, J. C.: *On Poetic Interpretation of Nature.* Boston (Houghton Miffin) 1885.

SMILES, SAMUEL: *A Publisher and his Friends. Memoirs and Correspondence of the late John Murray.* 2 vols. London (John Murray) 1891.

SMITH, G. GREGORY: *Scottish Literature, Character and Influence.* London (Macmillan) 1919.

SOUTHEY, ROBERT: Letter to James Hogg. "Keswick. 19 Oct. 1821." N.L.S. Ms. 2245, p. 72.

SPENSER, EDMUND: *The Poetical Works of Edmund Spenser.* London, New York, and Toronto (Oxford U.P.) 1947.

STEPHENSON, H. T.: *The Ettrick Shepherd: A Biography.* Indiana University Studies, IX, No. 54 (Sep. 1922).

STROUT, ALAN LANG: *The Life and Letters of James Hogg, the Ettrick Shepherd.* Vol. I (1770-1825). Lubbock (Texas Tech. Press), Texas, 1946.

THOMSON, THOMAS: "Biographical Sketch of the Ettrick Shepherd," in *The Works of the Ettrick Shepherd,* Vol. II, pp. ix-lvi. London, Glasgow, and Edinburgh (Blackie) 1865.

VEITCH, JOHN: *The History and Poetry of the Scottish Border.* Glasgow (James Maclehose) 1878.

VIRTUE, GEORGE: *The Wilkie Gallery.* London and New York (n.p.) n.d.

WELBY, T. EARLE: Intro. to James Hogg, *The Private Memoirs and Confessions of a Justified Sinner.* London (A. M. Philpot) 1924.

"Willie and Keatie," in *Scots Magazine,* LXIII (Jan. 1801), pp. 52-4.

WILSON, JOHN: "An Hour's Talk about Poetry," in *The Works of Professor Wilson of the University of Edinburgh,* ed. Prof. J. F. Ferrier, Vol. IX, pp. 201-6. Edinburgh and London (William Blackwood) 1857.

——: WILLIAM MAGINN, J. G. LOCKHART, JAMES HOGG, and OTHERS. *Noctes Ambrosianae.* Ed. R. Shelton Mackenzie. 5 vols. New York (W. J. Widdleton) 1863.

——: "On Hogg's Memoirs," in *Blackwood's Edinburgh Magazine,* X (Aug. 1821), pp. 43-52. Review of *The Mountain Bard* ; probably by John Wilson.

——: "Some Observations on the Poetry of the agricultural and that of the pastoral Districts of Scotland, illustrated by a comparative View of the Genius of Burns and the Ettrick Shepherd," in *Blackwood's Edinburgh Magazine,* IV (Feb. 1819), pp. 521-9. An early version of "An Hour's Talk about Poetry."

WITTIG, KURT: *The Scottish Tradition in Literature.* Edinburgh and London (Oliver and Boyd) 1958.

WORDSWORTH, WILLIAM: *The Poetical Works of William Wordsworth.* Edd. E. de Selincourt and Helen Darbishire. Oxford (Clarendon Press) 1946.

Index

"Abbot M'Kinnon, The": 25, 85.
"Adam Bell": 120, 162, 167-8.
"Adam Scott": 145-6, 159.
"Adventures of Basil Lee, The": 21, 95, 112, 202; autobiographical manner of, 113-14; improbable episode in, 118; style of, 121, 122; peasant character in, 134; synopsis of, 138-41; supernatural episode in, 159.
"Adventures of Captain John Lochy, The": 114, 141-3.
"Adventures of Colonel Peter Aston, The": 118, 151.
Agricola, Johannes: 170.
Altrive: 28-9.
Altrive Tales: 49, 141.
Anderson, Robert: 31.
"Andrew the Packman": 101.
Anniversary, The (periodical): 111.
Antinomian controversy: 171.
Antinomianism: 192 n., 196.
Antinomians: 170-3.
Athenaeum: 195.
Auchterarder Creed: 171.
"Auld Maitland": 54.
"Author's Address to his Auld Dog Hector": 102.
"Autobiography": 24, 26 n.; primary source of information on Hogg, 4; childhood described in, 8; first verses described in, 11; on residence in Edinburgh, 28; on meeting with Wordsworth, 31; "Triumphal Arch" episode in, 32; comments on Scott in, 43, 45; views of aristocracy in, 88; Hogg's opinions of his work in, 91; comments on *The Poetic Mirror* in, 96; Hogg's estimate of "The Bridal of Polmood" in, 152.

"Bailiff's Daughter of Islington, The" (traditional ballad): 76.
Ballads: collection of, by Hogg, 53, 54; definition of, 53, 55; history and

collection of, 53; imitations of, by Hogg, 54-5; form of, used by Hogg, 55; language in, as used by Hogg, 56-59; faults displayed by Hogg in, 60-1.
"Baron St. Gio, The": 122, 146.
"Basil Lee": *see* "ADVENTURES OF BASIL LEE."
Batho, Edith C.: 5; opinions of, on Hogg, 4, 14, 34-5, 40, 43, 81; on Hogg and Burns, 13; on Scott and Hogg, 15; on Hogg at Altrive, 28; on "Triumphal Arch" episode, 32 n.; on Hogg's collection of ballads, 54; on Moore and Hogg, 79; on "Basil Lee," 141; on *The Brownie of Bodsbeck*, 149 n.; on the "Edinburgh Baillie," 150; on authorship of the *Justified Sinner*, 192, 196.
Bible: 125.
Blackwood, William: 5, 24, 33, 34, 37, 152.
Blackwood's Edinburgh Magazine: 5, 111, 185; first appearance of, 33; Wilson editor of, 34; review of *Mountain Bard* in, 37; publishes Hogg's songs, 74; Keats on reviewers in, 78; literary practices in, 80; publication of "Ringan and May," 94; and sources of "Julia M'Kenzie," 153.
Boston, Thomas: 171, 196.
"Boy's Song, A": 131.
"Bridal of Polmood, The": 116-17, 119, 120-1, 124, 136, 152-3.
British Poets, The (Anderson): 31.
Brown, P. Hume: 63.
"Brownie of the Black Haggs, The": 112, 159; plot of, 115; style of, 122; synopsis of, 163-4; use of psychology in, 164-5; demon in, 166, 196, 197.
Brownie of Bodsbeck, The: 152; publication of, 42; opposition of Scott to, 42-3; re-use of scene from, 118; pastoral characters in, 132; synopsis of, 147-9; the supernatural in, 158;